Multiple Moralities and Religions in Post-Soviet Russia

Multiple Moralities and Religions in Post-Soviet Russia

Edited By

Jarrett Zigon

berghahn

NEW YORK · OXFORD

www.berghahnbooks.com

Published in 2011 by

Berghahn Books

www.berghahnbooks.com

©2011, 2014 Jarrett Zigon
First paperback edition published in 2014

Library of Congress Cataloging-in-Publication Data

Multiple moralities and religions in post-Soviet Russia / edited by Jarrett Zigon.
    p. cm.
    Includes bibliographical references and index.
ISBN 978-0-85745-209-2 (hardback) -- ISBN 978-0-85745-210-8 (institutional ebook)
-- ISBN 978-1-78238-053-5 (paperback) -- ISBN 978-1-78238-054-2 (retail ebook)
    1. Anthropology of religion—Russia (Federation) 2. Social ethics—Russia
(Federation) 3. Social values—Russia (Federation) 4. Post-communism—Russia
(Federation) 5. Russia (Federation)—Religious life and customs. 6. Russia
(Federation)—Social conditions. 7. Russia (Federation)—Moral conditions.
I. Zigon, Jarrett.
    GN585.R9M85 2011
    306.60947—dc22

                                                            2010052231

British Library Cataloguing in Publication Data

A catalogue record for this book is available from the British Library

ISBN: 978-1-78238-053-5 paperback
ISBN: 978-1-78238-054-2 retail ebook

Contents

List of Illustrations and Tables   vii

Part I. Introduction

CHAPTER 1
Multiple Moralities: Discourses, Practices, and Breakdowns
in Post-Soviet Russia   3
Jarrett Zigon

CHAPTER 2
Exploring Russian Religiosity as a Source of Morality Today   16
Alexander Agadjanian

Part II. Multiple Moralities

CHAPTER 3
Post-Soviet Orthodoxy in the Making: Strategies for Continuity
Thinking among Russian Middle-aged School Teachers   27
Agata Ładykowska

CHAPTER 4
The Politics of Rightness: Social Justice among Russia's
Christian Communities   48
Melissa L. Caldwell

CHAPTER 5
An Ethos of Relatedness: Foreign Aid and Grassroots Charities
in Two Orthodox Parishes in North-Western Russia   67
Detelina Tocheva

CHAPTER 6
"A Lot of Blood Is Unrevenged Here": Moral Disintegration
in Post-War Chechnya   92
Ieva Raubisko

CHAPTER 7

Morality, Utopia, Discipline: New Religious Movements and
Soviet Culture   119
Alexander A. Panchenko

CHAPTER 8

Constructing Moralities around the Tsarist Family   146
Kathy Rousselet

CHAPTER 9

St. Xenia as a Patron of Female Social Suffering: An Essay on
Anthropological Hagiology   168
Jeanne Kormina and Sergey Shtyrkov

CHAPTER 10

Built with Gold or Tears? Moral Discourses on Church
Construction and the Role of Entrepreneurial Donations   191
Tobias Köllner

AFTERWORD

Multiple Moralities, Multiple Secularisms   214
Catherine Wanner

Notes on Contributors   226

Index   229

Illustrations and Tables

Illustrations

7.1. LTC. Spiritual circle. Krasnoyarskii *krai.*   139

7.2. LTC. Discussion of daily events with a priest.
Krasnoyarskii *krai.*   139

7.3. LTC. Spiritual circle at a funeral. Krasnoyarskii *krai.*   140

9.1. Pilgrims at St. Xenia shrine.   169

9.2. Icons in a church shop at the Smolensk Cemetery.   179

Tables

7.1. Ethical narratives of LTC members.   129

PART I
Introduction

 CHAPTER 1

Multiple Moralities

Discourses, Practices, and Breakdowns in Post-Soviet Russia

Jarrett Zigon

Since the mid 1980s the Russian people have been living through an histori-cally unprecedented period of social and political upheaval and cultural and epistemological questioning—what is often referred to as the post-Soviet transition. This process has been accompanied by, if not partly instigated by, a neoliberal version of globalization that has disrupted the social lives of innumerable peoples around the world. According to James Faubion, globalization has brought about an "increasing intensity of problematiza-tion" (2001: 101). The Foucauldian notion of problematization, like Hei-degger's breakdown (Heidegger 1996: 68–69), describes a reflective state in which such everyday unreflected practices and discourses are presented "to oneself as an object of thought and to question it as to its meaning, its conditions, and its goals" (Foucault 1984: 388). The so-called transition of post-Soviet Russia can be considered as a similar process of problematiza-tion or breakdown. One characteristic of this questioning is the struggle by individuals and institutions to articulate a coherent and widely acceptable notion of morality. Thus, the post-Soviet period has seen a cacophony of moral debate, argumentation, and questioning. The contributions of this volume show that in the post-Soviet period, religions have become one of the central social arenas in which these moral processes are taking place (see also Rasanayagam 2006; Steinberg and Wanner 2008).

The Russian Orthodox Church has been an integral part of Russian life for centuries (Boym 1994; Ellis 1998; Gutkin 1999). In the post-Soviet era the Russian Orthodox Church has reestablished itself as one of the most stable and influential cultural institutions in the Russian Federation (Pan-khurst 1996; Hann and Goltz 2010). In particular, the Church has become increasingly involved in public debates concerning such specific moral is-sues and concerns as bioethics and reproductive rights, HIV/AIDS and drug rehabilitation, the family, and human rights (Ellis 1998; Russian Or-thodox Church 2000, 2005, 2008; Zigon 2011). But as several anthropolo-gists, including Caldwell and Raubisko in this volume, have argued, there is a long history within Russia of other religious traditions playing a significant role in both the social and moral lives of Russians. This continues in today's Russia. Thus, for example, Judaism (Goluboff 2003), Islam (Johnson, Stepaniants, and Forest 2005; Raubisko, this volume), Protestantism (Caldwell 2004, this volume), and Old Believer Orthodoxy (Rogers 2008, 2009) have all been and continue to be major religious traditions central to Russian notions of identity and morality (see also Pelkmans 2009).

A particularly insightful anthropological study of the relationship between non-Russian Orthodox religion and morality in Russia has been done by Douglas Rogers (2009), who has done research on the moral practices of persons living in a predominantly Old Believer village in the Urals. Rogers argues that the context of socio-political transition in the post-Soviet years has allowed for the renewal of negotiations and debates over the constitution of moral relations guided by Old Believer values in a time of capitalist transformation. These conversations and conflicts, so Rogers argues, are in a dialogical negotiation with historically informed Old Believer dispositions and sensibilities, which, in turn, leads to the kinds of ethical transformations he writes about. What makes this dialogue and transformation possible is that "what one thinks of as 'right' or virtuous usually exists in many shades of similarity and difference to what one's neighbors think" (Rogers 2004: 36). I find Rogers' observation on the importance of these "shades of similarity and difference" significant for understanding how morality is articulated, negotiated, and embodied in post-Soviet Russia in general, and particularly so for those negotiating the often competing moralities of religion and capitalist market relations (see Zigon 2008a, 2009, 2010).

As already pointed out above, one way of describing contemporary Russia is as a place where there is much open and public debate and negotiation between competing moralities of both the sacred and secular variety. Although post-Soviet Russia has been characterized as a society of *bespredel*, or a society without moral limits (Kon 1996: 205), I hesitate to make such a characterization and instead would say that in today's Russia there is a struggle over competing moral conceptualizations. In this sense, contemporary Russia is not a place without morality, but rather a place of multiple moralities where various sacred and secular moral discourses and ethical practices have become, to varying degrees, legitimate options (Wanner 2007: 10, this volume).

This multiplicity of morality and the concern of its potential danger to a perceived social and moral cohesion of collective life is not unique to the post-Soviet period and, in fact, seems to characterize much of the post-Stalinist years. For example, during the late-Brezhnev years many Russians, using a discourse very similar to that heard in the post-Soviet period, showed constant concern for the immorality of Soviet youth, the increasing negative effects of materialism and Western entertainment on Soviet morality, and a shocking rise of publicly expressed sexuality, the response to which was a widespread call for a return to traditional Russian and Soviet family values (Binyon 1983). Similarly, the Communist Party's promulgation of "The Moral Code of the Builder of Communism," a kind of communist ten commandments that was eventually taught in schools and spread door to door by members of the Komsomol, was conceived as a response to a perceived breakdown of morality in the early 1960s (De George 1969). Therefore, what Kon sees as an erosion of morality in post-Soviet Russia, and what I see as a cacophony of moral debate and questioning, is in large part a continuation of a public discourse that has been voiced for generations. In fact, it could be argued that one of the primary differences between post-Soviet Russia and the previous moral questioning of the post-Stalinist years is the emergence of various religious traditions in the public arena of moral debate and contestation.

A significant part of this moral questioning, and one shared by several sacred and secular moralities in contemporary Russia, has been an emphasis on individuals ethically transforming themselves into new moral persons (Ries 1997: 119; Fitzpatrick 2005: 304). As I have shown elsewhere through the life-historical portraits of post-Soviet Russian Orthodox believers, religions of various sorts have been central to this process of self-transformation (Zigon 2008a, 2009, 2010). This process is also clearly seen in the chapter by Panchenko, among others in this volume. Interestingly, however, this post-Soviet emphasis on working on the self (*rabota nad soboi*) has roots in the Soviet discourse of creating the New Soviet Man by means of individual self-disciplining (Etkind 1996: 107–09; Kharkhordin 1999; Fitzpatrick 2005). Kharkhordin (1999), in turn, has argued that Soviet emphasis on working on the self had its roots in the pre-revolution Russian Orthodox Church and continued well into the late-Soviet years. These practices continue in the post-Soviet period. Pesmen argues that tropes of self-analysis and suffering are central to the ways in which her informants spoke of working on themselves, and that they believe such practices are the necessary "work of *dusha*" (2000: 54n). Similarly, Rivkin-Fish shows that among reproductive health activists in Russia, there is a "common tendency to construe their work for reproductive health as a mission to promote moral changes in interpersonal relationships and the development of personality (or what might be called 'work on the self')" (284). As can be seen, then, although the moral discourse and ethical practices of work on the self are central to various religious traditions in contemporary Russia, this discourse and practice has much wider secular and historical cache, rendering it, perhaps, the most powerful moral concept in contemporary Russia.

Anthropology of Moralities and Religion

The recent explicit focus of some anthropologists on local moralities constitutes a theoretical and conceptual shift in attention of the anthropological gaze (e.g., Heintz 2009; Robbins 2007; Zigon 2008b, 2009). It has been argued that anthropologists, as well as social scientists in general, have not explicitly studied moralities because of a deep-seated Durkheimian influence that tends to equate the moral with the reproduction of social norms. In this sense, sociality as such is basically equated with morality. This Durkheimian perspective also tends to put significant emphasis on religious discourse, practice, and ritual for the maintenance and reproduction of this sociality as morality. While a number of contemporary anthropologists of morality tend to agree with this critique of the Durkheimian legacy, several of them have, nevertheless, researched and theorized local moralities through the lens of local religious life. In an attempt to explain this anthropological focus, Michael Lambek has argued that "religion provides objects and occasions, no less than models, 'of and for' meaningful, ethical practice" (2000: 313).

Despite this shared focus on the interrelationship between religion and morality, anthropologists have taken different approaches to their studies. Thus, for example, Steven Parish (1991, 1994) is primarily concerned with the ways in which Hinduism helps shape what he calls the moral consciousness and conceptions of his informants; Joel Robbins (2004, 2007) takes a structuralist approach shaped by the likes of Durkheim, Weber, and Dumont in his analysis of the moral torment that has resulted from the conversion of the Urapmin of Papua New Guinea to Pentecostalism; and Saba Mahmood (2005) has utilized a post-structuralist Foucauldian approach in her analysis of the ethical cultivation of virtue among women of an Islamic Piety movement in Egypt. Therefore, while these anthropologists agree that religion is an important and central social arena for the study of local moralities, each have approached this in very different ways.

These differences tend to reflect a basic distinction between two approaches within the anthropology of moralities. In my reading of the anthropology of moralities literature there are two predominant approaches: the moral reasoning and choice approach and the Neo-Aristotelian and Foucauldian approach. Howell and several contributors to her edited volume on the ethnography of moralities suggest that a cross-cultural study of moralities may best be served by focusing on the acting individual's process of moral reasoning, during which choices are made between alternative possible actions (1997: 14–16). Robbins agrees and claims that the moral domain is a conscious domain of choice (2004: 315–16; see also Laidlaw 2002). While to some extent attention to choices and reasoning are important, I am concerned that this position limits what Robbins calls the moral domain. This is so because it must be recognized that a person is not only moral when she must make a conscious decision to be so. Rather, the need to consciously consider or reason about what one must do only arises in moments that shake one out of the unreflective everydayness of being moral. This moment is what I will call in the next section a moral breakdown. What is often missing from the reasoning and choice approach, then, is an explicit framing of those moments of moral breakdown when one must find ways, and choosing and reasoning may only be two of the possible ways, to return to the unreflective state of being moral.

The other predominant approach taken by anthropologists to the study of local moralities is what we could call dispositional or virtue ethics (e.g., Hirschkind 2001; Mahmood 2005; Widlok 2004). These studies take Neo-Aristotelian and Foucauldian approaches in considering how people make themselves into properly attuned moral persons. While there certainly are differences between these two approaches, both share the notion that one becomes a moral person primarily by means of developing certain dispositional capacities. Mahmood describes this approach "as always local and particular, pertaining to a specific set of procedures, techniques, and discourses through which highly specific ethical-moral subjects come to be formed" (2005: 28). One becomes a moral person, in this way, not by following rules or norms, but by training oneself in a set of certain practices (Widlok 2004: 59). As will become clear below, I am also sympathetic to the dispositional/virtue approach. However, what is limiting about this approach is that the practices and techniques of moral training are too often restricted to certain local domains. Thus, this approach rarely allows us to see how persons can transfer and translate these dispositional trainings across various social contexts.

In my own work on morality in contemporary Russia I have been influenced by both of these approaches, as well as recognized the importance of religion in the shaping of public discourses and individuals' moralities. Nevertheless, taking a phenomenological approach to the study of local moralities, I am primarily concerned with the multifarious relationships between institutions, groups, and individuals within a society that come to constitute what *counts* as morality and ethical practice. It is also important to recognize that the various religions in Russia offer just one of several institutional and public variants of moralities that make up the assemblage of what we might call a local moral constellation. For this reason although religious discourses and practices of religion are highlighted within this volume, it is important to realize that they make up just one of several aspects of morality—for example, various secular, Soviet, and non-Russian/ Western moralities are also significant—that constitute the range of possible moral worlds in contemporary Russia. In the next section, an anthropological theory of moralities will be outlined that makes distinctions among different aspects of morality, as well as between morality and ethics. In taking this phenomenological approach it is possible to more clearly discern the varied and distinctive discourses and practices that come to constitute local moral worlds.

Moralities and Ethics

The anthropological study of moralities is best begun with a distinction between morality and ethics (see Zigon 2007, 2008b, 2009). The advantage of this distinction is twofold. First, it highlights the important existential fact of the difference between morality as acted and articulated in either a nonconscious manner or discursively, and ethics as a conscious attempt to be moral in moments of dilemma and questioning. Second, by making further distinctions between the different aspects[1] of morality, this approach recognizes that there is no one, totalizing morality in any society, but rather all societies consist of a range of possible moral discourses and practices that count as morality for particular institutions, groups, and individuals within particular situations and contexts. In the rest of this introduction I will show how this distinction brings some coherency to the diverse foci of the chapters of this volume.

Morality can be considered at three different, but certainly interrelated, aspects that are themselves pluralistic: 1) the institutional; 2) that of public discourse; and 3) embodied dispositions. I will consider each of these in turn. Institutions can be loosely defined as those formal and non-formal social organizations and groups that are a part of all societies and that wield varying amounts of power over individual persons (Foucault 1990: 141). It can be said that all persons have at least nominal contact with or participation in some of the institutions that make up their respective societies. However, most are intimately entwined within the overlapping influences of several different institutions within and beyond their own society.

As Alexander Panchenko and Melissa Caldwell show in their respective chapters, part of what it is to be an institution is to publicly claim the truth or rightness of a particular kind of morality. Thus, whether it is the moral condemnation of such characteristics as egoism and pride by the Last Testament Church described by Panchenko or the link Caldwell says the Russian Orthodox Church makes between theology and morality that often impedes the Church from participating in social work, institutions claim to have the legitimacy of knowing the sole moral truth and the authority to expect their adherents to follow it. But as several chapters in this volume show, those individuals entwined within any institution do not always follow to the letter the claimed morality of the institution. Furthermore, those who do not follow the institutional morality to the letter are not always punished or reprimanded for not doing so. In fact, it may oftentimes go unnoticed.

Additionally, all institutions, to some extent, consist of a range of moral positions that are debated and contested from within. This is clearly seen in the chapter by Melissa Caldwell, who shows how institutional moralities can become negotiable for the practical maneuvering through certain legal, social, and interfaith barriers. Thus, Caldwell argues that in the attempt by several Moscow-based parishes to work together in social charity programs, differences in institutional morality need to be negotiated and compromised for the more practical approach of what she calls the politics of rightness. Despite this internal and inter-institutional debate, however, institutions usually and for the most part publicly articulate a morality *as though* it were unquestioned.

Notwithstanding these contestations and pluralities within institutions and within societies, the influences that institutional moralities have on individual persons are clearly real and substantial. Thus, as Ieva Raubisko's chapter so interestingly shows, despite what she calls the moral confusion within Chechnya, certain institutional moralities, such as Islam, remain central despite the apparent contestation of particular values and competition among different moralities. Institutional morality, then, is a significantly influential moral discourse that is oftentimes supported by very real expressions of power, but which, nevertheless is not totalizing and is more akin to a very persuasive rhetoric than it is to a truth.

Closely related to institutional morality, yet not quite the same, is what I call the public discourse of morality. This distinction is similar to the distinction Voloshinov made between official ideology and behavioral ideology (2000), where the former is that which is upheld by official and state institutions, and the latter is the result of the everyday dialogical interactions between persons. Although these two kinds of ideologies, like the institutional and public discourse of morality, are separate and distinct from one another, they are in constant dialogue with one another. The public discourse of morality, then, is all those public articulations of moral beliefs, conceptions, and hopes that are not *directly* articulated by an institution. Some examples of the public discourse of morality are the media, protest, philosophical discourse, and everyday articulated beliefs, opinions, and conceptions.

An example of people's everyday articulations of their moral beliefs and conceptions is seen in Tobias Köllner's chapter, where he shows that persons articulate two different kinds of public discourses of morality concerning the reconstruction of Orthodox Churches. Indeed, these articulations can be understand as public discourses of morality in two distinct ways—first, as the interpretation of certain laypersons of Orthodox moral theology, or the Russian Orthodox Church's institutional morality, and second, as an articulation of a person's own moral conceptions. We see a similar process occurring in the chapters of both Kathy Rousselet and Jeanne Kormina and Sergey Shtyrkov, who show how different iconographic and narrative images are used as moral exemplars for guiding and understanding familial and gendered life. The complexity and diversity of public discourses of morality within contemporary Russia is clearly seen in Agata Ładykowska's chapter, which discloses the difficulties and inconsistencies that often occur when individuals attempt to articulate their moral world and understanding. Indeed, Ładykowska's chapter reveals the wide diversity of public discourses of morality within Russia that contribute to this difficulty. Thus, her chapter takes us on an interesting conceptual journey from the verbal articulations of school teachers' conceptualization of morality to authoritative dictionary definitions, and from school literature on morality to Russian Orthodox priests' writing on the subject.

The third aspect of morality is what I call embodied morality. This aspect of morality can be described in terms of a habitus, or unreflective and unreflexive dispositions of everyday social life attained over a lifetime of what Mauss called socially performed techniques (1973). Morality in this third sense, unlike the way morality is so often considered as rule-following or conscious reflection on a problem or dilemma, is not thought out beforehand, nor is it noticed when it is performed. It is simply done. Morality as embodied dispositions is one's everyday way of being in the world. It is because all persons are able to embody morality in this unreflective and unreflexive way that most persons most of the time are able to act in ways that are, for the most part, acceptable to others in their social world. A significant aspect of this embodied morality is, as Catherine Wanner points out in the afterword, the felt emotionality of being for and with others in certain ways and the commitment to particular practices and beliefs (see also Wanner 2007: 10).

It is, perhaps, such an embodied and unreflective morality that allows such different religiously affiliated persons to work together in what Melissa Caldwell calls the politics of rightness in the negotiation of institutional moralities. It is also this embodied morality that causes so many of Ieva Raubisko's Chechen informants to react as they do to the inconceivable violence in their lives, so similarly, in some cases, to the way Talal Asad has elsewhere described Oedipus' reaction to his own transgression (2003).

It is also this embodied morality that people hope to cultivate when they consciously work through the process of ethically transforming themselves into persons who are able to be moral in their world. It is this process that is particularly clear in Panchenko's chapter, which shows the detailed process by which self-transformation is enacted within a particular institutional context. Ethics, then, to distinguish it from the three aspects of morality, is what is done in those moments of a moral breakdown, when one calls into question any of the three aspects of morality or has his or her own embodied morality called into question. Ethics is a kind of stepping-away to question and work on any of the three aspects of morality. Indeed, ethics can very often question and work on more than one moral aspect, or all three, at one time. In stepping-away in this ethical moment, a person becomes reflective and reflexive about his or her moral world and moral personhood and what he or she must do, say or think in order to appropriately return to a nonconscious moral mode of being. What must be done is a process of working on the self,[2] where the person must perform certain practices on him or herself or with other persons in order to consciously be and act moral in the social world. Ethics, then, is a conscious acting on oneself either in isolation or with others so as to make oneself into a more morally appropriate and acceptable social person not only in the eyes of others but also for oneself. Thus, this moment of ethics is a creative moment, for by performing ethics, people create, even if ever so slightly, new moral personhoods and enact new moral worlds. It should be further noted that this process of ethics also refers to institutions and groups in that these bodies, as well as the individuals associated with them, also reflect, work on, and alter the institutional and public discourses of moralities by means of various forms of internal and public debates and negotiations.

While Panchenko's chapter perhaps most clearly reveals this process, ethics as conscious work to transform one's moral personhood, or the morality of a particular institution or public discourse, can be seen in several other chapters of this volume. For example, Detelina Tocheva's case of the woman who saw the need to provide clothes, shoes, and other necessities in her town was provoked by a social need to question her church and parish's moral discourse and practice and in so doing ethically worked to find new ways of morally being for and with others. Similarly, I suggest Raubisko's informants are constantly forced to reflectively step into a conscious ethical stance toward their social world in order to cultivate new moral ways of living in what might be called a societal-wide state of breakdown.

These cases show that this ethical moment of the moral breakdown is a moment in which the multifarious aspects of local moralities, which are all part of the three aspects of morality described thus far, come together to *inform* the ways in which a person, group of persons, or institutions works on themselves. I say *inform* because none of the aspects that belong to the institutional moralities, the public discourses of morality, nor a person's own embodied dispositional morality determine how this work will be done in the ethical moment. Rather, the ethical moment is a creative moment that although certainly influenced by the various trajectories of moralities already present, is never determined by them. Therefore, it is because of this moment, and the way it feeds back into the social world, that not only individual embodied moral dispositions change throughout a lifetime, but so too does the possibility arise for shifts, alterations, and changes in the institutional and public discourse of moralities.

✳ ✳ ✳

What I have tried to do in this last section of the introduction is to elucidate a particular distinction between morality and ethics that helps us find a way to bring together the diverse chapters of this volume. Because this anthropological theory of moralities recognizes not only the multi-aspectual nature of morality but also allows for the range of possible pluralities within each of these aspects, as well as within the range of possible ethical techniques available, it provides a way of conceptualizing the complexity of moral and ethical life as it is lived in everyday life in contemporary Russia. This framework is particularly helpful for understanding the various ways in which the chapters of this volume show that diverse religious and secular moralities intersect in institutional, public, and personal lives in today's Russia, and in so doing, allow us to move beyond notions of a society of a totalizing morality, and instead see that Russia, like all societies, is a social world made up of multiple moralities.

Notes

Parts of this chapter have appeared in other versions in *Morality: An Anthropological Perspective* (Oxford: Berg, 2008) and *Making the New Post-Soviet Person: Moral Experience in Contemporary Moscow* (Leiden: Brill Publishers, 2010).

1. I use "aspect" in the phenomenological sense of one of many that when together construct what is considered a whole. For example, the perception of two sides (aspects) of a cube allow for the cognitive construction of the whole of the cube although all the sides are never perceived at the same time.

2. I follow Critchley (2007: 11) in rejecting Foucault's notion of work on the self, which seems to aim at self-mastery, for a more open-ended and situational ethical process.

References

Asad, Talal. 2003. *Formations of the Secular: Christianity, Islam, Modernity.* Stanford, CA: Stanford University Press.

Binyon, Michael. 1983. *Life in Russia*. New York: Pantheon Books.

Boym, Svetlana. 1994. *Common Places*. Cambridge, MA: Harvard University Press.

Caldwell, Melissa. 2004. *Not by Bread Alone: Social Support in the New Russia*. Berkeley, CA: University of California Press.

Critchley, Simon. 2007. *Infinitely Demanding*. London: Verso.

De George, Richard T. 1969. *Soviet Ethics and Morality*. Ann Arbor, MI: The University of Michigan Press.

Ellis, Jane. 1998. "Religion and Orthodoxy." In *Russian Cultural Studies*, ed. Catriona Kelly and David Shepherd. Oxford: Oxford University Press.

Etkind, Alexander M. 1996. "Psychological Culture." In *Russian Culture at the Crossroads: Paradoxes of Postcommunist Consciousness*, ed. Dmitri N. Shalin. Boulder, CO: Westview Press.

Faubion, James D. 2001. "Toward an Anthropology of Ethics: Foucault and the Pedagogies of Autopoiesis." *Representations* 74: 83–104.

Fitzpatrick, Sheila. 2005. *Tear off the Masks!: Identity and Imposture in Twentieth-Century Russia*. Princeton, NJ: Princeton University Press.

Foucault, Michel. 1984. "Polemics, Politics, and Problemizations: An Interview with Michel Foucault." In *The Foucault Reader*, ed. Paul Rabinow. New York: Pantheon Books.

———. 1990. *The History of Sexuality: An Introduction*. New York: Vintage Books.

Goluboff, Sascha L. 2003. *Jewish Russians: Upheavals in a Moscow Synagogue*. Philadelphia: University of Pennsylvania Press.

Gutkin, Irina. 1999. *The Cultural Origins of the Socialist Realist Aesthetic: 1890–1934*. Evanston, IL: Northwestern University Press.

Hann, Chris, and Hermann Goltz. 2010. *Eastern Christians in Anthropological Perspective*. Berkeley, CA: University of California Press.

Heidegger, Martin. 1996. *Being and Time*. Albany, NY: State University of New York Press.

Heintz, Monica. 2009. *The Anthropology of Moralities*. Oxford: Berghahn Books.

Hirschkind, Charles. 2001. "The Ethics of Listening: Cassette-Sermon Audition in Contemporary Egypt." *American Ethnologist* 28, no. 3: 623–49.

Howell, Signe. 1997. *The Ethnography of Moralities*. London: Routledge.

Johnson, Juliet, Marietta Stepaniants, and Benjamin Forest. 2005. *Religion and Identity in Modern Russia: The Revival of Orthodoxy and Islam*. Burlington, VT: Ashgate.

Kharkhordin, Oleg. 1999. *The Collective and the Individual in Russia*. Berkeley, CA: University of California Press.

Kon, Igor S. 1996. "Moral Culture." In *Russian Culture at the Crossroads: Paradoxes of Postcommunist Consciousness*, ed. Dmitri N. Shalin. Boulder, CO: Westview Press.

Laidlaw, James. 2002. "For an Anthropology of Ethics and Freedom." *Journal of the Royal Anthropological Institute* 8, no. 2: 311–32.

Lambek, Michael. 2000. "The Anthropology of Religion and the Quarrel between Poetry and Philosophy." *Current Anthropology* 41, no. 3: 309–20.

Mahmood, Saba. 2005. *Politics of Piety: The Islamic Revival and the Feminist Subject*. Princeton, NJ: Princeton University Press.

Mauss, Marcel. 1973. "Techniques of the Body." *Economy and Society* 2: 70–88.

Pankhurst, Jerry G. 1996. "Religious Culture." In *Russian Culture at the Crossroads*, ed. Dmitri N. Shalin. Boulder, CO: Westview Press.

Parish, Steven M. 1991. "The Sacred Mind: Newar Cultural Representations of Mental Life and the Production of Moral Consciousness." *Ethos* 19, no. 3: 313–51.

———. 1994. *Moral Knowing in a Hindu Sacred City: An Exploration of Mind, Emotion, and Self.* New York: Columbia University Press.

Pelkmans, Mathijs. 2009. *Conversion after Socialism: Disruptions, Modernisms and Technologies of Faith in the Former Soviet Union.* Oxford: Berghahn Books.

Pesmen, Dale. 2000. *Russia and Soul.* Ithaca, NY: Cornell University Press.

Rasanayagam, Johan. 2006. "Healing with Spirits and the Formation of Muslim Personhood in Post-Soviet Uzbekistan." *Journal of the Royal Anthropological Institute* 12, no. 2: 377–93.

Ries, Nancy. 1997. *Russian Talk: Culture and Conversation during Perestroika.* Ithaca, NY: Cornell University Press.

Rivkin-Fish, Michele. 2004. "'Change Yourself and the Whole World Will Become Kinder': Russian Activists for Reproductive Health and the Limits of Claims Making for Women." *Medical Anthropology Quarterly* 18, no. 3: 281–304.

Robbins, Joel. 2004. *Becoming Sinners: Christianity and Moral Torment in a Papua New Guinea Society.* Berkeley, CA: University of California Press.

———. 2007. "Between Reproduction and Freedom: Morality, Value, and Radical Cultural Change." *Ethnos* 72, no. 3: 293–314.

Rogers, Douglas. 2004. *An Ethics of Transformation: Work, Prayer, and Moral Practice in the Russian Urals, 1861–2001.* Doctoral dissertation, Department of Anthropology, University of Michigan.

———. 2008. "Old Belief between 'Society' and 'Culture': Remaking Moral Communities and Inequalities on a Former State Farm." In *Religion, Morality, and Community in Post-Soviet Societies,* ed. Mark D. Steinberg and Catherine Wanner. Washington, D.C.: Woodrow Wilson Center Press.

———. 2009. *The Old Faith and the Russian Land: A Historical Ethnography of Ethics in the Urals.* Ithaca, NY: Cornell University Press.

Russian Orthodox Church. 2000. *Osnovy Sotsial'noi Kontseptsii Russkoi Pravoslavnoi Tserkvi.* Moskva.

———. 2005. *Kontseptsii Uchastiia Russkoi Pravoslavnoi Tserkvi v Bor'be s Rasprostraneniem VICH/SPIDa I Rabote s Liud'mi, Zhivushimi s VICH/SPIDom.* Moskva.

———. 2008. *Osnovy ucheniya Russkoi Pravoslavnoi Tserkvi o dostoinstve, svobode I pravakh cheloveka.* www.mospat.ru (accessed 12 February 2009).

Steinberg, Mark D., and Catherine Wanner. 2008. *Religion, Morality, and Community in Post-Soviet Societies.* Washington, D.C.: Woodrow Wilson Center Press.

Voloshinov, V. N. 2000. *Marxism and the Philosophy of Language.* Cambridge, MA: Harvard University Press.

Wanner, Catherine. 2007. *Communities of the Converted: Ukrainians and Global Evangelism.* Ithaca, NY: Cornell University Press.

Widlok, Thomas. 2004. "Sharing by Default?: Outline of an Anthropology of Virtue." *Anthropological Theory* 4, no. 1: 53–70.

Zigon, Jarrett. 2007. "Moral Breakdown and the Ethical Demand: A Theoretical Framework for an Anthropology of Moralities." *Anthropological Theory* 7, no. 2: 131–50.

———. 2008a. "Aleksandra Vladimirovna: Moral Narratives of a Russian Orthodox Woman." In *Religion, Morality, and Community in Post-Soviet Societies,* ed. Mark

D. Steinberg and Catherine Wanner. Washington, D.C.: Woodrow Wilson Center Press.

———. 2008b. *Morality: An Anthropological Perspective.* Oxford: Berg.

———. 2009. "Morality Within a Range of Possibilities: A Dialogue with Joel Robbins." *Ethnos* 74, no. 2: 251–76.

———. 2010. *Making the New Post-Soviet Person: Moral Experience in Contemporary Moscow.* Leiden: Brill Publishers.

———. 2011. *"HIV Is God's Blessing": Rehabilitating Morality in Neoliberal Russia.* Berkeley, CA: University of California Press.

 CHAPTER 2

Exploring Russian Religiosity as a Source of Morality Today

Alexander Agadjanian

When the Communist Party writers created the "Moral Code of the Build-ers of Communism," which became a part of the new party program ad-opted in 1961, it contained some unmistakable religious connotations. The creation of the "code" coincided with a harsh new wave of the Soviet anti-religious campaign. However, the "moral code" could not help not refer-ring, if only latently or mutely, to what it attempted to replace: religious morality. Whatever the design of the writers was, the communist "moral code" seemed to be *both* rejecting and retaining some religious meanings.

There were twelve points in this communist "moral code," not ten as in the Decalogue, yet the number twelve had, perhaps, its own symbolism. The text included at least one direct biblical citation, "He who does not work, will not eat" (from Paul's 2 Thessalonians 3:10: "If any would not work, neither should he eat"). Also, the short text of the code referred three times to the notion of brotherhood, with especially striking religious over-tones in article 6: "Everyone is a friend, comrade and brother to another man," and an appeal to universal brotherhood "with the working people of all countries and with all nations." The text emphasized strong family values (article 8), collectivism and mutual help (article 5), connoting an old Orthodox discourse of *sobornost'* or "togetherness," and it repeated the pious formulae of "honesty and truthfulness, moral purity, simplicity and modesty in public and personal life" (article 7). To be sure, the code also introduced some hard-core communist values such as "allegiance to the communist cause, the socialist Motherland and the socialist countries" (article 1). The militant formulae of intolerance, however ("intolerance" is repeated four times as *neterpimost'* or *neprimirimost'*), also encompassed some values with explicitly religious meanings, both positive or negative, such as justice, honesty, and greediness.

Thus, the ethos of an ideal "builder of communism" was consonant with the popular ethos of Eastern Christianity (or, indeed, of Christianity as such). I will omit here possible speculations about the affinity between the communist and Christian teachings as such. What is clear, however, is the sociological reality that this unusual consonance reflected a persistence of traditional values in the Soviet Union in spite of a few waves of dramatic modernization of people's social and personal lives, as well as direct anti-religious campaigns. Late Soviet society from the 1960s to the 1980s was largely (although not entirely) isolated from the cultural turbulence that occurred in the West during the same period. Therefore the Soviet moral system was much more traditional and conservative: it had substantially fewer opportunities for individual expression and permissiveness, a stronger collectivist emphasis and regulation, restrained sexual freedom, and an emphasis on family-oriented values and behavior. To be sure, at the apex of the entire system was the controlling and overseeing censorship of the State, which created what is well-known as a "double morality" along the lines of the public/private divide. Yet, I believe, there was a degree of congruence between officially promoted public values (such as the "moral code"), and those that were privately held.

As religion was largely not practiced in those times, this moral system might be seen, to some extent, as quasi-religious, or as a shadow of deeply persisting religious meanings—in a way, a shadow without an object. The "object"—real religious practice—started, however, to grow (or revive), latently and slowly, in the late Soviet era.

Then, after the turnover of the late 1980s, a twofold process took place. On one hand, there was a massive and rapid restoration of the institutional and social base for those types of morality we can call religious, particularly those related to Russian Orthodox values; on the other hand, there was an abrupt and precipitous opening of former Soviet lands (and psyches) to all kinds of other moralities, to moral pluralism, moral relativism, moral indifference or even cynicism, of openly immoral, "rugged individualism," and egocentric, success-oriented strategies. All of these modes of morality came either directly from the West, where similar challenges had been lived through a generation before, or they revealed much earlier and deeper secrets kept through the intricacies of Soviet "double morality," or switching between private and publicly prescribed moral judgments.

What we then saw in Russian society of the 1990s—and what the chapters of this book illustrate—was a new and previously unheard of diversity of moral strategies. Among these competing strategies, the growth (or re-growth) of *religious* morality became ubiquitous. Religion now became a direct, unhampered source of morality. It would be a gross exaggeration to say that in today's Russia religion *defines* the popular ethos; however, it is unquestionably a major factor not only for those who regularly practice and observe religion, but it is also an important and esteemed reference point for a massive part of the non-religious population. In Russia there is presently a "pro-Orthodox consensus"—a tacit or open assumption that

Russian Orthodoxy is a major part of the national identity and cultural idiom (Furman and Kaariainen 2007: 20ff.). Russian Orthodoxy is, in this sense, a "vicarious religion" which serves as a reference for all,[1] although we can certainly find similar morality quests in other major religions such as local Islam or Buddhism (see, for example, the chapter by Ieva Raubisko, this volume).

The Nature of "Religious Return": A Careful Look at Continuities and Breaks

It is unnecessary to refer here to the well-known and impressive statistics on the growth of religion in Russia since the end of the 1980s. What is more important is to be aware of the nature of this growth. The fundamental issue is whether this religious growth is a *return* to old models, an *invention* of new ones, or a combination of both? To put it differently, should we emphasize the *breaks* in religious tradition brought about in the last century, or should we emphasize *continuity*, and if so, what kind of continuity? These questions are at the very core of understanding today's religious practices in Russia.

The growth in the dominant religion, Eastern Orthodoxy, has been interpreted among clergy and regular believers as a "restoration" of an earlier model, particularly the pre-revolutionary nineteenth and early twentieth century "imperial" (or "Synodal") model of Orthodoxy. For many, this growth has been perceived as a Big Return, a decisive denial of the Soviet era which is treated as a dark and ready-to-be-forgotten interregnum.

The agenda of the Big Return was, of course, impossible to fully realise for several reasons. First, post-Soviet society was very different from the late imperial society; second, any direct official establishment of the Eastern Orthodox Church has become unreal and even unwanted; third, church piety and church life of the nineteenth century were quite different from how people presently think about them; and fourth, understanding the Soviet period that shaped the present state of affairs is essential to understanding the present. Let me stress this last point: When studying various manifestations of recent religious growth in Russia and its moral dimensions, the authors of this book have come across surprising affinities between religious and Soviet moral codes. This affinity is clear in Agata Ładykowska's account of moral discourses in education; in Kathy Rousselet's study of the moral and cultural preferences of Saint Tsar's devotees; in Alexander Panchenko's discovery of the Soviet moral idioms in the discourse of a New Religious Movement (the Church of the Last Testament); and in other cases.

The direct legacy of the Soviet ethos (which was obviously not completely uniform), as well as the latent religious content of some Soviet moral discourses, show that the breaks in the history of religion (and in the history of morality) in Russia have never been as definitive as they might be seen by today's cultural reconstructionists of what are considered "old and pure" Orthodox models. The surprising continuity between Soviet and present-day religious moralities is something the chapters of this volume have detected and that students of Russian religiosity need to explore further.

But can this moral continuity extend even further back in time? Is it possible that this moral flow leaked through the Soviet period, with possible metamorphoses, from pre-revolutionary Russia? It is mistaken to deny the effects of Soviet breaks: The very illusion of the Big Return has been caused by the lack of a free flow of religious culture through the seventy-year Soviet period. If there is an implicit continuity of some elements (like the conservative ethos I referred to earlier), there was also a blatant lack of elementary religious knowledge during the Soviet period, to say nothing about the lack of systematic religious education. It is this deep religious amnesia that has finally led to the present reconstruction or reification projects (and these projects are not confined to Russian Orthodoxy[2]).

However, acknowledging the deep amnesia and a hasty bricolage of the post-Soviet religious landscape, we should be careful not to miss some trends and characteristics of the *longue durée* which have certainly persisted, mutatis mutandis, over the century and, indeed, through a much longer period.

Overall, our strategy in assessing the dynamics of Russian religiosity in the early twenty-first century should follow a careful, balanced view of the continuities and breaks of the three main periods—pre-revolutionary, Soviet, and post-Soviet—thus more deeply historicizing the issue being analysed, for only such a complex framing can furnish us with appropriate explanations. The authors of this volume have invariably been aware of this complexity.

Two Complex Examples from Russian Orthodoxy History

In what follows I would like to illustrate this idea of a complex relationship between breaks and continuity, and among the influences (or legacies) coming from the three major periods listed above—in other words, the idea of a multi-layered process of historical causation. These two examples come from Russian Orthodox religious life only, but parallels with other religions could be made. I chose only two examples but certainly much more could be explored. Both my examples are closely connected to the production and legitimization of moralities. One deals with the issue of spiritual guidance within Orthodox tradition, and the second, with the issue of Church belonging or Church identity of individual believers.

My first example is the relationship of two types of authority, in line with well-known Weberian typology (1958): traditional priestly authority based on apostolic succession, that can be confronted with the charismatic authority possessed by the *startsy* (elders) (this quality may be also applied to some exceptional regular priests). Although some of the *startsys* are widely recognized and make up part of the monastic and liturgical tradition, others are accused by the Church of being *mladostartsys* ("young elders," sometimes, *lzhestartsys*, "false elders") who abuse their priestly power, introducing a strong authoritarian control over their flock's behavior and life decisions, especially in matters of marriage and sexuality; the Synod of the Church responded to this phenomenon with a particularly harsh condemnation in December 1998 (see Synod 1999). These charismatic persons create a strong community of highly devoted and dependant followers with a trend of operating as a sect in a Troeltschian sense (see Troeltsch 1960).

This model of split religious authority may remind us of phenomena we encounter in many early twenty-first century religions: from Islamist groups (for example, the Wahhabi) to Pentecostal Charismatics to some New Religious Movements; we can certainly draw a typological link between all these phenomena as bearers of a specific form of revivalism based on authoritarian leadership. Is the impact of this global charismatic effervescence visible in Russia today? Russia has certainly been exposed to such influences since the late 1980s, and non-Orthodox analogies certainly exist in the Russian religious landscape (for example, in the already mentioned Church of the New Testament [*Tserkov' poslednego zaveta*] or the Center of the Mother of God [*Bogorodichnyi tsentr*]). I think we can speak of an existing link or parallelism between the Russian and international examples.

However, the global impact (or parallel development) of charismatic religious authoritarianism seems to be only a part of the story in explaining the Orthodox phenomenon we are talking about. When we historicize the phenomenon and include the influence of the Soviet period, we can see the rise of charismatic authority as a compensatory response to the crisis of the *institutional* religious authority during the Soviet period. We know the crucial importance of elders, both male and (sometimes even more) female, in keeping religious tradition, otherwise cut off or oppressed, alive in the popular, folk religion of the Soviet times. The radicalism and the conservative rhetoric and practices found among both the priests and the flock of the post-Soviet era can be attributed to the radical fundamentalism of neophyte religiosity, opposed to the inertness and sluggishness of church institutions. In a way, this phenomenon of *mladostartsy* may be seen as a psychological syndrome of the *homo soveticus.*

Although these explanations add to the thickness of our understanding, they are still not sufficient. Our next step is to place the phenomenon of the importance of religious elders into a broader context of the Eastern Orthodox tradition and the very basic mechanisms of how this tradition operates. I do not mean the elders of the mid-nineteenth century Russia, who were immortalized by Dostoyevsky and Tolstoy and whom people frequently refer to now as part of the "reconstruction" project. Rather, I mean the fundamental pattern of spiritual guidance *(dukhovnichestvo),* which generates a circle, a network of intense relationships between "spiritual children" *(dukhovnye chada)* and the "spiritual father" *(dukhovnik).* This pattern, nourished by some of the fundamental images and symbols of the Christian tradition in general, took on a special form and importance in the Russian Orthodox tradition. It was, perhaps, one of the main focuses of the Orthodox life, along with the veneration of icons, popular saints and sacred objects. This relationship of "father and children" still remains a normal, ubiquitous pattern in today's Church, and is based upon guidance or obedience *(poslushanie),* linked to confession and penitence *(pokaianie)* and approval or disapproval (giving or not giving a blessing, *blagoslovenie*), and can be more or less unquestioning (and thus authoritarian). This guidance mechanism directly affects the moral choices of individual worshippers and creates a religious space within the practical ethos of those more or less involved with religion.

The *mladostartsys* we started with are but an extreme form of this broader pattern of religious guidance creating a paternal relationship, an extreme which may have been officially denounced by the Church, but one that is a part of a broader pattern integral to Church practices. Thus, through the process of historicizing, we can see the conflation of various sources of a particular phenomenon, related to various periods of religious history.

The second example of the multi-layered process of historical causation is the discourse about the borders of the Church. There is a permanent discussion about the criteria for being a Russian Orthodox believer (similar debates, within a different content, may be found in Russia's Islam, Judaism, or other faiths). Such a sense of belonging is an important reference point in defining a specific moral behavior. Yet, there are a large variety of interpretations of what this belonging means in practice.

The term for "belonging" that has the widest content would simply be "Orthodox" (*pravoslavnyi*), which is sometimes a synonym for cultural or even national self-identity for many Russians. The term Orthodox is used to add a spiritual or moral dimension to a more neutral or value-free ethnonym or a "cold" reference to a person's citizenship. However, being Orthodox has a very loose connection with religious observance, and very little requirement for it (unless the word is used inside the Church in a more narrow sense).

The next word—"believer" (*veruiushchii*)—is a generic and common word which may or may not imply regular observance. It still bears a sense of belonging to an isolated minority, a sense inherited from Soviet times. It is usually used in secular and mass-media contexts (again, unless it is used within the Church in a narrower sense).

However, clergy and laity prefer the term "churchliness" (*tserkovnost'* or *votserkovlennost'*) as the main indicator of Orthodox religiosity, as it implies belonging to the institution. Yet belonging to the Church may be many things: It may be interpreted as being a part of the mystical body of Christ, or as a membership in a bureaucratically structured corporation (what the Church certainly is). It may include regular participation in confession and communion, icon worship, or practices of holy water consecration (*vodosviatie*); pilgrimage to relics of the saints; apotropaic prayers and magic; worship of springs or stone traces; or, finally, any combination of the above. There is a nebulous array of Church practices beyond the Church norms and canons.

This leads to a flourishing casuistry that integrates various non-canonical or not-quite-canonical practices into what is supposed to be the Church tradition, without labeling them as deviations. The more inclusive term "canonical space" (instead of "canon") can be used to describe these practices, and some would distinguish two levels of interpretation of Church norms: rules versus customs.[3] Another device to interpret and justify normative fuzziness of the notion of "churchliness" is through the canonical concept of "church economy" (οικονομια —*oikonomia*), or pastoral handling of Church matters based on a certain leniency with regards to disciplinary requirements. Yet another argument to explain (and justify) such fuzziness would be the acceptance of what is called "elements of traditional popular churchliness" (in those matters where the canons are silent); or even tolerating some "admissible prejudices" (*sueveria*) such as elements of magic or belief in spirits (Kozlov 2006: 262). Even straightforwardly anti-canonical practices (like astrology) can be construed as "ordinary sins frequently committed by the average Orthodox" or "human weaknesses" which are the result of bad influences, such as the mass media (Chesnokova 2005: 11) .

The flexibility in the terms for religious belonging contradicts the usual view of the Russian Orthodox Church as a huge monolithic institution (even though the current Patriarchy headed by Kirill certainly expects the Church to be evolving in this direction). How does one explain this flexibility? First, we can think of some late-modern trends such as the general crisis of belonging, which makes religion a volatile, self-made patchwork concept far from any normative consistency; the crisis of traditional religious institutions (everywhere, and not just in Russia); dogmatic and behavioral eclecticism; and the postmodern, patchwork style of mass media information (see Lambert 2000: 87–116; Roof 1999). However, once again we need to look for a Soviet trace. The diffuse nature of today's practices may be attributed to the specific effects of the transmission of religious knowledge and religious authority in Soviet Russia: the exceptional role of the semi-underground folk religiosity, its non-priestly keepers, and its non-institutional and informal structure.

The said interpretative devices explaining the flexibility of Church belonging, often elaborated *within* Church tradition, are quite helpful; however, to give our understanding of religious belonging greater historical depth, these late-modern and Soviet explanations seem to be insufficient. Historical evidence shows that this picture of normative flexibility has deeper roots and is inherent to the Russian Orthodox tradition (in contrast, for example, to the Roman Catholic Church). In the historical records all the way through nineteenth and early twentieth centuries we find a similar fuzziness in the application of the canons, in the definition of churchliness and of orthodoxy as such, and a similar acceptance of some practices that cannot be directly supported by canonical rules (see Kivelson and Greene 2003). We should recognize this inclusiveness as a particular ethos of the Eastern Orthodox tradition that has continued over generations and historical periods (perhaps indirectly impacted by the fact that the Church has long been dependent on temporal authorities).

The relative vagueness of normative borders in the Russian Orthodox Church is something which leads to the loosening of relations of authority and affects the definitions of what is considered right and wrong within the tradition. This has the effect of further loosening the epistemological, aesthetic and, not least, ethical code of Church adherents, something we need to always keep in mind when speaking of the religious sources of morality in today's Russia.

* * *

Similar examples of historical and semantic deconstruction may be numerous (and, once again, also found in other religions). There is continuity in the Eastern Orthodox ethos which partly defines the present situation and trends in religion and morality. Understanding such continuity is crucial, yet it is very different from the revivalist fantasies or mythological reifications based on the premise of essentialist Orthodoxy. As we have seen, a variety of factors old and new, external and internal, have made the present situation. Working with these multi-layered meanings gives us a more authentic and palpable perception of today's religiosity. This approach also gives us a key to explain the multiplicity of religious identities that presently exist within each denomination—a multiplicity that stems from the numerous sources of today's religious experience, in all their possible combinations. Based on such scrutiny, this volume provides a nuanced picture of how religious norms are interwoven into the moral zeitgeist of Russia today.

Notes

1. "Vicarious" is the term used by Grace Davie in reference to the Church of England (see Davie 2007).
2. Compare with Shtrykov's account (2008) of the religious revival in North Ossetia.
3. See an interesting discussion in Kozlov 2006: 256ff.

References

Chesnokova, Valentina. 2005. *Tesnym putiem: protsess votserkovlenia naselenia Rossii v kontse XX veka* [Following a Narrow Path: The Process of Inchurchment of the Russian Population in the Late Twentieth Century]. Moscow: Akademicheskii proekt.

Davie, Grace. 2007. "Vicarious Religion: A Methodological Challenge." In *Everyday Religion: Observing Modern Religious Lives*, ed. Nancy Ammerman, 21–37. New York: Oxford University Press.

Furman, Dmitrii, and Kimmo Kaariainen. 2007. *Starye tserkvi, novye veruiushchie. Novye tserkvi, starye veruiushchie.* Moscow/St. Petersburg: Letnii Sad.

Holy Synod. 1999. *"Opredelenie Svyashchennovo Sinoda ob uchastivshikhsia v poslednee vremia sluchaiakh zloupotrebleniia nekotorymi pastyriami vverennoi im ot Boga vlast'iu viazat' i reshit'"* [Ruling of the Holy Synod about Frequent Recent Cases of Abuse by Some Priests of the God-given Authority of Binding and Loosing]. *Zhurnal Moskovskoi Patriarkhii* 1.

Kivelson, Valerie, and Robert Greene. 2003. *Orthodox Russia: Belief and Practice Under the Tsars.* University Park, PA: Pennsylvania State University Press.

Kozlov, Father Maxim. 2006. *Klir I mir: kniga o zhizni sovremennogo prikhoda.* Moscow: Khram Sv. Muchenitsy Tatiany.

Lambert, Yves. 2000. "Religion, Modernite, Ultramodernite: Une Analyse en Termes de 'Tournant Axial.'" *Archives de Sciences Sociales de Religion* 109: 87–116.

Roof, Wade Clark. 1999. *Spiritual Marketplace: Baby Boomers and the Remaking of American Religion.* Princeton, NJ: Princeton University Press.

Shtyrkov, Sergey. 2008. "Constructing an Ossetian Ethnic Religion: Ethics of Ethnicity." Unpublished paper presented at Conference on Multiple Moralities: Globalization and Religion in Contemporary Russia, Max Planck Institute for Social Anthropology, Halle/Saale, Germany (September).

Troetsch, Ernst. 1960. *The Social Teaching of the Christian Churches.* New York: Harper.

Weber, Max. 1958. "The Three Types of Legitimate Rule." *Berkeley Publications in Society and Institutions* 4, no. 1: 1–11.

PART II
Multiple Moralities

 CHAPTER 3

Post-Soviet Orthodoxy in the Making
Strategies for Continuity Thinking among Russian Middle-aged School Teachers

Agata Ładykowska

> The Russian language is very much about terms or notions.
> And in general—before you start talking about something—
> you have to reach an agreement on the terms you are using.
> Because people here call one thing this, another that. In order
> to avoid dissonance, rift, in order to understand each other
> correctly. It is when we talk about terminology.
> —Irina (30, school teacher)

The aim of this chapter is to illustrate how different local notions of morality are used in order to build a sense of continuity among the middle-aged school teachers with whom I did research, and who have experienced both socio-political and individual ruptures and transformations. One such transformation is conversion to Orthodoxy. Continuity and change have a specific articulation in post-Soviet and post-atheist Russia, which is undergoing what is described as "a religious revival" over the past two decades. The prominent feature of this articulation is the Church's emphasis on, and people's subjective view of, an encompassing continuity straddling the period of transformation (cf. Benovska-Sabkova et al. 2010). By focusing on how notions of morality are being conceived of and utilized, I intend to illustrate how middle-aged teachers, who were formerly actively engaged in the Soviet system of atheist education but are currently equally actively involved in the religious education of young people, construct their identity and legitimacy. Anthropological investigations of how continuity and change are interconnected in emic understandings can help to illuminate how post-Soviet Russians build their religious commitment and their identity as Orthodox Christians. Examples provided in this chapter, and the emic perspective on conceptions of morality emerging from these examples, correspond with and supplement Jarrett Zigon's theory of moral breakdown (2009).

The central role of education in the grand Soviet project of creating a new society and a "new man" has been described well in the field of history, especially for the Stalinist period. Equally well-known is the role of teachers and schools in the process of forming so-called Soviet morality, implemented partly by means of a special pedagogical approach: *vospitanie* (which can be roughly translated as "moral education" or "social upbringing"). However, there is little ethnographic data on contemporary Russian schooling or the professional practice and private life of teachers, especially those currently engaged in teaching religion; many of these teachers' professional biographies are rooted in the Soviet context, where they were officially required to educate pupils in the spirit of communist atheism. The so-called post-Soviet period has been marked (among other things) by a great change in religious practices as massive number of Russians have converted to Orthodoxy.[1] This change has resulted in the introduction of religiously oriented study into some public schools, a move which is still much debated across society.

This chapter draws on twelve months of fieldwork conducted in Rostov-on-Don, Russia, which aimed at exploring the ideas and practices connected to religious education (both in religious and secular contexts) in contemporary Russia. The research concerned the ways in which post-socialist transitions have involved the endurance and reproduction of Soviet ideologies and discourses pertaining to morality, or, as it is sometimes discussed, the ways in which people recycle skills and habits for contexts in which they were not intended (Luehrmann 2005). The aim of this chapter, however, is to investigate the problematic terminology surrounding the moralities and moral discourses I encountered during my research—terminology which provides an entry into the issue of moral and religious education and the practices of forming the moral self, as applied by Russian teachers.

An "Orthodox Atheist"?

My main concern at the beginning of my research was the question of how people think it is possible that teachers with Soviet training can now teach religious subjects. When the idea of introducing religious subjects in schools emerged, it was thought that the most suitable people for doing this kind of job were the priests. However, the constitutional separation of state and church, supported by voices from the secular part of Russian society, made this role for priests officially impossible. A compromise was reached: Religiously-oriented school subjects as taught in courses such as "Foundations of the Orthodox Culture" (*Osnovy pravoslavnoi kul'tury*, or *OPK*) may appear in secular schools, but they should be taught by experienced, secular teachers. The church wanted the subject to at least be taught by religious people, but this did not always occur.

Larisa Ivanovna (age 46)[2] was one of the first such teachers I met in Rostov, in the early autumn of 2006. She was held in high esteem for being an excellent teacher with a long professional career. Several years earlier she had become an Orthodox believer, and since then she had pursued her own religious education at a theological university. As the school assistant head (*zavuch—zaveduiushchii uchebnoi chast'iu*) she was responsible for the introduction and promotion of the course "Foundations of the Orthodox Culture" among both children and teachers. Her biography was exemplary for the research project I have outlined, and, as I discovered over the course of my fieldwork, she was representative of many teachers of her generation. Recent converts—often former Party or Komsomol[3] activists—are usually engaged in a process of self-education through reading religious literature or attending religious courses at any available level of education, including the elite option of theological university. Such converts are also usually involved in spreading the gospel to younger generations, a process motivated by feeling the necessity of bringing future citizens to Orthodox teachings.

During our first conversation, which was casual and did not go into much depth, I asked Larisa Ivanovna how it was possible that teachers with a Soviet or atheist background were engaged in teaching the OPK. She answered that "the most important thing is that these people should be *nravstvennye*"[4] (*Glavnoe, chtoby eto byli nravstvennye liudi*). This answer did not help me at the time—especially after looking up the word she used in the dictionary. Russian-English dictionaries offered one interpretation: "moral." As we had many occasions to talk during our frequent meetings and as we got to know each other better, I later asked Larisa Ivanovna to explain what she meant by *nravstvennye,* but she replied that "these teachers should be simply good people who love children"—an answer which did not help much either. When asked if there was some difference between *moral'nyi* (moral) and *nravstvennyi,* she repeatedly confirmed the dictionaries' definition by saying that "these are synonyms, and they mean the same thing."

Indeed, these two Russian terms—*moral'nyi* and *nravstvennyi*—are commonly used when one is speaking of morality, moral behavior, moral precepts, and values. According to the Russian to non-Russian dictionaries (primarily those translating to English, but not exclusively) both words have the same meaning. Similarly in experience of many Russians of all backgrounds, including the intelligentsia, who insist that the two words should be treated as synonyms. However, one quickly finds that the word *moral'nyi* is more frequently used in reference to phenomena of Soviet times, such as *Moral'nyi kodeks stroitelia kommunizma* (The Moral Code of the Builder of Communism), and the word *nravstvennyi* always appears when one is talking about Orthodoxy. This suggests that these two terms can stand for secular and religious conceptions of morality. However, such a conclusion would be misleading, as the term *nravstvennost'* is not exclusively reserved for religious discourse. Moreover, the word *nravstvennyi* is also used by non-believers and in secular contexts, such as the "spiritual-moral education"—*dukhovno-nravstvennoe vospitanie*—which was explained to me by a representative of a local division of Ministry of Education as the strictly secular form of spiritual development of the individual (such *vospitanie* involves, in her words, visiting theaters and museums, playing chess, developing an interest in ecology, playing sports, and "strengthening the spirit" by focusing one's attention on care for one's hygiene and the avoidance of slovenliness).[5]

All this was not very useful for understanding Larisa Ivanovna's answer, which, with help of the dictionary and the explanation she later provided, I could translate to myself as: "There is nothing unusual and suspicious about the fact that people who used to actively subscribe to one morality are now equally active in engaging with a seemingly opposite morality, as long as they are moral."

The ambiguity of these terms, which I will try to trace and unpack in the next few sections, is crucial to the point I am making in this chapter. My argument is that it is exactly the ambiguity of the terms *moral'* and *nravstvennost'* which allows for a strategy of constructing a new moral person, while at the same time presenting the appearance of continuity on a moral trajectory. This usage also serves as an important means for legitimizing ex-Soviet teachers as moral authorities for teaching religion.

The statement made by Larisa Ivanovna suggests a sense of continuity expressed both in the narratives of individuals and in the rhetoric of the Russian Orthodox Church; this perspective on the continuity of Orthodoxy seems to be a general feature of the post-Perestroika attitudes to religion, which are otherwise in flux. There is a general discourse, reproduced by both believers and non-believers, that says Russia has always been Orthodox: "The Moral Code of the Builder of Communism is nothing else but a disguised Ten Commandments," I was told many times. The idea that the communist system was built on a religious pattern, and was actually a reversed form of religion, was a common conviction repeatedly articulated and illustrated with examples of communist rituals borrowing their form from Orthodox ones. Whenever people were asked about transformations, they pointed to the structural similarities between communism and Orthodoxy (and sometimes ideological similarities too, such as the frequently invoked values of sharing or justice) and used them as examples to support the idea of continuity between these two ideological systems in their lives.

Comparisons of the Soviet doctrine with religion, and an understanding of Bolshevism as a civil religion,[6] are common topics of debates among not only the Orthodox intelligentsia, but also among common believers reflecting upon their recently embraced faith.

Nravstvennost' and *Nrav:* The Individual and the Social Together

My initial concerns with exploring the realm of moral education in schools without a vocabulary I could rely on were only deepening.[7] Feeling not competent enough in Russian myself, I consulted my native-speaking Russian colleagues about the dual terms for morality. The most common explanation was that the variety of terms for morality is often a source of confusion in everyday usage, but it does not have any practical consequences. As such it is not only limited to the Russian language (in Russian there is the indigenous *nravstvennost'* and *moral',* and *etika* of Latin origin), but the confusion also exists in most Western languages (for example in English: "morality," "ethics," "etiquette"). For anyone without education in philosophy, or with only a basic knowledge of it, the terms morality and ethics seem to be synonyms and are often used interchangeably. This applies also to the Russian terms *moral'* and *nravstvennost',* understanding of which does not require any training in philosophy for the average Russian user. Moreover, in Russian, especially in the newspeak of the Soviet period, compound words are often used. *Etichesko-moral'nyi* ("ethical-moral") or *moral'no-nravstvennyi* ("moral-moral," if one follows the logic of the Russian-English dictionary) are frequently used phrases. It was suggested to me that as tautological expressions are a feature of various languages, such examples should not be investigated as having any distinct or different meanings.

The terms "ethics" and "morality" in English and most of the European languages (Russian *etika* and *moral'*) originally had the same meaning. "Ethics" has its origins in the ancient Greek word *ethos* (way of life, custom, habit), and "morality" comes from *mores* (pl. *mos*), which was simply the Latin translation of *ethos*. Both *ethos* and *mores* were translated into Russian as "*nrav(y), obychai, privychka, kharakter*" (Iaskevich and Mishatkina 2006: 10), which again more or less confirms the English understanding: custom and habit, but, interestingly—also adds character (or disposition). Thus, Russian authors explain ethics (*etika*) as a theory of *nravstvennost':* the Greek word *ethicos* means "referring to *nravy,*" so—*etika* literally means "the theory of *nravstvennost'*" (ibid.).

The root word for *nravstvennost'* (*nrav*) in turn has interesting connotations. Its primary meaning, according to the *Dictionary of the Russian Language* (*Tolkovyi slovar' russkogo iazyka*) (2003: 423), is "*kharakter*—

character, disposition, personality trait," which can be good or bad. However, in the second meaning *nrav(y)* relates to "custom, system of social life"
(*uklad obshchestvennoi zhizni*). This dual understanding is also confirmed
by the *Tolkovyi slovar'* of Vladimir Dal'—a famous dictionary of the Russian
language compiled by one of the greatest Russian linguists and ethnogra-
phers of the nineteenth century. Dal' defines *nrav* as "an expression of the
features of an individual," a character or disposition, which can be both in-
born and learnt or developed (*vyrabotannyi*). At the same time *nrav* is also
a "feature of the entire nation, population, tribe, not depending on each
individual, but conditionally accepted; ways of life, customs, habits" (Dal'
[1880] 2004: 464).[8] Dal''s account is also interesting because the examples
he uses allow the reader to track the meaning of terms in his contemporary
usage as well as the more distant past.[9]

The double meaning of *nrav* that Dal' describes—as encompassing both
the individual and the social—seems to be essential for understanding Russian notions of morality. In what follows I will provide examples of how the
entanglement of the individual and the social that *nravstennost'* encompasses is conceived of, and what it entails for the problem of continuity
thinking among teachers of different generations.

Morality from the Perspective of Orthodox Teachers of the Late Soviet and the Post-Soviet Generations

I avoided asking such questions such as "What is morality?" or "What is
moral behavior?" during my fieldwork. Nevertheless, talking about moral
upbringing, especially in the religious context, inevitably leads to issues
related to morality, proper and improper behavior, techniques of moral
education, and values. Unexpectedly, it was my informants who urged
me—a non-native speaker—to be aware of the differences between the
two terms *moral'nyi* and *nravstvennyi*. Their urging and their explanations
gave me some help in understanding Larisa Ivanovna's confusing answer,
in which she mentioned *nravstvennost'* and *moral'*—terms she claimed to
be synonyms.

Irina (who is quoted in the epigraph of this chapter) had just turned 30
when I met her. She was a very religious person, modest and shy, but she
was enjoying talking to people, which probably helped her to grow fond of
the teaching she did both in the state school and in the Orthodox Sunday
school. She lived with her mother, also a teacher, a recent convert in her
50s. Baptized at the age of 14, Irina developed an increasing interest in
Orthodoxy which resulted in continuous religious self-education. As Irina's
experience of post-atheist transformations was indirect, her life history is

strikingly different from that of her mother's and of Larisa Ivanovna's generation (but at the same time her religious experience also differs significantly from that of her Sunday school pupils, who were baptized in early childhood). Irina also had a different understanding of the relationships between *moral'* and *nravstvennost'* than the older generation had, as the following conversation illustrates:

> Irina: And well, they say, "Nobody is born a Christian; one has to become a Christian" (*khristianinom ne rozhdaiutsia a stanoviatsia*). This seed is not in everybody; I think that only some people have it. And then, if this seed grows. … But I think it is impossible for everyone. I think it is only with some people. There is even a parable in the Bible—I can't remember where now. And then there is *moral'* and *nravstvennost'* …
>
> Agata: Could you say more about this seed? Does it mean that Christian morality does not depend on a person, at all?
>
> Irina: No. Nobody is born as a Christian; one has to become a Christian. And this needs a lot of effort, a lot of work on oneself (*nado deistvitel'no rabotat' nad soboi*). And we can only suggest, that is, to sow this seed. And they will either adopt it or not. And then again there is a parable, that it is impossible to *vospitat'* [educate or socialize] someone. Never, if someone doesn't want to learn—the teacher is unable to do anything. Precisely the same goes for *vospitanie*. That is, the teacher can only [have an influence] outwardly, on the surface. Just like one of our teachers [says to the children], "You shouldn't swear and quarrel. You shouldn't spit." And this will happen [i.e., the child will not spit nor swear]. But then he will go out of the school and will do all that. This is precisely what I am talking about. Teachers can only show and tell, and how will they [the children] take it? Will he want to make effort, work on himself? This is another question. And this depends only on his will. And then *moral'* and *nravstvennost'*—these are different words in Russian; you are aware of it?
>
> Agata: Could you explain?
>
> Irina: *Moral':* It is the way of regulating the relationships between people, that is—this is a moral act, and that is an immoral act. There is a Constitution, and everything is prescribed there. How we should live. If we violate it then this is immoral (*amoral'no*). If one has been insulted then one goes to the court. In principle we have a right to do that. That is an immoral act. But, this is only on the surface; it is only an external coating, and what is inside,

what an individual is like inside—this is *nravstvennost'*. This is precisely the work on the self (*eto rabota imenno nad soboi*). This is *nravstvennost'*.

Agata: The one who is *moral'nyi*—is he *nravstvennyi* at the same time?

Irina: Well, here we have a little nuance, a small nuance. *Moral'*, well, of course, you can be *moral'nyi* in the inside and on the outside. That is, for example the child who behaves as good both in and out of the school. That is positive. He behaves positively. But, he can be *moral'nyi* in the school, but he leaves the school—and he is immoral (*amoral'nyi*).

Agata: I don't think I understand. Is he then *nravstvennyi* or *bez-nravstvennyi* [the opposite of *nravstvennyi*]?

Irina: One moment. *Moral'* is a way of regulating the relationships between people. And here everything is written—how to behave. And we all know how. And *nravstvennost'* is when one works on the self, alone.

Agata: Does not such person need the rules?

Irina: Such person knows [what is right] from the inside.

Agata: But the law regulates these relations on the basis of the punishment.

Irina: Yes, punishment.

Agata: And *nravstvennyi*?

Irina: Yes, a person who is *nravstvennyi* doesn't need this anymore, it has this way of regulation inside itself, and it wouldn't allow itself. It feels what is wrong or right, and it doesn't need to read all these laws. It doesn't have to be preached to about all these laws. And it feels itself, that it cannot do this.

Agata: Can an atheist be a *nravstvennyi* person?

Irina: A real atheist—not really (*iaryi, istinnyi ateist nemnozhko net*). No.

Agata: Why do you think so?

Irina: In the first place, because he rejects God.

Agata: Well, it rejects God but it probably would not kill?

Irina: All these laws and *moral'* exist precisely for all those communists. This is *moral'*. For all those who do not live according to Christian Commandments. For them there are laws. This is *moral'*—law.

I have presented this long excerpt from the interview with Irina in order to show how she arrived at the topic of morality. We had been talking about the idea of *vospitanie*, and her answer ("nobody is born a Christian; one has to become a Christian") was actually a response to my question, "Can the school influence *vospitanie*?" The quotation she uses is a very unusual one for an Orthodox believer to use, but, on the other hand, it is very telling of her and her mother's attitude to religious education and conversion. The quotation itself comes from the writings of Tertullian, an early Christian philosopher, long acknowledged to be a heretic. Tertullian is rather little-known, and his words[10] are seldom discussed in contemporary Orthodox writings (as his works are considered "not fully accurate" (cf. Afanas'ev 1993). Also for Irina, I suppose, the origin of the citation remains obscure. However, I hope that the few existing discussions available in popular literature may serve as auxiliary material for the discussion of continuities and discontinuities in belief among contemporary Orthodox believers. Unlike the main arguments of Tertullian's writings,[11] which are almost ignored, the historical context in which he lived is highlighted when discussing contemporary ruptures in Orthodox faith: The first Christians were exclusively converts (mostly Jewish). These converts were never born into Christian families, and, therefore, an act of conversion for them was necessarily reflexive and processual. Such an interpretation exists in the writings of an important contemporary cultural and philosophical author, Averintsev (2006: 650, 765), who makes an analogy between the first Christians and contemporary post-atheist Orthodox converts, arguing that both "fiunt christiani." Similarly, 30-year-old Irina, a convert who chose to be baptized, just like the converts of her mother's generation, is reproducing the model of reflexive self-education as part of the act of becoming a good Christian. Irina's concern with developing children's *nravstvennost'*, understood as necessary "work on the self," echoes her own work on the self, which comprises the self-educational practice of "becoming a Christian." The description of *nravstvennost'* she gives, especially given her biographical context, corresponds to Jarrett Zigon's theory of moral breakdown (2007). "Moral breakdowns"—the ethical dilemmas, difficult times and troubles, or a change in life in which people do on occasion find themselves—force one to move to a state of moral questioning, in Zigon's terms, "to step-away and figure out, work through and deal" with the new situation. It is the moral breakdown, "the ethical moment" according to Zigon, when ethics must be *performed*. Ethics, then, is a process, a tactic performed as a response in the moment of the breakdown of the ethical dilemma. Conceived in this way, ethics corresponds to Irina's understanding of *nravstvennost'* as work on the self, an effort that needs to be done in order to alter one's ways (2007: 137–38). Significantly, "becoming" a *nravstvennyi* person for her exclusively involves becoming a Christian: an atheist or communist cannot become *nravstvennyi*. It is in this understanding of *nravstvennost'* where Irina differs from the middle-aged teachers of Larisa Ivanovna's generation.

In the conversation quoted earlier, Irina reflected on the role of the teacher, the qualities that are internal to a person, and the possibilities for changing or developing them. I am guessing that she referred here to the Biblical parable of the Sower (Mark 4:1–20; Matt. 13:1–23; Luke 8:1–15), which is about "the sowing" and its different outcomes.[12] So the seed can fall on different grounds and the prerequisites for the growth of the seed comprise the combination of the favorable conditions for growth and the grounds together, and not just "the sower" (in the parable the teacher is of course Jesus). Moreover, not everyone is even given the seed ("This seed is not in everybody; I think that only some people have it").[13] By this she meant that school or a teacher has in fact little or no influence on moral upbringing: "It is impossible to educate or socialize [*vospitat'*] someone," she said. "Never, if someone doesn't want to learn, the teacher is unable to do anything. Precisely the same goes for *vospitanie*." Irina thinks of the school as of a micro-social world, guided by moral and social rules. But for her such moral upbringing takes place only "on the surface" of a child, who simply adjusts to the desired norms of conduct "for others," but after leaving the school becomes "himself" and shows his genuine, authentic *nravstvennost'* by choosing to do what he feels like he wants to do, and not what he was told to do (what he should do). Moral growth can be accomplished only by the children themselves. They can adopt and embody these social rules and make the choice to behave according to them, if they want to make the effort and work on themselves in order to become *nravstvennye* persons. *Moral'* in her explanation is the same as written or prescribed rules or laws ("the Constitution"), which are easy to follow, as following them does not require any effort from people. In situations of conflict and of the violation of a law, the rules are clear, as they are externally established and guaranteed by means of punishment. People then act not out of their own individual choice (reflectively and reflexively) to behave in the correct way, but because they want to avoid punishment. The effort for her is the individual work of learning how to make a choice to act according the requirements of high *nravstvennost'*. It is this work that is supposed to be done in the process of learning, as nobody is *born* a Christian, or *nravstvennyi*, person. The role of the teacher ("the mission of the teacher" as she expressed it) is "to sow," which for her means "to show and to tell" examples of a good life, and *to assist* the children, who *freely choose to make an effort* and in this way develop their (desirable) high *nravstvennost'*.

This understanding of *nravstvennost* is very much in line with Orthodox ideas about *vospitanie,* which draw on the Orthodox concept of the person. The Orthodox "anthropology" encompasses four key principles: (1) the presence of God's image in humans allowing for the human potential of God-likeness (*bogopodobie*); (2) human freedom; (3) human nature as contaminated by original sin; and (4) salvation as possible only through the collaboration of God's grace and human free decision (cf. Shmalii 2001; Skliarova 2003). Points (2) and (4) are crucial for understanding the Orthodox approach to socialization: the free will to decide—and to work on oneself—is a condition for a person's moral growth, a process in which the teacher plays only the role of an assistant or a partner. Such an approach—named the "pedagogy of collaboration" (*pedagogika sotrudnichestva*) or the "pedagogy of support" (*pedagogika podderzhki*)—is seen by the Orthodox pedagogical theorists as standing in sharp opposition to Soviet pedagogy. Marxist materialism laid the ground for a concept of the person as determined exclusively by biological and social factors. Such an approach allowed for developing ideas about *vospitanie* as a process which is fully controllable and predictable. The process of "fashioning" (*formirovanie*) became increasingly understood as a process of orienting the individual by influencing her *from the outside* (Skliarova 2003: 3). Such an approach, according to Irina, is often present among teachers. Founded on the belief that a person can be molded from the outside, from Irina's perspective it is incomplete or ineffective, as it is working only on the surface.

It may seem that the ambiguities of the relationship between *moral'* and *nravstvennost'* are not often acknowledged in everyday life. However, they become a topic of discussion in the classroom as well, which shows the increasing need of attending to the distinction among teachers. Maria Ivanovna, a teacher from the generation of middle-aged devoted Orthodox converts, reported on how she posed the intricacies of this relationship as a question to her pupils:

> Maria Ivanovna: I had classes with the children. I divided the group into halves: One was to describe a *moral'nyi* person and the other one a *nravstvennyi* person. Well, it was my point of view then [that there might be a difference]. And this was also the result of the exercise—children thought that *moral'* would be shown on the outside, and *nravstvennost'* on the inside.

> Agata: So *nravstvennost'* is not about following the rules?

Maria Ivanovna: No, one moment. I will give you an example that we discussed in the classroom. I am standing on the road. A *babushka* approaches; she is crossing the street. And next to us there is my pupil, right? He sees me standing here—he helps *babushka* to cross the street. Is his act good? Yes, good, *moral'nyi*. But what is inside of him? He says: The teacher will praise me. Well this is not good. *Nravstvennost'* has suffered damage in that moment. He didn't have enough of the good, *nravstvennoe* feeling. And *moral'*?—everything is according to the rules. *Nravstvennost'* is more rigid, more intimate. Well, but many treat these words as synonyms, especially in the Soviet time. Well, these are only my findings. Although *moral'*, *nravstvennost'*, *etika* seem all as synonyms, in principle. And also children, when they were trying to describe a *moral'nyi* and a *nravstvennyi* person, and then we were trying to understand the difference, and we arrived at the conclusion, that yes, [there is a difference]. *Moral'* is for others, and *nravstvennost'* is within one's own conscience.

The distinction between outer and inner that emerges from the interviews with Maria and Irina becomes more complicated when it is confronted with the explanation given by 21-year-old Yurii. Yurii's biography is unlike the Orthodox teachers, yet the example he gives is also very telling:

Yurii: I'll give you the example of my father, because I know him as a spiritual-*nravstvennyi* (*dukhvno-nravstvennyi*) man, because he knows that there are poor people, who are in need. It's an example, ok? That there are disabled people and nobody should laugh at them ...

Agata: Would such a person be called *nravstvennyi*?

Yurii: Well, look, we consider that this is spiritual-*nravstvennyi* (*dukhovno-nravstvennyi*) you see, when this comes from your soul. ... But he [the father] has his own belief. He'll never enter the Orthodox church, because he considers it *pokazushnichestvo* [a "cheap" demonstration, a "cheap" show]. ... And the difference between *moral'* and *nravstvennost'*? Of course there is [a difference]. It can be expressed in a phrase, for example: A monk is a *nravstvennyi* man, right? When you say this, it is true, right? And even spiritual-*nravstvennyi*—this is how it is. I—for example, have never allowed anyone to violate my freedom for the sake of religion, to impose some religious beliefs, right? This is *moral'no* [adverb]. But my spiritual *moral'* is totally different—a different aspect. This is a spiritual *moral'*. *Moral'* is about principles, right? And belief is already a set of totally different precepts.

Agata: Is *nravstvennyi* connected to religion, then?

Yurii: Well, I don't know what you have in mind. About Stalin we may say that he was ... (pause) ... *Beznravstvennyi* [opposite to *nravstvennyi*], but *moral'nyi*.

Agata: What do you mean?

Yurii: Of course, he was *moral'nyi*. He had his own morality. The *moral'* he had was great.

Agata: What kind of *moral'* did he have?

Yurii: Well, he would never allow snow to remain on the streets, or that there was any dirt. When the snow fell, he understood what has to be done. He had principles; he was a man of principles. And he never went against his principles. But, he was *nravstvennyi*. Well, in some cases he maybe wasn't *nravstvennyi*. Well, but he wasn't spiritual-*nravstvennyi* for example. Well, we cannot judge him, right? Perhaps he showed remorse?

I chose the fragments from conversations with Maria Ivanovna and Yurii, as they illustrate well the contradictions that arise when one tries to compare these two notions: An act can be at the same time *moral'nyi* and *beznravstvennyi*, depending on the internal motivations of those who perform it. They both seem to share the view that *moral'* can be equated with the rules.

The terms with which I deal here are *almost* synonyms, but at some point they are opposed. By contrasting them, my informants articulated that they could stand for two different concepts of morality. *Moral'*, "an external coating," is related to externally imposed or prescribed social norms, which is what Maria Ivanovna meant by saying that *moral'* is "for others." In contrast, *nravstvennost'* rests "inside" and is related to the conscience, to reflexivity, and to the conscious choices that people need to make. The first term refers to acting "on the surface", and the second refers to the personal sphere and is related to self-discipline and authenticity. This distinction is also visible in other narratives, not quoted here, that recalled the example of Pavlik Morozov. As the story has it, Pavlik Morozov, a young Pioneer, denounced his own father for trying to cheat the Soviet government by hoarding grain. Throughout the Soviet period Pavlik remained the exemplar of a virtuous Soviet child who put public interest above private and family loyalty (cf. Fitzpatrick 2005: 207). Pavlik's story was often presented to me as an example of someone being "*moral'nyi* and *beznravstven-*

nyi" at the same time, where "*moral'*" was referred to as "*obshchestvennaia moral'*," the "morality of society," opposed to *nravstvennost'*, which is "intimate morality." For an Orthodox person the more rigid *nravstvennost'* is opposed to *moral'*, as the latter is rule-based and therefore easy to follow. These two concepts can sometimes "*idti v razrez*": they can split, or diverge, and lead to a "double morality" (*dvoinaia moral'*). The fact that these two terms—which some claim to be synonyms—are sometimes opposed in a dichotomy between the social and the intimate clearly relates to the dual notion of *nrav*, understood as both habits and customs, as well as personal qualities and dispositions.

Moral' and *Nravstvennost'* in Contemporary Textbooks on Ethics

Student textbooks on ethics also make a distinction between the notions of *moral'* and *nravstvennost'*, although in a different manner. Here, *moral'* is treated as a "socially formed set of norms and principles, the system regulating people's consciousness and conduct given in a concrete society, also the relations between them (relations between individuals, groups of individuals, individual and society, etc.)" (Druzhinin and Demina 2005: 16). *Nravstvennost'* "primarily reflects the deep dispositions (*ustanovki*) in the consciousness of an individual, which include reflection and the intuitive-*nravstvennyi* world" (18). However, one's *nravstvennye* convictions may not overlap with the universally accepted *moral'*, and they may even be contradictory, the textbook explains. In such cases people must themselves control their acts and their thoughts with the help of their conscience, and the norms of *nravstvennost'* are followed without external control, voluntarily. In the view of Druzhinin and Demina, *nravstvennost'* cannot exist outside of personality. It is the *nravstvennyi* choice in which *nravstvennost'* and individual responsibility for each unique act is created. In the view of the authors, the terms *nravstvennost'* and *moral'* must be treated separately: that is why in giving characteristics of an individual it is necessary to describe either her *moral'nye* or *nravstvennye* qualities, for which the compound term *moral'no-nravstvennye* seems to fit best (ibid.).

According to another textbook (Iaskevich and Mishatkina 2006), *moral'* refers to the system of ideal notions of norms and principles of desirable conduct, while *nravstvennost'* is understood as a set of norms and principles which guide people's behavior in practice, "hence *moral'*—is related to what *ought to be* (*dolzhnoe*), and *nravstvennost'*—to what actually *is* practiced (*sushchee*)" (10). This definition meets Irina's understanding of these concepts: *moral'* is the domain of what is prescribed, and what should be, and *nravstvennost'* is the domain of authentic, genuine behavior, the fact.

This textbook uses interesting examples. Introducing the subject of ethics, the authors emphasize the constant reflective activity of moral consciousness. They explain:

> [Moral consciousness] often finds itself in a situation of crisis, when *moral'* loses its obviousness, and people cease to understand what is good and what is evil. This happens, for example, when different cultures or different eras meet, or when new generations radically break with traditional norms. In order to find an agreement and to be able to communicate, people are forced to re-answer the question of what morality is, to justify its necessity and its new meaning. (12)

Throughout the book its authors illustrate ethical issues and possible clashes of moralities, with their interpretations drawing on examples from Soviet times, Perestroika, Orthodoxy and "current conditions," as well as questions raised by their students. The difference between the ideal and the practice is most telling for the authors when it comes to the structure of *moral'*. The main characteristic of the structure of *moral'* is its contradictions. Since an individual has internalized and learnt moral relationships that are consciously established, their practical realization (*nravstvennost'*) always involves reflexivity. No *nravstvennyi* act can be unconscious. But the contradictory nature of the structure of *moral'* provokes contradictions between the different elements of *moral'*: consciousness, (social) relationships, and behavior. This way an individual can hide his or her genuine feelings and opinions, or demonstrate behavior which counters the expectations of others. Hiding genuine feelings could happen for many different reasons, both of external (such as violence or force) and internal origins (such as ideas of one's safety, comfort, or career, or the desire to give nice impression). The dissonance between one's moral consciousness, relationships and behavior is expressed in the separation of words and deeds, in a specific *nravstvennyi* "camouflage," which is mostly about adjustment, conformism, and its consequence: a double morality, one "for oneself" and one for others (Iaskevich and Mishatkina 2006: 96).

The idea of "moral camouflage" could be linked to Oleg Kharkhordin's notion of dissimulation and deception, as a popular practice of the Soviet period, and "the central unofficial means of self-fashioning" (1999: 270). The practice of dissimulation in that period was a simple consequence of separation of public and private representations under conditions of official surveillance. For Kharkhordin, the Bolsheviks, who found themselves in situation "of life broken into two parts—the hidden private, and the visible official" started to individualize themselves with the practice of closure, so that "retracting or hiding suspect behavior became the only practice that they practiced on their own, individually, without any recourse to collectively approved skills and with little, if any, guidance from dominant ideology" (272). Separation of public and private was a dominant feature of life under socialism (or, more precisely, of life under a totalitarian regime), and it certainly must have provoked the practices of "moral camouflaging" understood as *deception*. What is of interest in this case, however, is how the *reconciliation* of apparently incongruent moral messages within people's everyday life is possible and how one finds a sense of coherence and continuity despite contradictions and disruptions.

"Moral Breakdown and Ranges of Possibilities"

Jarrett Zigon's theoretical framework for an anthropology of moralities (2009) helps to provide an answer to the problem of multiple and seemingly incompatible moralities reconciled in everyday experience, such as in the case of Russian teachers who are formerly atheist but currently devoted to Orthodoxy. Within the theory of moral breakdown, multiple and incompatible moralities do not pose a problem to people, because the theory views morality as multi-aspectual and characterized by plurality. Such an understanding becomes clearer, argues Zigon, when morality is considered as three different, yet interrelated, aspects: (1) the institutional; (2) that of public discourse; and (3) embodied dispositions (258). Within each of these aspects of morality a range of possibilities is always available. The institutions (such as, for example, the Russian Orthodox Church or the Soviet government) wield varying amounts of power over individuals, and "most human persons are intimately entwined within the overlapping spheres of influence of several different institutions within and beyond their own society" (ibid.). It is banal to say that not all persons that have some nominal contact with, or participate in some of the institutions that make up their society, always follow their prescribed morality. For an anthropologist asking what morality is, it is not uncommon then to be offered a version of the Ten Commandments, or the law, or the Moral Code of the Builder of the Communism, or other similar institutional prescriptions.

The public discourse of morality consists of all those public articulations of moral beliefs that are not directly articulated by an institution. These two, however separate, are in a constant dialogue with one another, and therefore may not only support and authorize one another but at times may also undermine or subvert one another. People's everyday articulations of their moral beliefs often offer an alternative voice to institutional morality, which is sometimes acknowledged and at other times also articulated by the same persons.

These everyday articulations are a part of public moral discourse but at the same time are an articulation, or a reflected verbalization, of what Zigon calls "morality as embodied dispositions" (260). In this sense, morality is not thought out beforehand, nor is it noticed when it is performed, unlike the way morality is sometimes considered as rule-following, or conscious reflection on a dilemma. Thus, unreflective dispositions, according to Zigon, allow people to consider themselves moral *most of the time,* despite the plurality of moral questioning voiced in the articulations of the institutions or public discourses. The contradictions of the moral articulations that anthropologists face in their field sites are then inevitable, for people "nonconsciously shift between various aspects of morality, as well as pluralities that constitute these aspects, within one context" (261). In everyday life it is only occasionally that one has to stop and consider how to act or be morally appropriate. Within Zigon's theory of moral breakdown this situation, an "ethical moment," is called ethics (260).

In this scheme, a set of moral guidelines or articulations is something that is both fixed and shifting. The sense of such dynamics is given by James Faubion, who describes an action of bending "a given set of rules without breaking them" (2006: 205), for which he offers a coinage: "paranomic." "Paranomic" is a hybrid composed of the Greek *para-*, a prefix indicating being beside or parallel to, and the Greek *nomos*, designating law or convention or rule or principle or standard. It relates to a property of existing in parallel to the rules of practice typical in a given convention. Paranomic actions are not transgressive, claims Faubion, but they constitute "a relativization in practice of the very rules from which they distance themselves, a questioning in practice of principles and standards that 'go without saying'" (ibid.). Paranomic actors are thus potential agents of what Michel Foucault calls "problematization" (2000), and Zigon calls the "ethical moment": the process of becoming intellectually detached from who one is or what one does, of constituting one's being or one's actions as an object of thought.

It is the first two aspects of morality that Zigon describes that are thought of by Irina as the "external coating," as "working on the outside." She describes the third aspect of morality—embodied disposition, in Zigon's terms—as *nravstennost'.* As *nravstvennost'* needs "a lot of work on the self," it could be conceived of as a process of embodying morality by children, who learn the ways of being in a society. Yet, it can also be conceived of as a process of ethics when it is applied to Irina's own experience of becoming a Christian.

An interesting set of ideas—relating to multiple reflexive stances and the way they are being connected to ruptures and perceived continuities—can be found in Ilana Gershon's ethnography of Samoan migrants in New Zealand who join evangelical churches (2006). In this account Samoan morality is described as sociocentric and context-dependent, where motivation is only partly linked to the actor's internal qualities or decisions: "[T]here is no such thing as private morality—morality exists only when one is judged by others" (158). She argues that these Samoans, who were leaving behind mainline churches, left also ways of presenting themselves as moral beings through exchange, where focus was placed on external, public display, a match between contextual demand and appearance. When they entered new congregations, they found an alternative to this form of morality in the church's focus on the labor of self-making and the so-called "*effort* to be good." In born-again churches the creation of meaning occurs through one's reflexive management of oneself as a moral being. These conversions, argues Gershon, entail shifts in morality but in the first place shifts in reflexivity, through which people learn to carve out different personhoods. People learn how to develop a self that can be regulated and managed. The shifts in reflexive stances allow for resolving the pressures brought about by the disruptions, and in consequence, for building the sense of coherence. By shifting morality from its social construction to an internal management of emotions, and demonstration through emotions, Samoans move from having morality defined through contextual selves to having morality defined through the continuous selves (160). Continuity, as it is imagined, works here thanks to and through the focus on the self.

Conclusion

In the Russian case, the relation between the secular and the religious present in ideas about morality prompts different understandings of the idea of *nravstvennost'* by believers of different ages and with different experiences of joining the Church, such as Larisa Ivanovna and Irina. However, there is clearly a strong sense of continuity between Soviet and post-Soviet notions of *moral'* and *nravstvennost'*, which are understood by both generations as a dichotomy between inner and outer. This understanding allows previously atheist teachers to identify themselves with new ideologies, such as Orthodoxy. Moreover, these specific local notions of morality allow for the building of individual continuities, and for presenting the new Orthodox selfhood as coherent with the Soviet one.

The idea of continuity works thanks to and through *nravstvennost'*. This, perhaps, gives more clarity to Larisa Ivanovna's answer presented at the beginning of the text. It also reveals that it is *nravstvennost'*, not *moral'*, that middle-aged teachers try to instill by their own example. This focus on *nravstvennost'* renders their subscription to a particular institutional or public *moral'* irrelevant.

This deep sense of continuity is notable especially when compared with the case of the ruptures acknowledged by Protestant converts, as analyzed by Joel Robbins (2007a; 2007b). It is possible that an emphasis on continuity distinguishes the anthropologist's perspective on the category of time and belief from local perspectives (as Robbins himself suggested for the case of the ideal-typical Protestant Christians [2007b]). However, the research presented in this chapter allows for a somewhat different conclusion. A radical opposition between the categories of continuity and change is not particularly relevant in the case of post-Soviet Orthodox converts, who, above all seek to emphasize the links between past and present. The post-Soviet case of continuity and change seems to be forming one nexus, where evident contradictions within a person's claimed moral identity can be reconciled.

Notes

1. Conversion is usually defined as abandoning one religion and turning to another. This kind of conversion can be traced in the post-socialist world as well; however, it is important to bear in mind that people in the former Soviet Union grew up with almost no involvement in religious life. Despite the difference, this process too can be defined as conversion (Pelkmans 2010).

2. All names used in this text are pseudonyms. I have preserved the formality of names that is standard in colloquial Russian. Thus, individuals of my own age group are given only the first name, while those of an older generation are given a name and a patronymic.

3. Komsomol is an organization for young people aged 14 to 28 that was primarily a political organ for spreading communist teachings and preparing future members of the Communist Party.

4. I will use original terms in the text, and will try to translate and explain them. The primary terms I deal with are the Russian nouns *moral'* (the adjective *moral'nyi*) and *nravstvennost'* (the adjective *nravstvennyi*).

5. The relationship between the moral and the spiritual, and between secular and religious conceptualizations of the spiritual, is not only a topic of debate in Russia, and certainly deserves attention and more detailed analysis (cf. Halstead 1994). Here I would only like to rely on my informants' interpretations, which suggest that *nravstvennost'* could belong to both religious and secular spheres.

6. These ideas are discussed in political and philosophical writings, such as in Nikolai Berdaev's (1955), a classic example here (cf. Luke 1983: 592–93). Berdaev was an émigré Russian philosopher who was the first to give a thorough rendition of the thesis. His 1955 volume was reedited in the 1990s, and became more and more popular among the intelligentsia, especially its Orthodox sections.

7. *Tolkovyi slovar' russkogo iazyka* (2003)—*The Dictionary of the Russian Language*— offers three possibilities for understanding the noun *moral'* (morality): (1) *Nravstvennye* norms of conduct and of relationships between people, also *nravstvennost'* itself; (2) logic, instructive/enlightening deduction (i.e. moral); and (3) moralizing

(*nravouchenie*), preaching. For the adjective *moral'nyi* (moral) the same dictionary provides also three possible definitions: (1) related to *moral'* (as described in definition (1) above); (2) *vysokonravstvennyi* (i.e., of high *nravstvennost'*), corresponding to moral rules; (3) internal, spiritual (2003: 365). For the noun *nravstvennost'* one finds in the same dictionary the following definition: "internal, spiritual qualities, which guide a person, ethical norms; rules of conduct defined by these qualities;" for the adjective *nravstvennyi*: "fulfilling the requirements of high *nravstvennost'*" and "related to consciousness, internal life of a human" (2003: 423). These explanations shed some light on the topic, as they do make some distinction between the terms, but still describe one term with help of another, which makes their somewhat tautological relationship difficult to grasp.

8. Hence *nravopisatel'nyi*, meaning "describing the habits and customs," is the old term for ethnographic description and *nravopisatel'*, meaning "the one who describes ways of life of some population (*narod*)" could be understood today as similar to an ethnographer (Dal' [1880] 2004: 464).

9. For example: "*nravstvennost'* of our religion is superior to the civil one (*grazhdanskaia*): the civil one requires only rigid fulfillment of the laws, the religious one has both conscience and God as a judge" (Dal' [1880] 2004: 464).

10. The original version of this quotation, in Latin, reads: "Fiunt non nascuntur christiani."

11. The context of this quotation is quite surprising. It considers a philosopher, who in a rational way discovers the truth and becomes a Christian. However, the quotation follows another equally famous one: "anima naturaliter christiana" (the soul is Christian by nature). The philosopher in question is such a soul.

12. The text from the King James version of the Bible (Gospel of Mark) is as follows:
   Behold, there went out a sower to sow: And it came to pass, as he sowed, some fell by the way side, and the fowls of the air came and devoured it up. And some fell on stony ground, where it had not much earth; and immediately it sprang up, because it had no depth of earth: But when the sun was up, it was scorched; and because it had no root, it withered away. And some fell among thorns, and the thorns grew up, and choked it, and it yielded no fruit. And other fell on good ground, and did yield fruit that sprang up and increased; and brought forth, some thirty, and some sixty, and some an hundred. And he said unto them, He that has ears to hear, let him hear.

13. This is reflected in the antonym of *nravstvennost'—beznravstvennost'*, which literally means "without *nravstvennost'*." One can, then, possess the seed and act in a good, *nravstvennyi* way or not, and then—act in a wrong way out of lack of it. Perhaps this is what Irina meant when she criticized the *beznravstvennost'* of atheists and communists, who need laws to guide them because of their lack of internal qualities to make the right choice.

References

Afanasiev, Nikolai. 1993. "Khreshchenie Detei." In *Vstuplenie v Tserkov*. Moskva: Palomnik (available online: http://www.golubinski.ru/afanasiev/vstuplenie9.htm).

Averintsev, Sergei. 2006. *Sofiia—Logos: Slovar'*. Kiev: Dukh i Litera.

Benovska-Sabkova Milena, Tobias Koellner, Tünde Komàromi, Agata Ładykowska, Detelina Tocheva, Jarrett Zigon. 2010. "'Spreading Grace' in Post-Soviet Russia." *Anthropology Today* 26, no. 1: 16–21.

Berdaev, Nikolai. 1955. *Istoki i Smysl Russkogo Kommunizma.* Paris: YMCA-Press.

Dal', Vladimir. [1880] 2004. *Tolkovyi slovar' zhivogo velikorusskogo iazyka,* vol. 2. Moskva: Olma-Press.

Druzhinin, Viktor, and Larisa Demina. 2005. *Etika: Kurs lektsii.* Moskva: Ekzamen.

Faubion, James. 2006. "Paranomics: On the Semiotics of Sacral Action." In *The Limits of Meaning: Case Studies in the Anthropology of Christianity,* ed. M. Engelke and M. Tomlinson. Oxford: Berghahn.

Fitzpatrick, Sheila. 2005. *Tear Off the Masks! Identity and Imposture in Twentieth-century Russia.* Princeton, NJ: Princeton University Press.

Foucault, Michel. 2000. "Polemics, Politics, and Problematizations." In *Ethics: Essential Works of Foucault, 1954–1984,* ed. P. Rabinow. New York: Penguin Books.

Gershon, Ilana. 2006. "Converting Meanings and the Meanings of Conversion in Samoan Moral Economies." In *The Limits of Meaning: Case Studies in the Anthropology of Christianity,* ed. M. Engelke and M. Tomlinson. Oxford: Berghahn.

Halstead, J. Mark. 1994. "Moral and Spiritual Education in Russia." *Cambridge Journal of Education* 24, no. 3: 423–38.

Iakhontova, Elena. 2005. *Osnovy etiki.* Saint Petersburg: Sankt-Peterburgskii Institut Vneshneekonomicheskikh Sviazei, Ekonomiki i Prava.

Iaskevich, Ia, and Tatiana Mishatkina. 2006. *Etika.* Minsk: Novoe Izdanie.

Kharkhordin, Oleg. 1999. *The Collective and the Individual in Russia: A Study of Practices.* Berkeley, CA: University of California Press.

Luehrmann, Sonja. 2005. "Recycling Cultural Construction: Desecularization in Post-soviet Mari El." *Religion, State & Society* 33, no. 1: 35–56.

Luke, Timothy. 1983. "The Proletarian Ethic and Soviet Industrialization." *The American Political Science Review* 77, no. 3: 588–601.

Pelkmans, Mathijs. 2010. "Introduction: Post-Soviet Space and the Unexpected Turns of Religious Life." In *Conversion After Socialism: Disruptions, Modernities and the Technologies of Faith,* ed. M. Pelkmans. Oxford: Berghahn.

Robbins, Joel. 2007a. "Between Reproduction and Freedom: Morality, Value, and Radical Cultural Change." *Ethnos* 72, no. 3: 293–314.

———. 2007b. "Continuity Thinking and the Problem of Christian Culture: Belief, Time, and the Anthropology of Christianity." *Current Anthropology* 48, no. 1: 5–38.

Shmalii, Vladimir. 2001. "Antropologiia." *Pravoslavnaia Entsiklopediia.* Moskva: Pravoslavnaia Entsiklopediia.

Skliarova, Tatiana. 2003. *Konspekt lektsii po vozrostnoi psikhologii i pedagogike.* Moskva: Pravoslavnyi Sviato-Tikhonovskii Bogoslovskii Institut.

Tolkovyi. 2003. *Tolkovyi slovar' russkogo iazyka,* ed. S. I. Ozhegov, N. Y. Shvedova. Moskva.

Zigon, Jarrett. 2007. "Moral Breakdown and the Ethical Demand: A Theoretical Framework for an Anthropology of Moralities." *Anthropological Theory* 7: 131–50.

———. 2009. "Morality Within a Range of Possibilities: A Dialogue with Joel Robbins." *Ethnos* 74, no. 2: 251–76.

 CHAPTER 4

The Politics of Rightness
Social Justice among Russia's Christian Communities

Melissa L. Caldwell

On 5 December 2008, Aleksei II, patriarch of Moscow and All Russia, passed away at his residence outside Moscow. The news quickly spread via telephone, text message, the Internet, and e-mail. Within hours, several Russian television stations were already broadcasting commentaries and retrospectives of Patriarch Aleksei's life and career. In both public and private conversations, succession seemed to be the issue of paramount importance and rampant speculation, as observers debated who would assume the role of patriarch and in what direction the new leader would take the church.

The issue of succession especially concerned Russia's non-Orthodox Christian community, as clergy and parishioners alike wondered about the impact of this transition not only on the status of their own congregations and religious practices, but also on the interfaith partnerships they had forged with one another. Within the Protestant community at the center of my own field research in Moscow, clergy, church staff, and parishioners alike seemed certain that the next patriarch would be either of two men who were highly placed clerics and patriarchate insiders. Although my informants regarded both men as effective and charismatic leaders, they were more concerned with the clerics' personalities and perspectives on Orthodox theology and tradition, including the Church's role as a national institution. While informants viewed one man as progressive, amiable, and supportive of a broader ecumenicalism in Russia, they viewed the other as somewhat mercurial and aligned with a more conservative, traditionalist vision of Orthodoxy and religious exclusivity.

In January 2009 Metropolitan Kirill of Smolensk and Kaliningrad was chosen as the next patriarch. Accounts of Metropolitan Kirill's selection furthered the uncertainty over the future of the Orthodox Church's attitudes and policies toward non-Orthodox Christian religions. While Metropolitan Kirill was described as a supporter of religious tolerance, he was also lauded for his dedication to promoting Orthodox tradition and heritage in Russia. Religious communities both within Russia and abroad pondered whether these two orientations could work productively together to foster simultaneously the continued revival of the Orthodox Church and a greater ecumenicalism within Russia, or whether this "tolerance" would be reserved for Orthodoxy within Russia and ecumenicalism would be promoted only with denominations outside Russia.

Since the late 1980s, the field of religion in Russia has been transformed both by the expansion of Christianity and by the shifting relationships of cooperation and competition that have emerged among Christian denominations. Most notable in accounts of these changes are the doctrinal and political issues that have at different moments simultaneously divided and united Christian communities, particularly the complicated relationships of sympathy and hostility, cooperation and competition, that reportedly exist between the Russian Orthodox Church and non-Orthodox Christian denominations (Knox 2005, 2008; Wanner and Steinberg 2008: 13–17). Because scholarly and popular accounts of the complicated relations among Christian communities have primarily highlighted antagonistic relations between Orthodox and non-Orthodox communities on the one hand, and among non-Orthodox Christian denominations on the other, little attention has been given to the cooperative efforts that have brought Russia's religious communities, Orthodox and non-Orthodox alike, into conversation and action around a common set of interests beyond those of theology and ritual. What is particularly noteworthy is the extent to which diverse Christian denominations and communities are forging collaborative relationships to pursue social welfare objectives that are removed from any particular religious orientation.

This chapter explores interfaith collaboration among Russia's Christian denominations as congregations work together in pursuit of social welfare and social justice goals. Specifically, it is concerned with how Orthodox, Catholic, and mainline Protestant denominations creatively move beyond their theological and historical differences to forge common practices of social action. These common practices of social action invite a reinterpretation not only of the nature and place of moral systems in a religiously pluralistic Russia, but also of the dimensions of that religious pluralism. As will become apparent, these interfaith collaborations produce a form of morality that requires the proper enactment of both practice (*praxis*) and belief (*doxa*).

The subject of interfaith collaboration illuminates a somewhat unfamiliar perspective on the nature of religious life in Russia today. Studies of post-socialist religious life have typically been framed around individual religious traditions, an analytical tendency that highlights and reinforces the idea that religious traditions are set apart by unique beliefs, rituals, and denominational histories and that theological or doctrinal features are the most significant elements of ritual life (e.g., Hann and Goltz 2010; Steinberg and Wanner 2008; cf. Caldwell 2005).

An alternative strand in accounts of Christian communities in Russia rests on a largely unproblematized dichotomy between Orthodox and non-Orthodox denominations, a move that homogenizes an incredibly diverse set of Christian traditions into a generic category often presented as "foreign," which in turn is a gloss for "evangelical," "fundamentalist," and other explicitly proselytizing movements. Thus an unintended result of these orientations is that religious pluralism is frequently presented either in terms of doctrinal or theological distinction and separateness or in terms of religious homogeneity, rather than through accounts that acknowledge religious syncretism or overlap.

In contrast, this chapter explores how Christian religious life emerges and flourishes in the spaces of intersection and negotiation among diverse religious traditions and how members of these communities forge a broader and more flexible notion of Christian practice through their collaboration on social justice projects. The congregations and religious associations that are the focus of this discussion are mainline non-Orthodox Christian groups—Lutheran, Baptist, Anglican, and Catholic, among others—that have forged collaborative partnerships to support ongoing social justice and relief work in Russia. These groups have at times been joined by Orthodox communities, although the visible participation of Orthodox clergy and parishioners can be politically problematic in Russia's religious sphere, an issue that will be discussed below.

This chapter draws on long-term ethnographic research among Moscow's faith-based social services communities. Since 1997, I have been working closely with several Christian congregations based in Moscow and following their worship and social welfare programs. Reflecting the transnational dimension of religious life in Russia today, particularly among non-Orthodox Christian communities, these worship and social welfare programs draw together a diverse community of clergy, parishioners, recipients, and community activists from Moscow and across the globe. Thus, one of the intriguing features of these communities is their internal demographic, national, and theological diversity. This diversity, in turn, directly complicates the creation and implementation of moral codes, as participants in these communities draw on different backgrounds and belief systems to inform their moral practices.

Reconciling Orthodoxy and Orthopraxy in Christian Justice Work

In order to place the religious denominations discussed here in proper context, it is important to clarify several points concerning religious life in Russia today. The denominations that will be described—Lutheranism,

Catholicism, Anglicanism, and other mainline Protestant traditions—occupy an ambiguous position in Russia's religious hierarchy. Both popular opinion and official legal codification have endowed the Russian Orthodox Church with the formal status of "official" national religion (Agadjanian 2001; Dinello 1994; Garrard and Garrard 2008), thereby making it akin to a state church. What gives the Russian Orthodox Church the most political traction in this sphere are Russian cultural practices that associate ethnicity with religion. Russian Orthodoxy is associated with ethnic Russianness, whereas Lutheranism is associated with ethnic Germans and Scandinavians, Catholicism with ethnic Poles and, increasingly today, with Asians, and the other Protestant denominations with other European ethnicities. Consequently, even as non-Orthodox religions have typically been categorized in both local and official practice as "foreign" and are positioned lower in Russia's religious hierarchy, the denominations listed above have, in fact, long been part of Russia's "indigenous" religious landscape—in some cases for several centuries.

Negotiations over moral systems are embedded within ongoing debates and conflicts about managing Russia's diverse religious landscape (Garrard and Garrard 2008; Steinberg and Wanner 2008). Although religious institutions have never been the sole sources of morality in Russia, especially during the Soviet period when the state promoted its own vision of a secular morality, in the post-Soviet period morality has emerged as an important venue through which religious traditions and religious practitioners can articulate their roles in this new society and attract followers (e.g., Caldwell 2010; Rogers 2008; Zigon 2008). As religious institutions and traditions assume status as the repositories and conduits of moral sensibilities, practices of theological distinction are being reframed as practices of moral distinction. In other words, individual religious communities are distinguished from one another through the particular moral systems with which each is associated. Conflations of moral particularity and theological particularity occur through assertions by clergy, religious practitioners, and observers alike (Caldwell 2008; Hann and Goltz 2010; Mitrokhin 2004; Rogers 2008; Zigon 2008).

Ultimately, what is at stake here is the extent to which any particular religious institution or tradition can lay exclusive claim to a particular moral system. More important than the efforts of religious communities to stake out their claims within a field of moral systems, however, are their efforts to stake a political claim as the most legitimate, perhaps even sole, authority of morality in today's Russia. The Russian Orthodox Church has been particularly active in asserting its moral authority through extensive morality campaigns covering such diverse issues as sexuality, abortion and reproductive politics, family relations, drug and alcohol use, gambling, immigration reform, and national security, among many others. Debates over moral authority also shape efforts by such institutions as the Russian Orthodox Church and the Russian state to determine legally and socially the status of the many different religious traditions that exist in the country.

Within the Christian realm alone, Russian Orthodox, Anglican, Lutheran, Methodist, Baptist, and many other congregations and clergy are engaged in extensive public relations outreach efforts to introduce their specific visions of the moral and good life to potential followers. These efforts to promote religious movements are reflected not just in the increase in the number of churches and church services, but also in the recent surge in religious publishing of Bibles, prayer books, meditation guides, spiritual self-help manuals, and other guides for denominationally or spiritually specific moral living, television and radio programs devoted to instructional conversations about religion, and more informal person-to-person outreach. Such guides are meant not simply to introduce potential followers to a particular religious tradition, but to provide them with a coherent framework for orienting their beliefs and practices to that religious tradition. Muscovites in my own field site stated that they found it useful to buy religious tracts and "how-to" books so that they would know how to act and what to believe in particular denominational settings.

Contestations over defining and legitimating particular combinations of religious and moral sensibility, coupled with the attendant issues of how individuals align their personal beliefs and actions "correctly" in accordance with theological policy and practice, comprise what I am calling a "politics of rightness." In other words, practitioners are concerned not simply with fulfilling the conditions of their respective religious traditions, but with fulfilling them properly, according to the rules of how that fulfillment should occur.

The concept of rightness is used in this discussion for three reasons. First, it is an ethnographic marker, because it is the concept that emerged most frequently in conversations with Christian social justice workers. A common response to questions to informants about why they do the work they do was the simple statement, "It is the right thing to do."

Second, the notion of rightness redirects the analysis of the values informing social action beyond a dichotomy between doxa (beliefs) and praxis (practices), and between the ethical and the moral, to focus instead on the norms of both doxa and praxis. Jarrett Zigon (2007) argues that the difference between the ethical and the moral is a distinction between doxa and praxis. That is, the moral refers to repertoires of knowledge that shape actors' beliefs and perspectives. These repertoires are deeply embedded systems of knowledge, whether subconscious or unconscious, and thus not immediately knowable or accessible to actors even as they shape their beliefs and actions. The ethical, by contrast, pertains to the moments and processes of awareness and reflection in the repertoires of knowledge and the circumstances in which they are evoked and engaged. In contrast to Zigon's perspective, the discussion here distinguishes between doxa and praxis in order to show how they are both entangled in the politics of rightness, but does not separate out one as moral and the other ethical. They are both parts of the same whole.

Third, and most important, my consideration of rightness in the present discussion draws inspiration from James L. Watson's insightful distinction between orthodoxy as a system of "correct belief" and orthopraxy as a system of "correct practice" (Watson 1988). With this distinction, Watson calls attention to the fact that there are coherent, delineated forms and procedures inherent in both belief and ritual systems. For religious rituals or beliefs to have meaning and efficacy, followers must adhere to the proper or correct enactment of these forms and procedures. Thus, I am interested in how the proper enactment of belief and practice reflects the moral order of Christian social justice work, because social activists are careful to create a common framework of rightness underlying their activities and the values they attach to those activities.

The issue of efficacy raised by Watson (1988), and similarly by other theorists of ritual (e.g., Turner 1969), is critical for understanding not just how Christian social justice activities work, but also whom they serve. Anthropological studies of religion emphasize the ways belief and performance are directed at the self, at a deity, or at both simultaneously. Fenella Cannell argues that "personal interiority" is a recurring theme in understandings of Christianity, and more particularly Protestantism, so that the motivation for Christians is a process of self-making as an expression of efforts to imitate God, to become Godly (Cannell 2006: 20; see also Miller and Yamamori 2007: 2). Redemption, salvation, and transcendence are all states oriented to particular relational configurations between the self and a deity. Curiously, anthropologists and other scholars of religion have not fully considered how orthopraxy and orthodoxy might be directed toward others beyond the self or a deity—most notably other members of society and society itself. This orientation to society confuses conventional distinctions between this-worldly and other-worldly religions (e.g., Weber 1946). Although such practices as tithing, alms-giving, and charity may be framed as a means to articulate and attain a presumed relationship between the giver, in this case a religious practitioner, and the deity, the same activities are also directed, whether explicitly or implicitly, to a this-worldly social community of real individuals (Caldwell 2008; Coleman 2006; Parry 1986). Thus social action presents a possibility for a simultaneous orientation to both an other-world and a this-world larger than the self.[1]

The efforts of religious communities and their supporters to help other people thus present a different way of understanding conventional categorical distinctions between worlds and participants. In their work on Pentecostal Christian social justice projects, Miller and Yamamori use the term "Progressive Pentecostalism" to denote the overlaps: "Pentecostalism has often been otherworldly, emphasizing personal salvation to the exclusion of any attempt to transform social reality, whereas the movement we are describing continues to affirm the apocalyptic return of Christ but also believes that Christians are called to be good neighbors, addressing the social needs of people in their community" (2007: 2).[2]

At the same time, the rules and expectations that may frame and guide the presumed relationship between self and deity may be different from those that frame and guide the presumed relationship between self and fellow person. To put it in concrete terms, while parishioners at one non-Orthodox Christian church in Moscow were encouraged to express their spiritual relationship to God through regular tithes to the church, they were encouraged to express their social justice commitment by making the tithes in the form of food and other items that could be used in the church's ministry to the homeless. Parishioners who generously make inappropriate donations present a delicate and profound quandary to clergy who must decide whether to accept a gift that cannot be used or to reject or dispose of it. In the weeks leading up to a special worship service dedicated to the presentation of material goods to the church for subsequent distribution to a local charity, the church's minister repeatedly warned congregants that if they did not adhere to the restrictions on the types of food items that could be donated (canned goods only), their gifts would be discarded.

Framed within these perspectives, rightness can thus be understood as proper adherence to a set of practices and beliefs about social action in order to bring about benefits simultaneously to oneself, to others, and to a higher being. These interpretations of rightness are crucial for constructing the pathways that allow religious communities to forge a shared set of social justice orthodoxies and orthopraxies.

Forging Interfaith Ties and Common Rightness

Over the past five years, Russia's religious communities have quietly launched an explicitly collaborationist approach to charity and social advocacy. Previously, there was something of a specialization of charitable work among congregations. Whereas the Christian Church of Moscow specialized in feeding programs, primarily for elderly pensioners and veterans, and, more recently, in monitoring race relations and supporting victims of racist violence (Caldwell 2004), the Anglican Church focused on the homeless and on drug and alcohol rehabilitation. The Korean Methodist community actively cared for orphans and the disabled, while the Catholic Church provided extensive support for refugees and asylum-seekers, and the Baptist Federation worked with ex-prisoners and children, among others. Russian Orthodox churches supported a broader set of initiatives—feeding programs, elder care, homeless support, and drug and alcohol rehabilitation, to name a few. This diversity seems to reflect both the fact that there are more Orthodox congregations and the fact that the institutional structure of the Orthodox Church facilitates more diverse activities.

Currently, congregations representing diverse theological orientations are increasingly pursuing cooperative ventures across denominational differences. In some cases, congregations from one denomination support the charitable projects of a congregation from another denomination by providing money, material goods, and volunteers. In other cases, several congregations have joined forces to operate welfare programs together. Clergy, church staff, and lay people meet regularly to share ideas and strategies and to help one another on projects. Local interfaith initiatives are supported at the international level by international and transnational ecumenical institutions and funding organizations. The denominational affiliations and histories of these local initiatives are not always matched by the denominational diversity of the ecumenical organizations, as when the Presbyterian Church supports the Baptist Church with funds and staff expertise and when support from Lutheran World Relief finds its way to individual Catholic congregations.

Through these interactions, a wider community of individuals devoted to relief and social justice concerns has emerged in Russia. This community is manifested in both face-to-face encounters, as clergy, staff, congregants, and other volunteers gather for meetings and work activities, and in virtual encounters, as people meet and communicate through Livejournals, blogs, and other online networking programs. Young people have been particularly active in using religiously oriented Internet discussions to coordinate spontaneous acts of public service voluntarism akin to "smart mobs."

Despite the Russian Orthodox Church's official stance of theological separatism from other Christian denominations, some individual Orthodox congregations are very much part of these new interdenominational collaborations. One of the more progressive Orthodox churches in downtown Moscow has long enjoyed close relations with its Protestant counterparts. For many years this Orthodox church sponsored a feeding program that operated in the same space and at the same time as a feeding program sponsored by the Christian Church of Moscow. The two churches ordered the same meals for their clients, and their clients were drawn from the same demographic of elderly and disabled pensioners living in the same neighborhood. The only visible sign that there were two separate programs operating simultaneously in the same place was that staff from the two programs were seated at separate tables. The registration cards that clients from the two programs presented to receive their meals were so similar in shape and style that at first glance it was difficult to notice the difference.

In Moscow, Christian clergy and congregants have actively pursued opportunities to bridge denominational differences in order to create a more unified and cohesive sphere of interfaith social action. In spring 2007, the newly arrived pastor at the Christian Church of Moscow set up a series of appointments to meet his counterparts at several other of the city's Christian congregations. Several factors motivated the pastor's networking. First, as an American, he had only recently arrived in Moscow and was interested in understanding the larger religious landscape. Second, he had quickly discovered that Moscow lacked the tight community of religious professionals he had enjoyed in his previous posting, and he was particularly interested in establishing closer ties with fellow clergy in hopes of initiating pulpit exchanges and joint fellowship events with other congregations.

A third factor was that the pastor's congregation, the Christian Church of Moscow, had long sponsored several charitable programs in Moscow and was in the planning stages of a new one. Members of the congregation felt strongly that their newest project should be a more ecumenically collaborative venture. At the congregation's urging, the pastor wanted to meet with clergy in other congregations in order to gauge whether they would be interested in joining with his church in charitable programs.

By mid-summer, he had met with many of his counterparts throughout Moscow—not just with clergy serving congregations with large non-Russian populations, but also Russian clergy serving Russian congregations, notably the Baptist Federation, the Russian Lutheran Church, the Russian Catholic diocese, Russian Korean Methodists, Russian Korean Presbyterians, and Russian Orthodox clergy. He and his colleagues had also already begun visiting one another's church services in pulpit exchanges, and congregation members were visiting with one another through shared fellowship activities, including excursions to local monasteries and other tourist sites.

At the same time, the congregations had also begun working closely with one another on charitable projects. In one case, a Protestant church and several Russian Orthodox parishes had joined forces to expand their homeless outreach programs. Members of the Protestant congregation had previously donated time, services, and money to assist programs sponsored by several Orthodox churches. One reason for these forms of assistance was that the Protestant church was not able to provide the same services in its own church building because of legal restrictions. Now, however, church members were interested in pursuing the possibility of setting up programs for shelter and medical assistance in their own building. Clergy and members of the Orthodox churches began contributing their own expertise and resources to reciprocate and help the Protestant congregation pursue these objectives. In other cases, youth groups from several congregations served as volunteer support staff in summer camps for underprivileged families operated by another religious community.

Collaborative ventures of these kinds require congregations and religious institutions representing different theological perspectives to find common ground in how they structure their programs, determine eligibility for recipients, provide services, formulate their expectations of volunteers, and even how they present service programs to the public. When clergy, staff, and volunteers from different congregations meet to discuss joint activities, conversations typically revolve around how to reconcile their denominational and theological differences in pursuit of a common goal.

An excellent example of how congregations have worked together comes from a charitable initiative launched by the Christian Church of Moscow, the Russian Lutheran Church, and the Russian Catholic community. In summer 2007, representatives from three different communities—the Catholic charity Caritas, the Lutheran Church of Russia, and the Christian Church of Moscow—held a series of meetings to explore opening a joint feeding program to serve single mothers with large families. This was a completely new program for each of the three communities, for the Christian Church of Moscow specialized in working with the elderly, the Catholic community provided support primarily to low-income families and refugees, and the Lutheran church was most proficient in small-scale parish outreach programs such as work with the homeless and educational support. Together the three communities hoped to mobilize their respective contacts among Moscow's social workers and welfare officials, local businesspeople, and their volunteer and donor pools.

Over the course of several planning meetings, clergy, staff, and volunteers worked together to blend their communities' respective strengths. Talking with one another through translators (Russian, German, and English were the three languages at play), the participants discussed how their respective religious communities approached such issues as defining need and the appropriateness of assistance, personal responsibility, and commitments to help others, both theologically and practically.

In most cases, denominational differences arose in the guise of institutional structures and experiences. Participants quickly agreed that they shared similar, if not identical, views on the need to help the less fortunate; such assistance was seen as an essential part of the spiritual journeys of their respective congregations, even as they admitted that their own denominations had different degrees of experience with the practical implementation of such projects. For instance, the Christian Church of Moscow was the most experienced congregation in terms of knowing how to procure funding and volunteers for welfare projects, attract and motivate volunteers, and ensure the long-term oversight and maintenance of active welfare programs. Although the staff of Caritas had far less experience starting and managing formal welfare programs, including administration and staffing issues, they had established strong working relationships with social workers and other administrators in the city administration, connections that the Christian Church of Moscow lacked. Staff from the Lutheran Church, meanwhile, had little experience operating welfare programs or working with local administrators, but they did have connections with state-level public officials and politicians and with officials of international religious bodies.

Although the Baptist Federation had been invited to participate, it did not play an active role in establishing the project. Senior pastors and the outreach director of the Baptist Federation had all admitted that their community was not yet experienced in social welfare work, and so they could not take a leadership role in the initiative, yet they reassured their colleagues that they and their members were committed to the idea of the program and pledged to help in any way they could.

Doctrinal differences rarely emerged during the course of planning meetings, except as interesting points of comparison among the denominations represented. Conversations typically entailed comparative parsing out of minute differences in the meanings of words or practices in their respective liturgies and prayers. Throughout the meetings, participants repeatedly reassured one another that these theological differences were so minor as to be inconsequential and thus not an impediment in the larger task of collaboration.

Although every meeting began and ended with a prayer led by one of the clergy members, with each participant following the prayer in his or her own way—such as making the sign of the cross, invoking Jesus or the Holy Trinity, or using gender-inclusive or gender-exclusive language—these performances of denominational difference seemed to be relatively inconsequential to the participants. In fact, the recitation of the Lord's Prayer was conducted in multiple languages and cadences. The prayers became a means for participants to affirm their common practical objectives while recognizing their different religious traditions. On one occasion, a Lutheran minister and the assistant to the Russian Lutheran Bishop suggested that perhaps the social work programs should also include a more explicitly mission-oriented approach. His colleagues politely acknowledged this idea but then moved quickly to non-religious themes in their plans, and the issue was dropped. Thus, for the most part, the planning meetings of Christian Church of Moscow, Lutheran, and Catholic clergy and volunteers focused almost exclusively on the concrete issues at hand—locating a cafeteria to provide food services, compiling a list of eligible recipients, training volunteers, and ensuring sufficient funding.

The opening festivities for the new feeding program were also an overtly ecumenical affair. Clergy and congregants from the Christian Church of Moscow, the Lutheran Church, the Catholic Church, the Anglican Church, and the Baptist Federation, among others, attended the opening celebration. Although officials from the Russian Orthodox patriarchate had been invited, they declined to attend. At first glance, this could be interpreted as evidence of the Orthodox Church's concerns about non-Orthodox Christian congregations, but the reason was far more significant.

Unofficially, the patriarch's office sent word to the Lutheran Church that it supported the venture but regretted that it could not send anyone to attend the festivities publicly because of ongoing political problems with the Russian Orthodox Church Abroad and not because of theological or political differences with the non-Orthodox Christian communities in Moscow. In other words, while the patriarchate's position on social justice activity was aligned with that of these congregations, the larger political issues surrounding theological differences prevented the Russian Orthodox Church from demonstrating its support publicly.

The ecumenical diversity displayed by the feeding program plays out in many other interfaith activities across Moscow and Russia more broadly. Catholic-inspired social programs, such as the Sant'Egidio street ministry and Sisters of Mercy, attract a theologically diverse set of volunteers who either set aside doctrinal differences or find ways to reconcile them as they work side-by-side. Similarly, social projects sponsored by individual Methodist and Baptist congregations attract not just people who identify themselves as belonging to many other Christian denominations, but also Jews, Muslims, atheists, and other non-practicing individuals. In the field of HIV/AIDS prevention and drug treatment, development programs encourage interfaith collaborations among Orthodox, Christian, and Muslim congregations, even though in some cases these collaborations take place informally and out of public view.

In each of these programs, clergy, staff, volunteers, and recipients alike described their activities in terms of aligning their personal beliefs and practices of social action into a set of tenets based on a common understanding of social justice. Rarely did informants explain their views in terms of religious motivations or theological requirements. Rather, they consistently framed their perspectives in the languages of socially correct action:

"human rights," "humanitarianism," "social justice," "love," "friendship," and more simply "the right thing to do."

This significance of common rightness is illuminated in informants' responses to questions about why they directed their time, labor, and other resources to one or another program. Although factors such as social networks, time constraints, and distance were important considerations in how clergy, staff, and volunteers made decisions about which projects to support and in what ways, these issues seemed in many ways to be secondary to another factor: the rightness of a particular social program.

More precisely, clergy, staff, and volunteers evaluated not only whether the interests, goals, and methods of social programs appealed to their personal sense of appropriate social work, but also whether these programs were consistent in how they pursued their objectives. For instance, one of the qualities of the food-sharing programs of the Christian Church of Moscow that appealed to volunteers was that the community consistently and reliably met its goals. This consistency gave its programs an appearance of stability that many volunteers, donors, recipients, and other supporters found reassuring. In turn, that stability imbued the Christian Church of Moscow with value as a successful and compelling leader in the field of Russian social justice work.

Attributes of consistency and reliability also informed the social value of other successful interfaith programs. Most notable are the activities of the progressive Orthodox church mentioned previously. This particular congregation had long sponsored a number of social work initiatives, often in partnership with non-Orthodox Christian congregations. Although it was rumored that the congregation had at times been under pressure from the patriarchate for not adhering to church policy regarding theological interpretation and relationships with non-Orthodox congregations, the church continued its social work in partnership with a broader ecumenical community. The church's commitment to adhering to its own principles of social action appealed to observers who saw this consistency as evidence of the church's moral authority. Ultimately, the ability and willingness of faith communities and their participants to conform to norms of social action becomes in some ways more important than theological orientation in how faith communities are evaluated in terms of their value and contributions to Russian society.

In the logic of orthodoxy and orthopraxy proposed by Watson, these faith communities become meaningful in Russian religious life because they are properly adhering to the rules of doxa and praxis for social action. And by extension, it is this conformity to the norms of social action—rightness, in other words—that enables these communities to stake out claims in the field of morality.

Conformity as Moral Authority

The importance of rightness for constructions of morality emerges perhaps most strikingly in the views on social and moral decay in their country that appeared regularly in both public discourse and private conversations with informants (see also Zigon 2008). Citing such diverse issues as growing socioeconomic disparities, the plight of lower-income people, the intrusion of socially deviant activities such as graffiti and drunkenness into public spaces, piles of trash and other refuse, the lack of public decorum, environmental degradation, and political and financial malfeasance, Russians expressed concern that the transition from socialism to capitalism has damaged the social and moral fabric of the country (see, e.g., Caldwell 2004; Ries 2002; Patico 2008; Stephenson 2006). For their part, public institutions such as state agencies and the Russian Orthodox Church also lament the perceived social and moral decline through public campaigns to solve problems such as gambling, prostitution, human trafficking, and illegal immigration, among many others.

Discussions about moral decay and moral breakdown of Russian society are directed at ideas about the disarray and disintegration of the structures and codes of norms in society. In other words, concerns about moral decay are, at heart, concerns about rightness, as Russians debate the extent to which individuals and institutions conform to or deviate from social norms of appropriate behavior.[3]

For the specific case of social assistance and social action, Muscovites' concerns about immorality arise when they criticize those who are believed to be withholding assistance from family and neighbors. In this configuration, the immoral are individuals who violate social norms of mutual assistance and reciprocity by keeping money and other resources for their own purposes rather than sharing with people presumed to be in their social networks (Caldwell 2004: 86–99). In other words, selfishness is immoral because it fails to conform to cultural norms of mutual support. This understanding of immorality as a lack of conformity to norms is similarly evident in public attitudes, mostly negative, about New Russians, *biznesmen,* and other political elites who are suspected (or known) to have violated the standards of social and economic propriety. Intriguingly, Russia's mafia is often valorized because, unlike the state, it is believed to provide social order and stability (Ries 2002).

Moralizing discourses were evident in the frustrations of Muscovites who criticized state agencies and state workers for being apathetic or even hostile to the needs of the less fortunate, thereby deviating from expectations about compassion and care. Even aid programs risk criticism for not meeting public expectations about assistance. When I first began working with the feeding programs of the Christian Church of Moscow in the late 1990s, donors frequently gave the community small food and personal hygiene items (e.g., candy bars, instant soup packets, soap, toothbrushes) to distribute to recipients. On some occasions, there were enough donated items for every client to receive more than one; on other occasions, items were limited to one per person. Clients became accustomed to receiving these free items, and on days when supplies were limited or, even worse, were depleted early in the morning, it was not unusual for them to become angry and berate staff and volunteers for treating them improperly and unfairly. Clients who manipulated the system to receive more than their fair share were similarly accused of impropriety by other clients.

Curiously, Russian Orthodox churches have been sharply criticized as immoral and, more precisely, corrupt because of their social action policies. Despite a long tradition of charity as an essential mission and responsibility of the church (see Kenworthy 2008; Lindenmeyr 1993, 1996), a stance made manifest in a separate administrative unit within the patriarchate that is dedicated to developing and promoting the church's charity and humanitarian activities, practical realities prevent Orthodox churches (like most religious institutions) from providing assistance to every person who requests it. Yet many Russians have singled out the Russian Orthodox Church as an especially immoral and corrupt institution because of its presumed violation of a sacred trust with the Russian nation (Caldwell 2010). In other words, the Russian Orthodox Church is seen as having violated proper norms of social action, and thus failing to conform to rightness.

Hence it is the ability of institutions and individuals to conform to orthopraxies and orthodoxies of social action that determines whether they are moral or immoral. And despite the public criticisms of Orthodox churches as failing to conform to cultural norms of social action, Russians by and large see faith communities as the institutions most likely to meet the standards of rightness. Interfaith projects seem particularly well positioned to demonstrate their moral authority, because all of their efforts to create truly collaborative partnerships are ultimately oriented to minimize individual differences in the mission of achieving conformity with a shared set of values and practices about social action. Through careful negotiation of theological and political differences, churches forge a new common ground, a consensus in Habermasian terms (Habermas 1987) that, in turn, sets standards to which they can adhere and demonstrate their moral authority.

Reconsidering Christian Moral Exceptionalism

As a result of these projects of alignment, social justice activities have become the arena where Russians look to a set of cultural guidelines and social norms regarding proper actions and beliefs. This attention to qualities of correctness, appropriateness, and rightness is important for understanding the complicated nexus of morality, religion, and spirituality not just in Russia, but also in studies of Christianity and other religious movements more generally.

For the case of religious life in Russia, interfaith social justice projects challenge and complicate more familiar accounts of religious institutions as moral authorities by investigating how the qualities of morality come into being and how authority is achieved. Interfaith communities directly challenge perceptions of Christian moral exceptionalism in which some denominations or congregations are accorded special legitimacy as sources and arbiters of moral authority, a tendency that is particularly relevant for popular and scholarly attitudes toward Russian Orthodoxy. It is important to note, however, that these legitimizing attitudes are not exclusive to Orthodoxy, as is illuminated by the ongoing tensions among Russia's religious communities as congregations use moral differences in their competitive efforts to attract members. Morality is very much both an ecumenical phenomenon and a collaboratively constructed venture.

Attention to interfaith social action projects also reveals that Christian communities are not necessarily moral in and of themselves. That is, it is not their status as religious institutions that endows them with the status of moral authority. The enactment of particular norms through the realm of religious activity may give them greater cultural valence, but their value is not derived specifically or exclusively from religion. Rather, morality is a state that must be achieved through a process of conformity. When seen from this perspective, morality is disarticulated from religion. The movement of morality outside the exclusive domain of theology and doctrine thus facilitates ecumenicalism. For the case of Russian Orthodoxy, the disentangling of theology and morality enables Orthodox churches to resolve the conundrum of Christian exceptionalism. Individual churches from diverse denominations can work together for a common project of moral action separate from the issues of faith, belief, ritual, and identity that would otherwise divide them.

Attention to the codes of doxa and praxis for social justice presents an important reminder that the entirety of religious activity encompasses both practical, this-worldly interests and spiritual, other-worldly interests. Fenella Cannell suggests in her work on Christianity (2006: 7) that there is a tension between the theological positions that churches accept as orthodox and the positions that remain unorthodox.

While Cannell makes an important contribution by explicating the need for adherence and conformity as the means to empower and enliven theological, liturgical, and doctrinal positions, she overlooks the ways in which more practical, and not necessarily theologically unique or specific, aspects

of religious life are embedded within just as significant systems of orthodoxy and orthopraxy. Finally, even as Cannell's call to reconsider "the idea
of Christianity as a religion of radical discontinuity" (2006: 8) critically in-
tervenes in monolithic accounts of a universal Christianity, consideration
of the non-theological aspects of religious social action open new inter-
stices and spaces for considering how and where both common Christianities and common moralities might take shape. Interfaith social justice
activities remind us that multiple orthodoxies and orthopraxies pertaining
to different registers of religious life are always at work. And just as rituals do not have meaning and transformative power in and of themselves
but only through their proper enactment (Turner 1969), morality acquires
power and significance only through its proper enactment.

Notes

Research for this chapter was supported in part by funds provided by the National
Council for Eurasian and East European Research through the U.S. Department of
State under Title VII (the Soviet–East European Research and Training Act of 1983, as
amended). Additional support was provided by the Committee on Research and the Division of Social Sciences, University of California, Santa Cruz. An earlier version of this
chapter was presented at the conference "Multiple Moralities in Contemporary Russia"
at the Max Planck Institute for Social Anthropology Halle, Germany. The author thanks
colleagues at that conference, especially Jarrett Zigon, Tünde Komaromi, Detelina
Tocheva, Cathy Wanner, Doug Rogers, and Chris Hann, for comments and suggestions.
Another version of this chapter appeared as an article in *Problems of Post-Communism*
56, no. 4 (July/August 2009): 29–40.

1. See Scott Kenworthy's discussion (2008) of this for the case of the Russian Orthodox Church.
2. Miller and Yamamori also write that "Progressive Pentecostals…are attempting to
   build from the ground up an alternative social reality" (2007: 4).
3. See Stephenson's discussion (2006) of Soviet and post-Soviet attitudes about the
   immorality of homelessness. Homeless people are often officially labeled with
   moralizing terms such as "parasite" and "criminal," because they are presumed to
   violate social norms about proper residence and labor patterns.

References

Agadjanian, Alexander. 2001. "Revising Pandora's Gifts: Religious and National Identity
   in the Post-Soviet Societal Fabric." *Europe-Asia Studies* 53, no. 3: 473–88.
Caldwell, Melissa L. 2004. *Not by Bread Alone: Social Support in the New Russia.* Berkeley, CA: University of California Press.
———. 2005. "A New Role for Religion in Russia's New Consumer Age: The Case of
   Moscow." *Religion, State & Society* 33, no. 1: 19–34.
———. 2008. "Social Welfare and Christian Welfare: Who Gets Saved in Post-Soviet
   Russian Charity Work?" In *Religion, Morality, and Community in Post-Soviet So-*

cieties, ed. Mark D. Steinberg and Catherine Wanner, 179–214. Washington, D.C.: Woodrow Wilson Center Press.

———. 2010. "The Russian Orthodox Church, the Provision of Social Welfare, and Changing Ethics of Benevolence." In *Eastern Christianities in Anthropological Perspective*, eds. Chris Hann and Hermann Goltz. Berkeley, CA: University of California Press.

Cannell, Fenella. 2006. "Introduction: The Anthropology of Christianity." In *The Anthropology of Christianity*, ed. Fenella Cannell, 1–50. Durham, NC: Duke University Press.

Chaplin, Vsevolod. 2006. "Post-Soviet Countries: The Need for New Morals in Economy." *The Ecumenical Review* 58, no. 1: 99–101.

Coleman, Simon. 2006. "Materializing the Self: Words and Gifts in the Construction of Charismatic Protestant Identity." In *The Anthropology of Christianity*, ed. Fennella Cannell, 163–84. Durham, NC: Duke University Press.

Dinello, Natalia P. 1994. "Religious and National Identity of Russians." In *Politics and Religion in Central and Eastern Europe: Traditions and Transitions*, ed. William H. Swatos Jr., 83–99. Westport, CT: Praeger Publishers.

Garrard, John, and Carol Garrard. 2008. *Russian Orthodoxy Resurgent: Faith and Power in the New Russia*. Princeton, NJ: Princeton University Press.

Habermas, Jürgen. 1987. *The Theory of Communicative Action*, vol. 2: *Lifeworld and System: A Critique of Functionalist Reason*, trans. Thomas McCarthy. Boston: Beacon Press.

Hann, Chris, and Hermann Goltz, eds. 2010. *Eastern Christianities in Anthropological Perspective*. Berkeley, CA: University of California Press.

Hondagneu-Sotelo, Pierrette. 2008. *God's Heart Has No Borders: How Religious Activists Are Working for Immigrant Rights*. Berkeley, CA: University of California Press.

Kenworthy, Scott M. 2008. "To Save the World or to Renounce It: Modes of Moral Action in Russian Orthodoxy." In *Religion, Morality, and Community in Post-Soviet Societies*, ed. Mark D. Steinberg and Catherine Wanner, 21–54. Washington, D.C.: Woodrow Wilson Center Press.

Knox, Zoe. 2005. *Russian Society and the Orthodox Church: Religion in Russia after Communism*. New York: RoutledgeCurzon.

———. 2008. "Religious Freedom in Russia: The Putin Years." In *Religion, Morality, and Community in Post-Soviet Societies*, ed. Mark D. Steinberg and Catherine Wanner, 281–314. Washington, D.C.: Woodrow Wilson Center Press.

Lindenmeyr, Adele. 1993. "Public Life, Private Virtues: Women in Russian Charity, 1762–1914." *Signs* 1, no. 3: 562–91.

———. 1996. *Poverty Is Not a Vice: Charity, Society and the State in Imperial Russia*. Princeton, NJ: Princeton University Press.

Miller, Donald E., and Tetsunao Yamamori. 2007. *Global Pentecostalism: The New Face of Christian Social Engagement*. Berkeley, CA: University of California Press.

Mitrokhin, Nikolai. 2004. *Russkaia Pravoslavnaia Tserkov': Sovremennoe Sostoianie i Aktual'nye Problemy*. Moscow: Novoe Literaturnoe Obozrenie.

Parry, Jonathan. 1986. "The Gift, the Indian Gift, and the 'Indian Gift.'" *Man* (New Series) 21, no. 3: 453–73.

Patico, Jennifer. 2008. *Consumption and Social Change in a Post-Soviet Middle Class*. Stanford, CA: Stanford University Press.

Ries, Nancy. 2002. "'Honest Bandits' and 'Warped People': Russian Narratives about Money, Corruption, and Political Decay." In *Ethnography in Unstable Places: Everyday Lives in Contexts of Dramatic Political Change,* ed. Carol J. Greenhouse, Elizabeth Mertz, and Kay B. Warren, 276–315. Durham, NC: Duke University Press.

Rogers, Douglas. 2008. "Old Belief between 'Society' and 'Culture': Remaking Moral Communities and Inequalities on a Former State Farm." In *Religion, Morality, and Community in Post-Soviet Societies,* ed. Mark D. Steinberg and Catherine Wanner, 115–47. Washington, D.C.: Woodrow Wilson Center Press.

Steinberg, Mark D., and Catherine Wanner, eds. 2008. *Religion, Morality, and Community in Post-Soviet Societies.* Washington, DC: Woodrow Wilson Center Press.

Stephenson, Svetlana. 2006. *Crossing the Line: Vagrancy, Homelessness and Social Displacement in Russia.* Aldershot, UK: Ashgate.

Turner, Victor. 1969. *The Ritual Process.* Chicago: Aldine.

Wanner, Catherine, and Mark D. Steinberg. 2008. "Introduction: Reclaiming the Sacred after Communism." In *Religion, Morality, and Community in Post-Soviet Societies,* ed. Mark D. Steinberg and Catherine Wanner, 1–20. Washington, D.C.: Woodrow Wilson Center Press.

Watson, James L. 1988. "The Structure of Chinese Funerary Rites: Elementary Forms, Ritual Sequence, and the Primary of Performance." In *Death Ritual in Late Imperial and Modern China,* ed. James L. Watson and Evelyn S. Rawski, 3–19. Berkeley, CA: University of California Press.

Weber, Max. 1946. "The Social Psychology of the World Religions." In *From Max Weber: Essays in Sociology,* ed. and trans. H. H. Gerth and C. W. Mills. New York: Oxford University Press.

Zigon, Jarrett. 2007. "Moral Breakdown and the Ethical Demand: A Theoretical Framework for an Anthropology of Moralities." *Anthropological Theory* 7, no. 2: 131–50.

———. 2008. "Aleksandra Vladimirovna: Moral Narratives of a Russian Orthodox Woman." In *Religion, Morality, and Community in Post-Soviet Societies,* ed. Mark D. Steinberg and Catherine Wanner, 85–113. Washington, D.C.: Woodrow Wilson Center Press.

 CHAPTER 5

An Ethos of Relatedness

Foreign Aid and Grassroots Charities in Two Orthodox Parishes in North-Western Russia

Detelina Tocheva

Most often, gifts made in the frame of personal relationships enhance people's solidarity and engender reciprocal exchange. Gifts made in Christian churches are most usually done with the intention to address God and the saints. This chapter will show that fully anonymous and unreciprocated gifts can also be the manifestation of social relatedness. The second objective of this chapter is to demonstrate that gifts made within churches, and more specifically gifts that can be called "grassroots charities" may completely ignore religious motives. Thus, this chapter explores how Russian Orthodox churches have come to be transformed into an arena of secular social relatedness.

In Russian society, networks of support and informal exchange have a strong reciprocal and personal character. The use of personal connections was a clear feature of the late Soviet and early post-Soviet periods (Ledeneva 1998), including when state resources served personal ends under Soviet rule (Grossman 1977, 1991). Post-Soviet Russians heavily relied on mutual help as well, especially among rural households from the same village (Rogers 2005) and within kin groups (Rousselet 2005). The ways in which Russians mobilize their acquaintances, neighbors and relatives for making ends meet have received great attention in sociological studies conducted by native scholars (see, e.g., Barsukova 2004; Fadeeva 1999; Gradosel'skaia 1999; Lylova 2002; Shanin, Nikulin, and Danilov 2002; Shteinberg 2002; Vinogradskii 1999). In various ways, these and other works all demonstrate that reciprocal support in the frame of personal relationships remains essential in the strategies of making-do for a large portion of the population.

Based on one year's field research (2006–2007) conducted in a city of approximately 80,000 inhabitants located in the region of Saint Petersburg, this chapter focuses on a slightly different logic of giving and receiving— one that engages anonymous and unreciprocated acts which, nonetheless, attest solidarity and relatedness. These can be called "grassroots charities" that take place within Orthodox churches. These "grassroots charities" raise the question: How should one approach contemporary Orthodox charities in Russia? Only a few Orthodox charities are well structured and regularly funded (Mitrokhin 2004). Their Protestant counterparts, in particular the proselytizing groups, who entered Russia after the fall of the Soviet regime, are usually better organized, more efficient, and seem to apply less discriminatory criteria when selecting the potential recipients than Orthodox charities do (Caldwell 2004). Some critics argue that the Russian Orthodox Church is self-interested rather than interested in alleviating suffering within society (Mitrokhin 2004). This opinion is supported by what is popularly conceived of as an equivalence between Russianness and Orthodoxy: Because the Russian Orthodox Church is commonly seen as the national Church, it is expected to take care of the Russian population (Caldwell 2010). And when it does not do so, it is accused of selfishness.

Despite the lack of Churchwide organized social programs, individual Orthodox churches are in fact involved in giving and receiving help at the local level—activities which are not restricted to activists and insiders of the religious community. I propose a more inclusive notion of charity in order to be able to account for more people's concrete experience within Orthodox churches.

Statistical data has shown for more than a decade that the number of active believers, identified in surveys as "practicing" members of the Orthodox Church, is quite low (Dubin 2005; Kääriainen and Furman 2000). This statistical category includes regular churchgoers who stick to strict theological notions of belief and practice. Most sociological surveys, when defining who is a "practicing" believer, refer to criteria such as: "Does her understanding of who God is fit the theological definition?" or "Does her personal conduct follow the highest requirements of religious observance?" Therefore, the category of "practicing" excludes the most widespread forms of flexible Orthodox religiosity (Filatov and Lunkin 2006). However, in various surveys taken since 2000, the proportion of practicing Orthodox Russians rose from 4 percent to 8.5 percent of those who declare themselves to be Russian Orthodox. In the scarce ethnographic literature on the life of post-Soviet Orthodox parishes, these people appear as the "core community" of the church (Sergazina 2006) or as the "church circle" (Tarabukina 2000). Although there is little doubt about the important role of the parishes' core members, it is necessary to look beyond them by extending the scope to those who come in contact with the churches without necessarily being identified as parishioners. I focus on the localities in which the churches are rooted and where what I call "the Orthodox grassroots charities" take place. These charities reflect the idea of an intrinsic relationship between the Russian national "imagined community" (Anderson 1983) and Orthodoxy.

I use an open notion of charity. My initial project was to look at what appears as support, help-giving, and help-receiving inside the parishes. This approach led me to pay attention to a large range of practices, logics, and ways of speaking; it revealed what is performed and lived out as support. Two complexes can be identified. The first are the networks within the core of the parish community—sometimes this core consists of various groups or, better, networks—that draw on both religious and secular views of sociality. The second complex is precisely what can be called grassroots charities. They depend upon the very existence of the church, but they reach out to a broader group of local dwellers, far beyond the parish community, and also involve people with no religious commitment. The term "charity" is appropriate here because it helps put the stress on the personal motivation I have encountered among participants: to give support without expecting reciprocity, and to receive support without giving anything back and often anonymously. Here "grassroots charities" is used as a term of analysis, and is not a translation of some Russian term. I will outline the relevant Russian terms and their local meanings below.

Some of the support for the various groups of needy persons established in Orthodox parishes, including some of the more spontaneous and informal forms of support, have already been outlined by Mitrokhin (2004). In examining the practical functioning of such support, my attempt is, firstly, to investigate it in depth using ethnographic methods, as well as to shed light on the points of view of the participants. Secondly, my approach should allow this chapter to go beyond the topic of charity itself in order to investigate the peculiar and intricate configurations of secular moralities and religious institutions that have emerged in the post-Soviet context.

In this chapter, I will first describe two parishes and provide some terminological details. Then, I will turn to the local reception, and domestication of, external humanitarian aid. This foreign aid was replaced by local grassroots charities. I will analyze their structural and dynamic aspects, as well as their logics of inclusion and exclusion. I will conclude by questioning the relevance of the impact of Orthodox teachings and religious notions on the underlying morality of this ethnographic case. I will, alternatively, suggest that the underlying morality is rather a secular ethos of relatedness.

The Parishes and Their Members

The Church of Saint Peter

The largest parish of the town, identified with its most important Church of Saint Peter,[1] is the center of the higher hierarchical level of the Russian

Orthodox Church, the *blagochinie,* and the rector of this church is also the rector of the *blagochinie* (*blagochinnyi*). The *blagochinie* was comprised of twenty-four parishes at the time of my field research. Built in 1852, the Church of Saint Peter has remained open ever since, with the exception of a four-year closure during World War II (called "the Great Fatherland War" in Russia). This main church employs about forty people. Only six of these employees, mainly the priests, work full-time. Two smaller churches belong to the same parish, one in the hospital and one in a school.

The Church of Saint Peter is located at the top of the main pedestrian street. Its visibility and its almost continuous operation mean the church is well-known by the local inhabitants. Indeed, this is the most visited of all the local churches. According to one of the priests, it has around 500 permanent parishioners. The number of occasional visitors is much higher but is difficult to estimate. According to the priests, during important feasts 4,000 visitors attend per day. Based on my observations, a slight majority of the parishioners are female. Most of those who visit the church at least once every two weeks are in their forties and fifties. There are also elderly women among the common visitors, but they do not constitute the core of the community and do not constitute the majority of visitors. The Church of Saint Peter has a reputation for attracting less radical believers who are more wealthy than others.

The Church of the Mother of God

The church in the other parish I conducted research in is situated a ten-minute walk from the central Church of Saint Peter. The construction of the Church of the Mother of God finished in 1914, when the church was blessed and opened. It was closed in the early 1930s after the priests refused to collaborate with the Soviet state.[2] It reopened in 1991 and remained under reconstruction for more than ten years. Today the parish has about 500 to 600 parishioners according to the rector (including those who go to church no less than every two or three weeks). An impressive influx of people attend the church for important religious feasts, people who usually never, or only occasionally, go to church. But the occasional daily visitors are fewer than at the Church of Saint Peter, first because the Church of the Mother of God is not centrally located, and second because it is open only a few hours per day on a few days of the week. As in other parishes, the most serious churchgoers refuse to consider these occasional visitors as parishioners or churchgoers (*prikhozhane*) and dismiss them as "passers-by" (*prokhozhane* or *zakhozhane,* those who pass through without staying in the church). The 500 to 600 people who regularly attend are considered by the clergy to be the "real" parishioners. The Church of the Mother of God is less well-off than the Church of Saint Peter. The prices of religious goods and rituals are lower, and it also seems to attract poorer and older visitors.

Insiders' Points of View on Giving Help

The parishes are the arena for various practices of giving help based on both religious and secular ideas, which are revealed as a form of social support through everyday practices and colloquial ways of speaking about such practices, although their degree of formalization is very low. Let me outline some local ideas, practices, and ways of speaking of help-giving. First, according to the dictionaries, the Russian *blagotvoritel'nost'* can be translated as "charity" and "philanthropy." *Miloserdie* means "mercy," "charity," or "clemency." The adjective *miloserdnyi* means both "merciful" and "charitable." From English, "charity" is translated as *blagotvoritel'nost'* and *miloserdie*. When people use the terms *blagotvoritel'nost'* and *miloserdie* (*miloserdie* is used less often) they usually refer to a publicized, sometimes even grandiose, act of giving in order to help the needy, an act of publicly committing oneself to support others. In the Orthodox milieu of my field site, *blagotvoritel'nost'* is understood as an act motivated by profound spirituality and moral purity. Because the charitable giver (*blagotvoritel'*) is spontaneously defined as a person possessing outstanding moral qualities, when I, or some of my interlocutors themselves, evoked the term, people invariably spoke of the pre-revolutionary era that they often presented as a quasi-mythical period when Russia was inhabited by highly moral people. From the local point of view, the terms *blagotvoritel'nost'* and *miloserdie* would seem pretentious if applied to current practices. Generally, religious and non-religious local dwellers say that charity does not really exist in the town.

Locals use the term *blagotvoritel'nost'* to include both donations to help the needy and donations to a church for renovation works and for the internal functioning of the parish. However, contemporary donations to the church are usually called sponsorship support (*sponsorskaia pomoshch'*) and less often *blagotvoritel'nost'*. Referring to a donor as a *sponsor* connotes modernity and less moral purity, and can imply that the person does not have any religious motivation. In contrast, the *blagotvoritel'* is seen as the ideal merciful and pious charitable giver.

An important practice of giving help is the mutual assistance that occurs inside the parish community, most often as interactions between the most engaged members, but also reaching beyond the community. These relationships can be identified as networking and informal reciprocal support. None of the participants and non-participants in parish life ever described such mutual assistance as "charity" (*blagotvoritel'nost'* or *miloserdie*). In colloquial language, such assistance is referred to as "mutual help" (*vzaimovyruchka* and *vzaimopomoshch'*). Often these interactions are simply not named at all. Although these forms of assistance are clearly effective in providing material and psychological support to the most active parish members, as these interactions are totally invisible from outside the community of parishioners, they are hardly identified as such by the larger public.

There is also invisible charity, performed by believers who wish their gifts and good actions to remain secret in order to be appreciated only by God, and consequently for the giver to be rewarded for these deeds in the afterlife. Such secret gifts are also totally informal and depend on individual decisions. By definition these gifts are meant to remain hidden and unspoken; the donors consider acting according to the gospel which says that the left hand should not know what the right hand does (*levaia ruka ne dolzhna znat' to chto pravaia delaet*). Unlike the mutual support realized through networking inside the communities, these gifts are explicitly conceptualized in Christian terms as help to a neighbor. They are invisible, and this is their raison d'être. These gifts occur in the context of the parish's core communities, as they are practiced only by the most committed believers.

Another understanding of giving help is a widespread notion that spiritual services (such as confession, the blessing of flats and cars, the distribution of holy water, prayers, and other religious rites) constitute help at least as much as food, money, and clothing do, and possibly even more. Indeed, I constantly encountered the conviction that real support goes beyond offering items for everyday use, food, and health care. This idea is largely shared by priests, church workers, and regular churchgoers. One of the most widespread religious practices consists of writing the names of acquaintances, friends, and family members on sheets of paper (*zapiski*) which are then read out in prayers by priests and church workers. For the numerous Russians who use the *zapiski*, many of whom often ignore much of the Church's doctrine and do not participate in church life, spiritual practice is indivisible from support and assistance.

There is also the explicit, although not highly formalized, material support intended for the larger public, support that I describe as grassroots charities. These grassroots charities are far from being as inclusive and efficient as some of the more large-scale soup kitchens, or some of the massive clothing, housing, and health programs established in larger cities, often by foreign organizations. These much larger charities formally define, for example, who is entitled to assistance, precisely how the specific project works in terms of staff, types of items and support provided, and official authorizations they hold (Caldwell 2004). Such formalization is absent from local charitable efforts. Nonetheless, in my field site the invention of the local grassroots charities began with such foreign aid.

From Foreign Aid to Local Patterns

When considering the models of charity of the Roman Catholic Church and those of the most established Protestant churches, one might assume that a strong Orthodox revival and a secure existence for the Russian Orthodox Church would also lead to a strong tendency for establishing similar stable formal frameworks for Orthodox charitable activities. Yet local examples contradict this assumption (see also Köllner, chapter 10, this volume). In fact, less formalization has been the dominant pattern in recent years. During the second half of the 1990s and in the very beginning of the 2000s, the town received humanitarian aid from its German twin-city, a town of 38,000 inhabitants situated in the Baden-Württemberg region.[3] Various local institutions (such as homes for elderly and disabled people) benefited from the aid. The Church of Saint Peter and the Church of the Mother of God also received aid that they redistributed through their own channels. The humanitarian support sent to the churches came from the German Diakonie services, the main charitable organization in Germany affiliated with the German Evangelical Church.[4] Today, many local dwellers recall this period of hardship and mention that everyone received some type of material support from the German twin-city.[5] In Orthodox milieus as well as beyond them, only the name of the twin-city is remembered, but nothing is said about the Diakonie and its Protestant affiliation. According to local dwellers, it was possible to order a specific item, such as a coat, shoes, or other items, from the German charities and even to specify the necessary size and type of item. Some received what they expected. Others received inappropriate clothing that they gave away to friends and acquaintances.

For example, in 2000, the Church of Saint Peter received 11,214 kilograms of clothing, shoes, books, and thermoses for the city from the German Diakonie. In 1999, ten wheelchairs reached the parish; consequently they were gifted to the local committee for social protection. The church served as a point of distribution for the aid. The parish archives hold detailed reports on the number of boxes and kilograms of aid given to local dwellers, to neighboring parishes that are part of the *blagochinie*, to a children's home, to the local society of former children deported to Nazi work camps during World War II, to a fund designed to support large families, and to the local military detachment. Many of the recipients wrote letters of thanks to the rector of the parish. Some letters also mention "the good people" who provided the packages. Some letters were written on behalf of the institutions receiving aid. I met the staff of one of these institutions, a children's home situated in a village (*poselok*) some ten kilometers out of the city. The staff members insisted on how helpful this aid was; all the children were dressed, thanks to the boxes of clothes and shoes they had received through the parish.

When the massive, one-sided Western support ended, no similar initiative followed. For the clergy, as for all local inhabitants, the influx of foreign aid remained a central point of reference. This generous unilateral aid was seen as an ideal form of charity. At the time of my field research, the local positive memories were a strong reminder of the fact that the larger public in Russia approved such aid. This larger public expected such an ideal form of charity from the Russian Orthodox Church as well.

"The Cleaners Know Who Is in Need"

Shortly after 2000, the unilateral foreign aid ended, but the clergy did not undertake any initiatives to replace these programs. Instead, foreign charity was totally replaced by local patterns of support. The supply of clothing was not such an acute problem in 2006–2007, but a range of basic foods had become too expensive for many to purchase, and people also suffered from the scarcity of affordable housing. There remained no trace of the central role that the Church of Saint Peter had previously played in providing clothing for a significant portion of the local population. There were no more visible activities of church poverty relief. The only visible reminders of the fact that churches were associated with charity were a few old women begging every day at the entrance of the church yard. However, many people, both churchgoers and non-churchgoers, brought bags of clothes, shoes, and other things like dishes, baby strollers, and other goods for everyday use to the churches. The shop workers and cleaners (*svechnitsi* and *uborchitsi*) distributed these goods to the people they knew to be in need of such things. This activity was not advertised. The workers of the Church of Saint Peter did not think of these activities as something valuable to the church. The priests were surprised when I showed an interest in these transactions. One of them told me that the clergymen did not supervise this activity. "The cleaners know who is in need," he said, indicating that these re-distributive activities were of secondary importance and that finding recipients was a totally informal affair. The church workers, but never the priests themselves, assigned themselves to the task of collecting what was brought to them and further distributing these items, primarily to their kin, friends, acquaintances, and networks of acquaintances. Those outside of church networks may also have had access to the gifts, but without any guarantee that they would benefit from those of the best quality. The shop workers and cleaners kept on redistributing in order to solve the problem posed by the unceasing arrival of bulky plastic bags, more numerous in feast days, but still a regular feature of ordinary days. There were no official rules on how to distribute the items and whom was deserving of them, as there were no high ideals of charity and support associated with this redistribution of goods. Similar practices were carried out in other neighboring parishes, with a similar lack of formality. During a Sunday morning service in a neighboring village, I inquired about the bulky plastic bags left in the entrance of the church and was immediately encouraged by the female shop worker to take for myself what I wanted. I was a completely anonymous visitor there. In another church the priest refused all donations apart from those explicitly solicited by the church for its own needs. This priest systematically directed those who tried to leave donations at the church to a home for the elderly. He explained to me that people bring mainly old clothes and broken things that nobody needs. He claimed that those who bring donations are merely acting according to the saying "God, take what we don't like" (*Na tebe, Bozhe, chto nam ne gozhe*). My observations in other churches showed that some of the donated items were really not useful anymore, but nevertheless many quickly found future users (about the clerical point of view on charity, see Köllner, chapter 10, this volume).

A horizontal rhizome-like pattern of grassroots charities appeared from below and expanded to the churches. As the economic situation of the population improved, people took the initiative of bringing things to the church in order to transmit them to future users. Similar initiatives of mutual support were typical in Russian kindergartens where parents of grown-up children gave to those who had younger children. The home for the elderly in the town also regularly benefited from gifts. Those places were perceived as needy; pensioners, the disabled, and children appeared to be natural recipients. Such recipients were, in the Soviet system, considered to be deserving of support, both by the official ideology and by the population. The current institutional categories of those deserving of help and the popular understandings of them largely follow the Soviet ones (Yates 2004).

It clearly appears that the population uses the churches as appropriate mediators between those who can give and those who receive. Why did people give them this role? In the first decade of the 2000s, almost every single local Orthodox church started to experience the phenomenon of bulky plastic bags left at the church by visitors and passers-by. The popularity of Orthodoxy in post-Soviet Russia partly explains why the churches started to be used for such non-religious purposes. First, the churches are open to everyone. Second, Orthodoxy is largely promoted by the state, in contrast to other denominations, especially to those labeled as "non-traditional" or "sects." Third, there is a lasting perception in Russian society that the Orthodox Church has a role in helping the needy. On one hand, the non-practicing Orthodox public believes the Church does not have adequate programs of social support, because it does not work according to the ideal of large-scale unilateral support. On the other hand, the churches have become integrated into local secular logics of support, sometimes against the will of church authorities. Thus, under pressure from the unceasing arrival of bulky bags, churches have become spaces of grassroots charitable efforts, whose practical modalities require a closer examination.

"People Bring, Others Take"

The churches are usually rather passive actors in the process of charitable redistribution. Most of the time, it is the church workers who face the problem of bags and bigger items left at the church by locals, and it is they who need to find ways to use them or to get rid of them. However, the following example from the Church of the Mother of God is a bit different. It illustrates, first, domestication of Western ways of providing charity and, finally, a total conversion to a local model with a higher degree of organization in comparison with the neighboring parishes.

The church was undergoing reconstruction work when, in the middle of the 1990s, German humanitarian aid began to arrive at this officially registered parish. The story I provide here is based on narratives of members of the parish who at that time were working to rebuild the church, or who were aware of the arrival of the packages of humanitarian aid. The twinned German town[6] sent boxes containing clothes, shoes, and, according to some informants, even umbrellas and blankets, all used but in good condition. During several summers young Germans came to help with the reconstruction of the church. All of those who remembered the young Germans said that these foreigners were helpful and happy to be visiting Russia. Packages of food were also sent from Finland to the local Red Cross.[7] But the German aid was far greater in volume and is now remembered more clearly. In the 1990s, all the packages were stored inside the church and distributed from there. First, those who worked for the reconstruction benefited from the packs, and after them all those who showed interest. By the end of 1999 (or in 2000), the German aid ended, but many items still remained undistributed.

There is a church shop, or *lavka,* in front of the Church of the Mother of God. In Soviet times it was a place where empty bottles were collected. The building had belonged to the church before it was closed in the beginning of the 1930s, so the small building was restored to the Church of the Mother of God in the beginning of the 1990s. By the end of the 1990s, this shop was already established as a normal church lavka, of about twelve square meters, selling various religious items, books, and booklets. The shop worker at that time, a woman in her seventies, spoke to people coming to the lavka who told her that they needed shoes or other essential items, but had no money to buy them.[8] She also heard other people say that they had some household items in good condition that they did not need anymore. The shop worker then suggested to the clergy, and in particular to the *starosta* (head of the parish lay council, a key person in this parish), that she could bring the undistributed German humanitarian aid into the shop. These remaining items had encumbered the activity of the church. The shop worker proposed that these items be displayed in the lavka in order to make them available to those who might need them. She also suggested that the people who told her they had some useful items at home should bring them to the lavka for display. Thus the lavka began its new charitable activities alongside the more conventional sale of religious objects. A joke circulated at that time emphasizing the crucial role of the shop worker who conceived of and managed the lavka's new charities. If someone admired another person's coat and asked where it came from, the lucky coat owner would often reply "From Ivanovna,"[9] and mimic the speech of a New Russian describing the latest Versace. This joke between acquaintances reveals an ironic attitude to experienced economic hardship, as well as gratitude for the shop worker's good idea. It also acknowledges a deep awareness of a system of "making do" created in order to survive in difficult times.

At the time of my fieldwork in 2006–2007, the lavka was well known in town. It was open almost every day. Around twenty people came each day to buy a cross, a candle, or another religious item, to request prayers, or to inquire about rituals (for example, what they needed for a baptism, how much it cost, and when it could be done). Some people came in order to drop off clothes, shoes, dishes, or shelves from home. Others came hoping to find some donated things they needed for free. While the former German and Finnish humanitarian aid was called "*gumanitarka*" (which can be translated as "humanitarian package"), these locally-based charities were not called by a specific name. Nevertheless, almost every single local inhabitant I talked to about this lavka expressed approval and many said that they had brought items there at least once. Although the church made no real effort to support these charitable activities, it did offer the use of the room and the assurance that the shop worker would look after donated items. In fact, the existence of this charitable redistribution totally depended on the parish.

Perceptions of the Lavka Activity

It is tempting to look for deeply buried religious motivations as being responsible for the process of integrating Orthodox churches into grassroots social support activities. One way of understanding the link between charitable activity and religious belief is to examine the actors' own interpretations by asking them whether they saw these activities as religious. Another method is to distance the analysis from these immediate responses by conducting it at a higher level and embedding the current logics in a historical perspective, and as part of a broader model of social self-representation. I will take this latter, analytic approach in the conclusion, but for now I will examine the direct responses given to the question of the link between religion and charity, drawing on the case of the church shop.

The donors and the recipients of items did not think of the lavka's charitable activity as religious. Usually people responded that this charitable activity had nothing to do with religion. Similarly, the lavka grassroots charities were perceived by parish workers and priests as extremely modest and simple efforts, and they never spoke of them as being based on some Christian motivation. Every time that I asked about charity (*blagotvoritel'nost'*) in this parish, I was told that, unfortunately, there was no such thing. The parish is considered poor and its parishioners are viewed as modest people; the clergymen, the parishioners, and other persons speak of it as a "village parish" (*derevenskii prikhod*), implying that it is not well-off and survives thanks only to its parishioners. The religious identity of the church shop is completely subsumed under the secular motivations for gifting and logics of redistribution. "People bring, others take" (*liudi prinostiat, drugie berut*) is the usual way it was spoken of. Expressed in such terms, for the clergy and the church workers this charitable activity was neither a source of pride nor a Christian argument for future salvation due to good actions. However, it would be misleading to say that the clergy and the church workers disregarded the lavka activity. Rather, they saw it as vaguely good but insignificant, deserving only the lowest attention. The priests were not even interested in what happened in the lavka. Only the lavka worker and the accountant of the parish were really involved. Therefore, the idea that the lavka would carry out acts of Christian compassion never crossed the minds of the local dwellers.

Gifting

In principle, everyone could donate items and everyone could take what he or she liked. In practice, the patterns of giving and redistribution reproduced some of the dominant social logics of discrimination and privilege, of moral evaluation and judgment. Sometimes when people brought items to the lavka, they stayed there for some time to check and see if there was anything available that they wanted. This checking can hardly be termed "barter," for there was no strong expectation that having donated something, a person would get something in return. If a donor did find something he wanted, this was simply considered good luck.

People from various social backgrounds and of different ages brought items to the lavka. Women and men were equally represented. Some said that they brought a sweater, or shoes, or dishes, or a suitcase, because they wished to make a useful gift to others. Others emphasized that donating was a good "opportunity to get rid of things" (*sposob izbavlenia ot veshchei*). Only one woman declared that she was motivated to give by her Christian faith, which she defined as "not especially Orthodox." She said she often checked her cupboards at home hoping to find something to donate to the lavka. Some people also brought garments to the homes for the elderly and for disabled people. All donors were animated by the desire that their things should become useful again, rather than end up in the garbage. But this did not mean a total disinterest in the future of the items they offered. Conversely, many persons, including those who wished to "get rid of things," expressed satisfaction when their donations were welcomed by the shop worker. When one woman brought in a plastic bag full of clothes, the shop worker said, "Thank you for bringing this." "Thank you for accepting it," the woman replied, appearing to be pleased with the very fact that her bag was welcome. Some people left their gifts and came back a couple of hours later to find out if someone had taken them. If someone heard that his or her gift had reached a receiver, he or she usually appeared quite satisfied. Although face-to-face donations were quite rare, many of the givers manifested a more or less open interest in the success of their gift, in particular if it successfully reached a needy person. As in other churches, the usefulness of their donation to another, usually anonymous, person was seen by donors as a criterion of the success of their action. When a recipient chose to take a donated item, it was seen as a recognition of the usefulness of the donor's gift and an accomplishment of the act of giving.

Privileged Recipients

Sociologically, there were several types of recipients. There was less diversity of social backgrounds in the recipients than in the donors. There were no well-to-do recipients; instead they were usually people who were ostensibly poor, as well as people with low incomes who considered themselves to be neither particularly poor nor rich. Working people, especially women in their thirties, forties, and fifties, as well as pensioners (both women and men), usually selected one or two items that they liked. Those who visited the lavka in order to buy candles or another religious item, to request a prayer or a ritual, or simply to seek advice from the shop worker whom they considered competent in religious matters, often had a look at the donated items, and sometimes choose one or two pleasing objects. Sometimes, a person who brought an item would also choose another one to take home. These occasional recipients constituted one group of the common users of the lavka. They had access to all the things that were displayed, and the shop worker was open and friendly with them.

But not all recipients were granted equal access to the donated materials. The shop worker played a key role here. She distinguished between the users, reproducing in her actions some widespread modes of discrimination and favoritism. A former factory and printing company worker, she had retired in 2004. Like many retired persons in Russia, she needed an additional income. As a trustworthy person, she was offered the job of shop worker after the sudden death of the previous locally famous creator of the lavka. Although she was Orthodox, she was not an ardent believer and only rarely attended church. Like others from her generation, she was nostalgic about many aspects of Soviet life. This woman privileged some recipients she considered deserving, while disadvantaging others. Two groups of shop users benefited from her special treatment: first, there were her acquaintances, friends, and family members, including some of the most engaged parishioners. This privileged group had no clear boundaries; it was rather a network of acquaintances. When the shop worker deemed an object to be nice and useful, she put it behind the counter.

Frequently, a person who wished to bring something to the lavka first came to the shop worker and asked if his or her item would be accepted. The shop worker immediately refused garments that were too old and encouraged people to bring in only what is particularly useful and nice. When an agreement was reached and the items were about to be delivered, the shop worker would inquire among her closest contacts about who might be interested in the items—particularly in the case of rare donations like baby strollers, or baby and children's clothes. If one of her contacts was interested, as soon as the object arrived, the shop worker would telephone the future owner. She was a key acquaintance who could potentially offer what was needed at the right moment.

The privileged persons were not always acquaintances; no reciprocity could be expected from many people, given that they usually remained as anonymous to the shop worker when leaving the lavka as they were before entering it. In those cases, the shop worker made her own evaluation of the moral qualities of persons seeking items from the lavka. She made decisions according to widely accepted social criteria of worthiness, the main ones being physical disability and work. Several times people simply addressed the shop worker to ask if a desired item had arrived. In such cases the shop worker proceeded to morally evaluate the person: Did he or she really need this item? Did he or she deserve it? Was he or she righteous? In these situations, it was crucial to have some convincing reasons to expect a favor. I witnessed one case of a blind woman who, because of her physical disability, received the requested garments directly at her home, carefully selected and delivered by the shop worker. Another woman, a single working mother ("She works a lot," the shop worker said), also received personally selected items at home. If one was a recipient who was previously unknown to the shop worker, it was fundamental to be recognized as deserving in order to have access to the best items. Physical disability and especially hard work have been lasting markers of human worth in the Soviet and post-Soviet periods (Vladimirova 2006; Yates 2004). The official Soviet categories of the "invalid," or the "pensioner" (one who is no longer able-bodied), still referred to the deserving needy. Similarly, participation in (or willingness to participate in) socially recognized work serves as a measure of the value of persons; in the Russian case, this understanding derives from Soviet ideology of labor (Vladimirova 2006) and permeates all social milieus of Russian society. Therefore, a good worker is always considered to embody high morality. But in the lavka, not everyone was given the opportunity to demonstrate how deserving they were.

A Procedure of Appropriation

In the very beginning of my fieldwork, when the shop worker considered me as a special visitor, she offered me a long thick winter coat assuring that it had been donated by a "clean woman," an acquaintance of a friend of hers, as I understood later. What I took then for an exceptional event came out to be a rather usual practice. Since Marcel Mauss ([1924] 1990), anthropologists have acknowledged that, in a multitude of cases and societies, things that are donated are marked by the person of the donor. While in some cases the appropriation of a donated thing did not involve any mention of the donor, in other cases this was a prominent feature of the grassroots charities. In particular, in the lavka, the transfer of donated items from a giver to a future recipient required a specific procedure. Cleanliness was brought into the procedure as an intermediate category which allowed the transfer. The shop worker selected items of good quality for deserving recipients. For her, the quality of the item was raised by the moral portrait of the giver. When she offered good clothes to close contacts and deserving recipients, she often mentioned that "this was brought by a clean woman" or "that was brought by a clean person" (*chistenkaia zhenshina prinesla, chistenkii chelovek prines*). As we know from Mary Douglas (1978), dirt and cleanliness are relative ideas. Indeed, the reference to cleanliness meant that the shop worker knew the donor, or that she considered him or her to be a good person. Thus, a positive moral judgment referring either to a close contact, or to an unknown but morally high-standing person, was voiced in terms of cleanliness. The donated objects appeared as an extension of the person; a moral portrait became instilled in the things that were given. Ultimately, this operation was meant to make the gift easily acceptable to the recipient.

When occasional visitors found something and decided to take it home, they often used the same phrases as the shop worker in order to acknowledge the donor's cleanliness, although they did not actually know who had donated the item. Admiring an item and saying, "This was given by a clean person" served as a kind of explanation for their choice and as an act of self-persuasion that the object was of good quality. The connection between the giver, the object given, and the receiver was built through these brief judgements of the donor's cleanliness. They signified a recognition and an acceptance of the moral self of the anonymous donor, and in this way they helped to neutralize the tension existing in the process of appropriating other people's objects. On one hand, the donors seemed to desire complete alienation of the items they had given. When some of them came back to check and see if somebody had taken their gifts, this was precisely because they wished their things to become other people's property. But on the other hand, complete appropriation did not seem immediately possible from the recipient's point of view. The appropriation required a special procedure of building a positive moral portrait of the anonymous donor through the category of cleanliness. The potential recipient achieved the transfer of the object by describing its cleanliness, a process which aimed to recognize the worth of the donor.

Lavka Users Who Were Discriminated Against

In Russian society, "Gypsies are hardly ever depicted as sincere players" (Lemon 2000: 4); they are considered "slippery by nature" (226), and their relation to money is suspect, at best (Lemon 1998). Alaina Lemon's observations found a poignant resonance in the everyday functioning of the grassroots charities. The lavka welcomed all visitors; no one was prevented from entering and everyone could see the items on display. Scorn and latent conflict became more explicit when *some* visitors made a particular request or when their behavior was considered inappropriate. The shop worker was clearly critical of those whom she called "the Gypsies" (*tsygany*) and of the resellers. Her negative opinion of these "misusers" was shared by the leaders of the parish community. (But these leaders did not intervene and even appeared disinterested in these matters.)

One day, a young Gypsy couple entered the lavka and had a look at the clothes and shoes on display. Then the man turned to the shop worker: would she have a pair of shoes "to sell" to his wife? The woman behind the counter got upset because the young man implied that she might have been selling the shoes donated to the shop. Then she replied that everything was displayed and that she had no other things available. This was in fact not true, although at that precise moment she did not have an appropriate pair of shoes behind the counter for the woman. After the man insisted, the shop worker told him, in quite a firm voice, that they should go to the second hand store where they could buy what they needed. When the couple left, the shop worker commented on the idleness of Gypsies that, she went on to explain, always meant that they tried to acquire things for free. Her comment was made despite the fact that the young man had offered to pay for the shoes, which was in fact an offending offer to her. On another occasion, she told me that the Gypsies have no money and therefore they need to find goods for free, "but one can see the golden teeth in their mouths." The conclusion that I was expected to draw was that Gypsies have an irrational relationship to money, and that it was totally natural for the shop worker to refuse to support their supposedly absurd way of life. Interestingly enough, criticism of the "Gypsy" use of money erupted in the shop worker's talk even when the Gypsy visitors did not mention money at all. She imputed their poverty to their "Gypsy" way of using money. But she never discussed in detail why ethnic Russians should have recourse to the lavka; for her, this was normal because "many have a hard life in today's Russia." Yet Gypsies were treated as suspect no matter whether they offered to pay or if they sought to acquire things for free; they were "the 'wrong' social type" not only when they wielded money (Lemon 1998: 45–46) but also when they lacked money. I cannot generalize that perceived Russian-ness was an immediate guarantor of worthiness. But it was definitely true that a perceived Gypsy origin always raised suspicion and resentment in matters of charity.

In addition to those with a perceived Gypsy ethnicity, the other group that was constantly criticised by the shop worker were those who were suspected of selling what they had acquired from donations to the lavka. The priests themselves were reluctant to become involved in these conflicts. Five or six of the regular lavka visitors were said to sell what they took from the shop for free. Of course, none of them openly declared that they engaged in such activity. In most cases, only their daily visits and the bulky bags they carried away from the lavka raised suspicions that they might be selling. Nevertheless, the shop worker never impeded them from gathering the displayed items. Gypsies and ethnic Russians took equal part in this unfair trade. One regular seller of lavka goods was a Gypsy woman in her early thirties, originally from Moldova.[10] She was the mother of two young children. She came to the lavka literally every day. The shop worker knew that she sold everything and that this was a way for her to get some vital cash. The shop worker had an ambivalent relation with her. On one hand, she denounced the young woman to me for her immoral behavior. Once, the Gypsy woman started selling lavka goods just outside the lavka. The shop worker got extremely angry, especially when she heard people gossiping that the lavka was selling things that people had donated. On the other hand, the shop worker supported the woman's ongoing transgression to some extent. The shop worker would regularly select clothes and other items she knew the young woman could easily sell, and would offer these to her in voluminous bags. The shop worker tolerated the reselling when the young woman sold the goods far enough from the lavka that nobody could guess the origin of the articles. Thus she admitted that the young mother's ostensibly immoral behavior was after all pardonable because of her hardship. However, she insisted that I not give money to this Gypsy; apparently reselling donated goods was a more acceptable way to give the woman access to money. The effort the young Gypsy was putting in the resale seemed, from the shop worker's point of view, to qualify as work, and therefore this effort seemed to bring legitimacy to the money acquired in this way. But when the Gypsy woman begged and received money as a result of begging, the shop worker heavily disapproved of both the procedure and the money obtained in this way.

The shop worker's disapproval of the young Gypsy was also mixed with empathy. Humor indicated complicity between the two women. For example, the shop worker joked with the young woman that she lied so frequently to find reasons for requesting money and services that she forgot what she had said on previous days. "I tell her: 'Your birthday is six times per year!'," she laughed, a half critical and half friendly remark. In addition, the young Gypsy and her children helped the shop worker tidy the shop by sorting through and throwing out old and unpleasant clothes and other items. The shop worker also offered candies to the children. Nevertheless, the Gypsy woman told me that the shop worker did not like her: "She advises people not to give me money," she said. This case shows the complexity in practice of the discrimination that occurred as part of the distribution process in the grassroots charities. While all unknown Gypsies and resellers were met with resentment, empathy became possible only by creating a closer relationship. Such a relationship, however, did not completely erase the initial mistrust and scorn.

Conclusion

The ethnographic account I have given aims to demonstrate the spontaneous and non-formalized giving, networking, and informal mechanisms of inclusion and exclusion that shape the grassroots charities. Current Russian high ideals about charity differ vastly from the grassroots charities. While the idealized forms of charity rest on ideas of unilaterality and the distance between the charitable giver and the needy recipient, the grassroots charitable re-distribution is made possible only by shared ideas of relatedness. I will now take a closer look at the forms of this relatedness.

Two distinct, but often entwined, logics of relatedness are at work: the first one characterizes the process of distribution; it implies networking, various forms of reciprocity, moral judgment, and discrimination. In this logic, horizontal and hierarchical, inclusive and selective, personal and anonymous relationships are brought to bear in practical transactions. Numerous sociological studies emphasize the social significance of networking and informal exchanges in urban and rural Russia for the late Soviet and post-Soviet periods. What has attracted less scholarly attention is what constitutes the second logic of relatedness present in the grassroots charities: spontaneous and often anonymous acts of altruistic giving. The donors act out of empathy and without much introspective self-examination of their deeper motives. The common motivation, even in the case of those who wish to simply get rid of things, is for their gifts to be helpful to others. Thus, instead of asking whether their acts are *really* altruistic or conceal shadows of interestedness, I prefer to trust my informants—following, then, John Davis (1992: 14–27)—and to argue that people become donors out of a mere desire to help. Discriminatory relationships and indiscriminate, most often anonymous, gifting all shape the overall model.

An intriguing element in this second logic of relatedness is the role attributed to and played by the Orthodox churches. As I showed above, no religious meaning is consciously attributed to the grassroots charities. These actions cannot be labeled religious "pure gifts" (Parry 1986); they are not intended to address the transcendent in any way, and even the clergy do not see any religious meaning in them. Neither do these donations show traces of almsgiving motivated by religious belief. Could we, then, advance the argument that traces of religion are embedded in the phenomenon of these modest donations, even though they are invisible at first glance?

A brief historical comparison between these grassroots charities and their possible historical precedents shows that the current practices do not reproduce earlier forms of giving in which religion was an underlying element. We can situate at the two extremes of a continuum the indiscriminate almsgiving, deeply rooted in pre-revolutionary Orthodox culture and practiced over centuries (Bernshtam 2005: 282–86), and the organized charities which emerged in the nineteenth century. The so-called "homes of industry" are prominent examples of the nineteenth-century charities, inspired by scientific philanthropy. They hosted poor people, prostitutes, and vagrants and, by putting them to work, aimed at improving their employability and morality (Lindenmeyr 1986, 1996). Some of these homes operated under the auspices of the Church. In addition, there were a wide range of other religious and non-religious charities. As Lindenmeyr has argued, even charity is too "frail" a concept to express the complex and multiple philosophies of giving that prevailed during the late imperial Russia (Lindenmeyr 1990: 689). Religion was pivotal to many pre-revolutionary forms of support to the needy. Religion is again important for some of the more recent Orthodox charities. However, it is deceptive to look for a revival of nineteenth-century models of giving in the shape of the recently created Church programs. Revivalist discourses often surround such charitable initiatives. But these discourses are part of the performance of authenticity, since a particular representation of pre-revolutionary Orthodoxy is meant to stand for an ideal of righteous religiosity. The grassroots charities themselves are an example of something radically different from all the nineteenth–century forms of almsgiving and philanthropy, and they also differ from any organized contemporary charity. They do not resemble the direct face-to-face relationships established in traditional Orthodox almsgiving, because they are indirect and anonymous most of the time, mediated by church workers, and their participants are rarely devoted Orthodox believers. Unlike almsgiving, they do not necessarily imply a hierarchy in the respective status of the giver and the receiver; in addition, the donor occasionally becomes a recipient of what other donors bring. Unlike the nineteenth-century initiatives, they do not rely on any idea about transforming society or reshaping the moral self of the recipient. They are something entirely new to the Church, or at least something that has not so far been acknowledged by historians.

If the donors do not expect any kind of reciprocity and there is no religious meaning attached to their acts, what relates them to the recipients of their gifts? The grassroots charities are an arrangement founded by the members of a society, an arrangement that involves their churches in the practical enactment of a social ethos of relatedness. This ethos permeates the churches from below with the singular impetus of unplanned spontaneous acts of giving. It holds together an imagined horizontal community of those in need, a category largely coincident with the imagined community of ordinary Russians. Giving and receiving, often in anonymous ways, puts the emphasis on one's belonging to a specific but large group in society: the group of the common people who experience need and those who are aware of, and physically in contact with, the massive presence of needy people. This imagined collective of the needy is historically constructed and anchored in popular self-images. For example, Nancy Ries (1997) reports that during Perestroika, Russians overwhelmingly perceived themselves to be those who suffer but still make do. In the period of Perestroika, the needy were to a very large extent defined as ordinary Russians who experienced chronic shortages of basic goods. More generally, the motif of material poverty and suffering is present in a large range of Russian poetry and works of literature. Hence, there is a lasting social self-representation of a community held together along horizontal lines of need. This self-image engenders concrete social dynamics, of which the grassroots charities are just one example.

Religious interpretations have sometimes given meaning to this self-image. One of the historically lasting ideological schemes in Russian Orthodoxy is the relation between physical suffering and poverty, and spiritual elevation. Traces of this were found even in the late Soviet period. For instance, in her rich description of "Russian talk" during the Perestroika years Nancy Ries mentions both implicit and explicit references to Orthodoxy; poverty was considered a source of spiritual merit and some associations with sanctity were established (1997: 126–60).

But such religious conceptualization cannot be found in the grassroots charities; the latter are modestly pragmatic, not spiritually emphatic. On one hand, the very fact that people use the churches for their grassroots charities indicates a lasting relation between Russian society and the Orthodox Church. But on the other hand, in the case discussed here, the ethos of relatedness is no longer articulated in terms of religious belief. When one turns to the larger public of those who use these charities and to the clergy, it is difficult to find any religious connotations to these activities. It is deceptive to search for traces of forgotten Orthodox teachings that could explain a phenomenon which is definitely secular. All donors share the conviction that the overwhelming majority of their fellow members of society face material hardship that they can help to alleviate (although only partly). All clerics try to delegate the problem of the management of donations to their subordinates who "know who is in need." No religious belief or implicit religious meaning emerges. As Kormina and Shtyrkov write in this volume, in some sense Soviet atheism has really won (see chapter 9).

One could object that the inequalities in the redistribution of donations examined above contradict the idea of a community of equals in need. Indeed, the everyday distribution of gifted goods includes practices of discrimination and favoritism. But this characteristic does not supercede the more comprehensive feature of giving practices: both disinterested giving based on empathy and the unconditional receipt of gifts, as well as discrimination and favoritism in distribution, involve people from various social backgrounds and operate in the general frame of an imagined collective of the needy. In this sense, the grassroots charities, though very limited in their efficacy, appear as an enactment of an ethos of horizontal relatedness. They draw on a specific awareness of being one of many, one among others, in the same society. This contemporary ethos of relatedness is unambiguously secular. It spills over into the churches and is enacted there in the form of grassroots charities. This secular ethos connects with a religious institution on the basis of the lasting idea that the Orthodox Church has some role in helping the needy. Thus local Orthodox churches become involved in the practical manifestations of this ethos of relatedness and no religious meaning arises in the process. Popular acts of giving turn the churches into a convenient ground for redistribution. Thus, we observe how, through these spontaneous enactments of a secular ethos of relatedness, a religious institution is being embedded into post-Soviet society. This is just one way in which Russians make the Russian Orthodox Church part of their social world. Religious belief is certainly crucial to other mechanisms of re-appropriation of the Church, although what originates from pre-revolutionary Orthodoxy and what bears the marks of the Soviet and post-Soviet periods, and contemporary Russian capitalism, are again other questions.

Notes

This research was fully supported by the Max Planck Institute for Social Anthropology, Halle, Germany. I am grateful to Kathy Rousselet, Melissa Caldwell, Doug Rogers, Alex Agadjanian, Jeanne Kormina, Sergey Shtyrkov, Tünde Komáromi, Tobias Köllner, Agata Ladykowska, Jarrett Zigon and Chris Hann for their inspiring comments.

1. The names of the churches are pseudonyms.
2. The priests refused to participate in the movement known as the *obnovlenchestvo,* or "renewal." Started in 1922, the *obnovlenchestvo* appeared to its clerical supporters to be the only possible way of rescuing Orthodoxy while under the control of the Bolshevik state since the revolution in 1917. However, for its opponents, the *obnovlenchestvo* was a betrayal of the Orthodox faith and the Church. For the wider flock of lay Orthodox and for a good part of the clergy, the "renewal" and its opposition took place in a general atmosphere of confusion as to matters of ritual and calendar (Freeze 1995). Eventually, in the 1930s, those who joined the movement endured the same bloody repression as those who opposed it.

3. German charitable organizations and NGOs were particularly active in Russia at that time.
4. The German Evangelical Church should not be confused with most other Evangelical churches, which feature a more proselytizing nature.
5. In 1998 the lives of Russians were shaken up by a sharp financial crisis which worsened the generalized economic hardship and social instability that began with the collapse of the Soviet system and was still visible by 2006 and 2007.
6. In the parish of the Church of the Mother of God I was never explicitly told that the aid arrived through the Diakonie services of the twinned German town.
7. Before the 1917 revolution, many Finnish speakers lived in the town and in the surrounding villages which are situated in the historical region of Ingermanlandia. Some of these Ingermanlandian Finns emigrated to Finland after the revolution. Many of those who stayed were deported by Stalin to Siberia, but later returned to their native region. Today the relations between Finland and the Finns who stayed in Soviet Russia are getting stronger. The Finnish humanitarian aid sent to the town was part of these strengthening post-Soviet Finnish ties.
8. The woman who told me this story worked in the lavka during my fieldwork and was a close friend of the previous shop worker, who had taken the initiative that I describe.
9. The real patronymic name of the shop worker is as common as the pseudonym Ivanovna that I have given her.
10. In the town, all those identified as Gypsies (*tsygany*) by ethnic Russians say they come from Moldova, although many have been rooted in the same neighborhood for generations.

References

Anderson, Benedict. 1983. *Imagined Communities. Reflections on the Origin and Spread of Nationalism.* New York: Verso.

Barsukova, S. 2004. *Nerynochnye Obmeny mezhdu Rossiiskami Domokhozhiaistvami: Teoriia i Praktika Retsiproknosti.* Moscow: GU Vysshaia Shkola Ekonomiki.

Bernshtam, Tatiana. 2005. *Prikhodskaia Zhizn' Russkoi Derevni: Ocherki po Tserkovnoi Etnografii.* Sankt-Peterburg: Ethnographica Petropolitana, Peterburgskoe vostokovedenie.

Caldwell, Melissa. 2004. *Not by Bread Alone: Social Support in the New Russia.* Berkeley, CA: University of California Press.

———. 2010. "The Russian Orthodox Church, the Provision of Social Welfare, and Changing Ethics of Benevolence." In *Eastern Christians in Anthropological Perspective,* ed. Chris Hann and Herman Goltz, 329–50. Berkeley, CA: University of California Press.

Davis, John. 1992. *Exchange.* Minneapolis, MN: University of Minnesota Press.

Douglas, Mary. 1978. *Purity and Danger: An Analysis of the Concepts of Pollution and Taboo.* London: Routledge.

Dubin, Boris. 2005. "Un 'fardeau léger'. Les Orthodoxes dans la Russie des Années 1990–2000." *Revue d'Etudes Comparatives Est-Ouest* 36, no. 4: 19–42.

Fadeeva, Ol'ga. 1999. "Khoziaistvennye Strategii Sel'skikh Semei." In *Sotsial'naia Traektoriia Reformiruemoi Rossii,* ed. Tatiana Zaslavskaia and Zemfira Kalugina, 426–47. Novosibirsk: Nauka.

Filatov, Sergei, and Roman Lunkin. 2006. "Statistics on Religion in Russia: The Reality Behind the Figures." *Religion, State & Society* 34, no. 1: 33–49.

Freeze, Gregory L. 1995. "Counter-Reformation in Russian Orthodoxy: Popular Response to Religious Innovation, 1922–1925." *Slavic Review* 54, no. 2: 305–39.

Gradosel'skaia, Galina. 1999. "Sotsial'nye Seti: Obmen Chastnymi Trasferami." *Sotsologicheskii Zhournal* 1–2: 156–63.

Grossman, Gregory. 1977. "The 'Second Economy' of the USSR." *Problems of Communism* 26, no. 5: 25–40.

———. 1991. "Informal Personal Incomes and Outlays of the Soviet Urban Population." In *The Informal Economy: Studies in Advanced and Less Developed Countries*, ed. Alejandro Portes, Manuel Castells, and Lauren A. Benton, 150–70. Baltimore: Johns Hopkins University Press.

Kääriainen, Kimmo, and Dmitri Furman, eds. 2000. *Starye Tserkvi, Novye Veruiushchie*. Moscow: Letnii sad.

Ledeneva, Alena. 1998. *Russia's Economy of Favours: Blat, Networking and Informal Exchange*. Cambridge: Cambridge University Press.

Lemon, Alaina. 1998. "'Your Eyes Are Green Like Dollars': Counterfeit Cash, National Substance, and Currency Apartheid in 1990s Russia." *Cultural Anthropology* 13, no. 1: 22–55.

———. 2000. *Between Two Fires: Gypsy Performance and Romani Memory from Pushkin to Post-Socialism*. Durham, NC: Duke University Press.

Lindenmeyr, Adele. 1986. "Charity and the Problem of Unemployment: Industrial Homes in Late Imperial Russia." *Russian Review* 45, no. 1: 1–22.

———. 1990. "The Ethos of Charity in Imperial Russia." *Journal of Social History* 23, no. 4: 679–94.

———. 1996. *Poverty Is Not a Vice: Charity, Society and the State in Imperial Russia*. Princeton, NJ: Princeton University Press.

Lylova, Oksana. 2002. "Neformal'naia Vzaimopomoshch' v Sel'skom Soobshchestve." *Sotsiologicheskie Issledovaniia* 214, no. 2: 83–86.

Mauss, Marcel. [1924] 1990. *The Gift: Form and Reason for Exchange in Archaic Societies*, trans. W. D. Halls. New York: W. W. Norton.

Mitrokhin, Nikolai. 2004. *Russkaia Pravoslavnaia Tserkov': Sovremennoe Sostoianie i Aktual'nye Problemy*. Moscow: NLO.

Parry, Jonathan. 1986. "The Gift, the Indian Gift and the 'Indian Gift'." *Man (New Series)* 21, no. 3: 453–73.

Ries, Nancy. 1997. *Russian Talk: Culture and Conversation During Perestroika*. Ithaca, NY: Cornell University Press.

Rogers, Douglas. 2005. "Moonshine, Money, and the Politics of Liquidity in Rural Russia." *American Ethnologist* 32, no. 1: 63–81.

Rousselet, Kathy. 2005. "La Famille Russe : Configurations des Relations et Evolutions des Solidarités." *Informations Sociales* 124, no. 4: 76–83.

Sergazina, Ksenia. 2006. "Dinamika Vozrozhdenia Russkoi Religioznoi Kul'tury." In *Religioznye Praktiki v Sovremennoi Rossii*, ed. Kathy Rousselet and Alexander Agadjanian, 106–25. Moscow: Novoe izdatel'stvo.

Shanin, Teodor, Alexander Nikulin, and Viktor Danilov, eds. 2002. *Refleksivnoe Krest'ianovedenie. Desiatiletie Issledovanii Sel'skoi Rossii*. Moscow: Moskovskaia Vysshaia Shkola Sotsial'nykh i Ekonomicheskikh Nauk.

Shteinberg, Il'ia. 2002. "Real'naia Praktika Strategii Vyzhivaniia Sel'skoi Sem'i: 'Setevye Resursy'." In *Kuda Idet Rossiia? Formal'nye Institutsii i Real'nye Praktiki,* ed. Tatiana Zaslavskaia, 183–274. Moscow: Moskovkaia Vysshaia Shkola Sotsial'nykh i Ekonomicheskikh Nauk.

Tarabukina, Arina. 2000. "Fol'klor i Kul'tura Pritserkovnogo Kruga." Unpublished Ph.D. thesis, A.I. Gertsen Russian State Pedagogical University, Saint-Petersburg. Available online: http://www.ruthenia.ru/folktee/CYBERSTOL/books/Tarabukina/arina_tarabukina.html (accessed 15 January 2009).

Vinogradskii, Valerii. 1999. "'Orudiia Slabykh': Neformal'naia Ekonomika Krest'ianskikh Domokhaziaistv." *Sotsiologicheskii Zhournal* 3–4: 36–48.

Vladimirova, Vladislava. 2006. *Just Labor: Labor Ethic in a Post-Soviet Reindeer Herding Community.* Uppsala: Acta Universitatis Upsaliensis.

Yates, Samantha Jane. 2004. *Living with Poverty in Post-Soviet Russia: Social Perspectives on Urban Poverty.* Unpublished Ph.D. thesis, London School of Economics and Political Science, London.

 CHAPTER 6

"A Lot of Blood Is Unrevenged Here"
Moral Disintegration in Post-War Chechnya

Ieva Raubisko

Aishat,[1] a seemingly jovial woman nearing sixty who received me warmly at her home in one of the villages in Chechnya, once had eight children: four daughters and four sons. Born in exile in Kazakhstan,[2] she lost both of her parents by the age of two, spent some time at an orphanage together with her two sisters, was then adopted by her father's cousin and returned to Chechnya in her late teens. She got married at the age of eighteen and gave birth to her first son, Magomed, soon after.

Aishat's eldest son is no more; he was detained, mocked and forced to undress, beaten and killed by Russian soldiers during the second war in Chechnya in 2000, while taking his friend by car to neighboring Dagestan. It took the family several months to find out what had happened and to get possession of Magomed's remains. Aishat's second son, Adam, died in a car accident before the wars started. The car fell into the local river when the small bridge over it crumbled. Adam had managed to save his two mates but was drowned in the process. Aishat's third son, Said-Magomed, was taken away from their home by military troops in masks in 2003 and has been missing ever since; Aishat still refuses to admit him dead. She is bringing up her grandson who was two months old when his father disappeared. Aishat's youngest son Khamid experienced serious illness during the period of the armed conflict and until recently spent most of his time at a hospital in Moscow. Aishat's elder daughter, Petimat, is a widow with two children whose husband died during the second Chechen war. The long unsuccessful search for the missing brothers was one of the reasons that Aishat's second daughter Mariam started studying law; perhaps that was her way of countering the unbearable loss and trying to help other families who experienced similar bereavement. Aishat's youngest daughter, Zargan, is married to a German man, a former employee of a humanitarian aid organization. She lives in Western Europe. "Our mother is not what she used to be before," Zargan told me during her visit to Chechnya last summer, "she still works a lot and keeps cooking but it's not like it was before—she has lost her joy. Her heart is not in it anymore." Zargan is not happy either.

Secluded in the comfort of her German flat, looking after her baby daughter and enjoying the support of a caring husband, she still misses her family and home and wishes to return and work in Chechnya.

Like many other Chechens, Aishat is worried about the loss of what she calls "traditions": a whole generation has grown up during the wars without a proper upbringing and education. These teenagers and youth do not respect the tradition, she says; they do not uphold the old values and rules of behavior, such as a reverence for elderly people and steady, hard work.

But the older generation has changed too, as have the previous communal practices—something Aishat and her daughters regret sorely. "In the old days, we used to visit each other for tea and spend long nights together chatting, playing music and dancing, sometimes even to 1:00 a.m. Kids were up in the street quite late," says Aishat. Nowadays people are at home by 11:00 p.m. "We do not visit in the same way anymore. We have lost the habit," she adds. During the war the movement of villagers was restricted by curfew, and the constant presence of Russian federal troops posed a great risk to their lives. "People were sitting in their own holes," Aishat recalls. It was dangerous to walk around. Every time Aishat went to use the water supply tap on the street, she thought about the possibility of being captured and killed. "They needed to catch the terrorists and show some results," she says, adding that the task of capturing a "terrorist" could be conveniently achieved when a person was going somewhere alone. Villagers also declined invitations to visit each other because they did not have much to offer—no food or anything else. Aishat, however, had stocked up on a lot of provisions which she would give out to her neighbors. Mariam tells me that during Soviet times her mother used to keep a considerable amount of livestock, including eighteen cows, as well as sheep and hens. Her tasty dairy produce—milk, cream and cheese—was stored in the large wooden barrels in her basement at home but most of it was distributed to other villagers. "That's how she always was," says Mariam of her mother. "She would work hard and then give what she made to others for free."

There is another thing Aishat misses—the collective work in the spirit of *belkhi*[3]: "Previously when someone had to do something, build something, others immediately came to help in a friendly manner. This does not happen anymore. Now one needs to call for help. Not many elders are left, and young people don't know now whether others need help and whether they should lend them a helping hand."

Yet even if so much has gone and changed and the wounds are slow to heal, Aishat does not give up. Her vigor is seemingly inexhaustible. "Our men and women are strong in spirit," Aishat once told me. When Zargan and her daughter arrived from abroad for a long visit at her parents' home in summer, "all pale and thin," Aishat immediately took matters into her own hands. She went to the local mullah and got an amulet (a small leather purse with Quranic verses in it) to be hung on the baby girl's neck. After that, Aishat said, the baby's nervousness abated and her appetite and sleeping patterns improved considerably. Aishat also planned to organize a *mawlid*[4] for her granddaughter, as she had not had one upon her birth abroad. The mullah helped now, just as he and many other respected and learned men (apart from those who denounced the members of their communities as "enemies"/ "*Wahhabis*") had helped people during the war, either by summoning the men and women of the village in the mosque and speaking to them about the necessity of patience and endurance, or by discussing the situation among groups of men who would then spread the advice among their families.

Aishat's story is the story of many families in Chechnya today: a story of destruction, vulnerability, suffering, and yet defiance. Since 1994 when the first war broke out between the Russian federal government and Chechen pro-independence forces, the majority of Chechen families have experienced either the loss of their loved ones, or their homes, or both. They have gone through the horrors of war, and have been, and still are, subjected to state violence. What is more, they have seen the ideals and standards, the laws and norms of their society disintegrate and dissipate, only to emerge in disturbing new forms in a process partly engendered by external agents and partly something in which they themselves have been involved. Now that active warfare is over, and many houses and main infrastructure have been rebuilt, an ambiguous feeling of normalization has taken hold. Yet underneath the pretence of normality are deep-seated traumas, suspended grief, and apathy—recovery from which is precluded by the current condition of violent unpredictability. However, it is not the endurance of suffering resulting from massive warfare—the artillery bombardment, the looting, the "cleansings," and the torture and killings of civilians caused by the seemingly unequivocal external enemy, the Russian army— that is required today. What is required is the stamina to notice and face the further moral corruption and affliction brought about by the local Chechen regime behind the façade of normalization, and the courage to make one's own painful and dangerous choice of where to stand in the current phase of power relations. Not many mullahs can be trusted in making the difficult decisions of today: most of them are members of the official Spiritual Board of Muslims of Chechnya, directly subject to Chechen President Ramzan Kadyrov. The advice of independent moral authorities is not easily available; the official public attempts to rediscover the *ought* and revive morality stand in stark contrast to the corrupt practices of what *is*, sustained by the same official circles.

This chapter focuses on the confusion ensuing from moral destruction at a time of major social upheaval in Chechnya, a time when moral ideals have partly lost their previous substance and a variety of fragmentary interpretations are emerging in a process of messy regrouping marked by the violent assertion of power.

An Anthropological Look at Morality amidst Violence

Many studies have focused on Chechnya in the last fifteen years, from journalistic accounts of Chechen wars and the history of Russian-Chechen confrontation (e.g., Gall and de Waal 1997; Lieven 1998; Smith 2000),[5] to predominantly historical-political analyses attempting to trace the causes and development of the recent conflict and its wider implications in the national and international context (e.g., Dunlop 1998; Fowkes 1998; Evangelista 2002; Sakwa 2005; Hughes 2007; Wood 2007; Russell 2007; Gammer 2006, 2008; Gilligan 2009).[6] Anthropological studies, however, have been scarce, and almost none of them have been based on prolonged fieldwork in Chechnya (among the few notable exceptions are Chesnov 1999 and Sokirianskaia 2005, 2008). Some authors have focused on the representations and modes of violence in Chechnya and other parts of the North Caucasus (Bobrovnikov 2002; Grant 2005; Rigi 2007), while Russian scholar Valery Tishkov has produced a comprehensive ethnography of Chechen war (2001, 2004), relying on what he terms "delegated interviews" carried out by colleagues and research assistants in Chechnya. While these works offer valuable insights into the themes of war, state and violence, sovereignty and ideology, what remains wanting is the ethnographic depth, a description of life as currently lived "from inside," which might potentially enrich and adjust theoretical concepts applied in the analysis. The physical distance of authors from the field seems to have produced a certain conceptual distance as well. Likewise, even if moral values and practices in Chechen society have been directly or indirectly discussed in terms of Chechen "ethnic character" (Chesnov 1999), kinship ties (Sokirianskaia 2005), or demodernization as erosion of social norms amid the chaos of war (Tishkov 2001, 2004), morality has not been the central focus of discussion.

In this chapter I aim to consider specifically the transformation of morality in a violent environment, thus responding to a growing interest and calls for a separate study of morality within the discipline of anthropology. Many have noted the long-standing absence of morality as an independent analytical theme, a consequence of its treatment as a thread permeating all social life (the two prominent early exceptions are Read (1955) and Edel and Edel (1959)). A consensus has been emerging that Durkheimian society-cum-morality (the view of society as governing the morality of its members, and the identification of social rules with moral rules (and thus treatment of morality as a system of social rules)) has hampered the examination of, and potential insights into such concepts as reflexive freedom, moral reasoning, and choice (see Parkin 1985; Laidlaw 2002; Widlok 2004; Zigon 2007). As noted by Parkin: "The Durkheimian view of morality as being socially sanctioned rules covers only one dimension. There are acts thought morally wrong which are neither breaches of rules nor socially punished. Conversely, many social rules, often codified as laws in modern society, may not always be regarded as part of society's morality" (1985: 5–6).

Several stimulating suggestions on how to treat morality and moralities have been offered in recent years. Laidlaw (2002) has insisted on the insertion of Kantian reflexive freedom into the conceptualization of morality; Carrithers (2005) has taken "moral agency-cum-patiency" to be a universal category of human thought; and Robbins (2007) has distinguished between the morality of reproduction in domains of culture where a stable hierarchy of values is in place, and the morality of choice in domains marked by a conflict of values and major cultural changes. Zigon (2006, 2007; see also chapter 1, this volume) has pinpointed the "ethical moment" of "moral breakdown" when morality is questioned, ethical dilemmas arise, and specific ethical techniques are applied by individuals in order to return to what he calls "the unreflexive morality of the everyday." Faubion (2001) has drawn on Foucault's treatment of reflexive freedom as a good starting point for a rehabilitated anthropology of ethics; Thomas Widlok (2004), expanding on Aristotelian thought as well as Gell's approach to art and Ingold's approach to skill, has proposed an anthropology of virtue which examines how basic human goods that are internal to social practices come to be realized. The Aristotelian legacy has also figured in the work of Michael Lambek who has accentuated Aristotelian *phronesis* (practical judgment), called for a study of "moral practice" (Lambek 2000), and, most recently, underlined the advantages of the "virtue" approach over the "value" approach when studying social and moral worlds (Lambek 2008). One benefit of such a focus on virtue, according to Lambek, is that it has helped to shift the anthropological discussion of morality away from a Durkheimian view of rules and obligations, and instead towards practice and the moral person.

The works on the anthropology of morality I have mentioned indicate a considerable diversity of, and little agreement on, the usage of various terms in the study of morality, starting with the concept of morality itself. Like other concepts of similar type, such as religion (see Asad 1993), morality has at times been taken for granted and treated as self-evident, without further consideration of its genealogies and meanings. This matter deserves a separate study that cannot be undertaken here. For now one need only note that students of morality have been especially challenged by the long-acknowledged difficulty of employing Western systems of knowledge in the analyses of societies of markedly different orientations elsewhere in the world. There remains the obvious challenge that any treatment of moral issues undertaken by Western anthropologists must inevitably be informed, and to some extent shaped, by their general cultural context and often, more specifically, by one or several prominent lines of thought in the rich history of Western moral philosophy. Thus, while trying to conceptualize the "moral" in his or her field of research, the anthropologist also has to assume a certain position within the theoretical field of philosophical knowledge. In addition to epistemological quandaries, anthropologists confront personal ethical problems as well: as Didier Fassin (2008) reminds us, we cannot, and should not, remain unaware of the judgments and values that constitute our own moral standpoint.

The difficulties in this area start as soon as one attempts to name the broad object or theme of one's study: is it morality or ethics? Even if these terms are assumed to have distinct meanings—with "ethics" generally denoting the overarching system/s of values and customs (as well as a subfield in philosophy), and "morality" designating particular system/s in concrete contexts—they are often used interchangeably and sometimes subsumed within each other. Anthropologists have either preferred one concept over the other, or applied both, proposing various distinctions between the two terms. Appreciating but not fully subscribing to any of these distinctions, I take the terms "moral" and "morality" broadly to mean ideas about what is good and bad, as well as the actions and practices, both individual and social, guided by these understandings. In other words, I use "morality" to describe the ways in which good and bad, and the categories in between, are conceptualized and played out in the everyday life of a society. The terms "ethical" and "ethics" are used to refer to a particular branch of moral philosophy—virtue ethics—and also to the specific notion of "good" as delineated by this school of thought. This distinction between morality and ethics differs from the one proposed by Jarrett Zigon in this volume in that mine joins both what Zigon terms "unreflective and unreflexive morality" and "conscious creative ethics" under the broader frame of morality. While I find Zigon's idea of "moral breakdown" occurring when ethical work is done in returning to unconscious morality insightful, I tend to view ethics as a more pervasive element of moral life which informs and activates moral choices in an ongoing process that cannot always be reduced to a particular moment.[7]

To clarify my epistemological leanings: I am inclined to follow Lambek and others who have drawn on Aristotelian virtue ethics, directly or indirectly, through the work of several philosophers and social theorists, of whom MacIntyre and Foucault have perhaps been the most influential.[8] I have hitherto found MacIntyre's interpretation of classical virtue ethics (MacIntyre 1988, 1997, [1967] 2000, [1981] 2007) most helpful in the analysis of the Chechen moral universe.

MacIntyre builds on Aristotle's view of virtues as qualities that enable people to achieve the *telos* (goal) of *eudaimonia,* a "state of doing well in being well, of a man's being well-favored himself and in relation to the divine" (MacIntyre [1981] 2007: 148). Virtues are seen not only as a means to accomplish the good life (or of flourishing) but also as an indispensable part of such life. Importantly, virtues have to be cultivated: learned and systematically trained and practiced, so that they become dispositions not only for acting, but also for feeling. Thus, "to act virtuously is not, as Kant was later to think, to act against inclination; it is to act *from* inclination formed by the cultivation of virtues" (MacIntyre [1981] 2007: 149, emphasis added).

MacIntyre's account of virtues proceeds in three stages: from virtues as qualities necessary to achieve "the good" internal to practices, to virtues as qualities ensuring the good of each entire human life, and, finally, to virtues as elaborated and contained within an ongoing social tradition ([1981] 2007: 273). By goods internal to practices, MacIntyre means progress and positive results (or excellence) that can only be achieved by engaging in a particular practice and can only be recognized by those who have participated in that practice (188). MacIntyre provides the example of a child learning to play chess, who begins with a wish to win by all means and receive remuneration, but gradually moves to an appreciation of the specific goods of chess: the analytical skill, the strategic imagination, and the competitive intensity. In this later stage, the child finds in the goods of chess his or her own reasons for trying to excel at the game. These kinds of internal goods are distinguished from external goods, for example, the prestige, status, and money that adults can achieve, not only by playing chess, but through many other practices as well. While external goods are outcomes of competitions in which there are winners as well as losers, internal goods benefit the entire community to which they are relevant. "Practice" is thus a "socially established cooperative human activity" through which goods internal to it are realized in the course of trying to achieve its specific standards of excellence, and which increases human powers to achieve excellence, and extends human conceptions of the ends and goods involved (187). Examples of such practices include the making and sustaining of family life, architecture, farming, and scientific inquiry. And as noted above, goods internal to practices and virtues exercised in their achievement are rooted in the wider context of tradition—a "historically extended, socially embodied argument" partly about the goods that pertain to a particular community (222). MacIntyre explains, "Within a tradition the pursuit of goods extends through generations, sometimes through many generations. Hence the individual's search for his or her good is generally and characteristically conducted within a context defined by those traditions of which the individual's life is a part, and this is true both of the goods which are internal to practices and of the goods of a single life" (ibid.).

MacIntyre's notion of tradition has proved to have great potential in anthropological investigations, with authors revising and expanding the concept. For example, Anand Pandian has recently argued that MacIntyre's ideas could be put to even better use if they allowed for more fragmentation of tradition within its continuities, as well as for less coherence in the narrative of a single life (2008).[9] Pandian nevertheless appreciates the sense of dynamism, of the possibility of arguments being defined and redefined within the MacIntyrean tradition.[10] The idea of inherent argument has also been welcomed by David Scott (1999) and Talal Asad (2006), although Asad has pointed out the disappointing absence of the body in Macintyre's thought on tradition. For Asad, tradition is not just a matter of argument; it is "primarily about practice, about learning the point of a practice and performing it properly and making it a part of oneself, something that embraces Mauss's concept of *habitus*" (2006: 234). Asad employs the concept of *habitus* as a predisposition of the body, its *traditional* sensibilities, and more generally as "that aspect of a tradition in which specific virtues are defined and the attempt is made to cultivate and enact them" (289). Such embodied traditional practices amount to what Asad has elsewhere called the ethics of necessity (2000), which in turn links to the notion of embodied morality Jarrett Zigon has offered in this volume.[11]

To summarize, the concepts of tradition, virtue and moral *habitus* as discussed above constitute the central analytical elements in this study of Chechen morality. The intention of what follows is not to compare the contents or the internal make-up of a Chechen virtue system. Rather, I will adhere to the MacIntyrean view that human behavior is guided by commonly held virtues which are embedded in a particular social context, and I will build on Asad's emphasis on the embodiedness of moral sensibilities in order to study some of the fragmented and depleted moral ideals and the related diverging and contradictory practices in Chechen society, as well as the attempts to reassemble and reassert a new disfigured and unstable Chechen moral framework. I focus particularly on respect for human dignity as a universal as well as a central Chechen virtue, and the virtue of justice closely linked to it. I argue that in the Chechen worldview, it is ultimately through the blood feud that human dignity can be restored and justice achieved. I start, however, with an analysis of Chechen tradition, especially the local discourses on the "loss of tradition" and the contradictory role of elders as bearers of tradition.

Disintegration of Tradition as a Space for Moral Quests

I consider social tradition in Chechnya as more centered on virtues than on the values of modern liberalism.[12] Hence I find compelling MacIntyre's argument about the incompatibility of his virtue-based approach with modern liberal individualism and the Enlightenment (and post-Enlightenment moral philosophy) at its intellectual core. However, I do not mean to neglect the transformation and diverse influences that Chechen moral tradition has undergone during the seventy-year existence of the Soviet industrial (some would claim "modern") state, and the subsequent social change and turmoil. Also, while I apply MacIntyre's idea of social tradition in the broad sense, on a more specific level I take Chechen tradition to be a dynamic synthesis of two prominent intertwined strands: indigenous socio-cultural ideas and practices often referred to as "Chechen laws" (or *adat*s), and Islamic discourses and routines.

From Aishat's story we can glimpse a deep-felt concern about the "loss of tradition" in Chechen society today. I encountered this anxiety on my first day of fieldwork in Chechnya when I joined some acquaintances on a trip from the Chechen capital Grozny to a family in a rural village who were holding a rite of remembrance (*sagha dakkhar*)[13] for a widely-respected and elderly man who had passed away a week before. I was sitting and eating in the room designated for village women, who shared with me stories of the past, of the recent warfare that had forced them to abandon their settlement in the mountains as refugees and to start an often desperate search for housing in the lowland areas, and of other unwelcome changes the past two decades had brought. Madina, a middle-aged woman, told me that "Chechen traditions" had slackened considerably, a process which she traced back to the late Soviet period and especially to the last ten to fifteen years. She talked about the young generation not knowing how to behave and particularly about young women not dressing properly nowadays. Just before leaving Grozny to attend this religious gathering, I had met a young woman named Luiza, who had also stressed the importance of "tradition" early on in our conversation and had voiced concerns about maintaining it in her own family. Her siblings had scattered around the world during the recent armed conflict, her sister's family staying in Belgium and brother's family settling in the United States. Luiza said she talked to her brother and twelve-year-old nephew on the phone frequently and kept asking herself:

what kind of Chechen will this boy be? However, the threat of losing tradition is considered to be as great in Chechnya itself as it is abroad. In Chechnya, former norms and practices are perceived to be fading away, just as they sometimes are in the mainly Western countries where Chechen emigrants attempt to retain their modes of life within often hostile frameworks of state and host communities, people in which subscribe to different ideals and engage in different practices.

However familiar they might seem, the frequent complaints about the ignorance and incivility of youth, the "war children" who do not want to work and do not know how to behave[14] cannot be dismissed as yet another mark of social transformation and a generational gap characteristic of so many societies. In Chechen society, it is also the elders[15] who face widespread criticism. "Not only youth, but the elders have also let things slide," noted Arbi, a man in late thirties and one of my hosts. His comment echoed many others who complained to me that "there are not many elders left nowadays." These people meant that elders cannot anymore be trusted to provide the best advice as they do not know well enough "how things should be done" and, more importantly, they are not always upright or virtuous in their deeds. "They are to blame for accepting the deal of the current times—they accept money and betray virtue," Arbi added.

It seems apt to see the "acceptance" of immoral positions by elders as part of a larger power balance in Chechen society today, and as an example of how power has corrupted morals. It is on this level that major moral contradictions emerge. In today's Chechnya, elders are present at all public gatherings such as the massive and necessarily televised *dhikr*s (Sufi rituals for the remembrance of God) performed as part of the general religious campaign of the government, or gatherings in village communities, again widely covered by the government-controlled media, aimed at solving the problem of youth joining the ranks of Wahhabi resistance.[16] Elders are employed as a sign of support for the current order, which is upheld by a brutal regime, and often as its mouthpiece. Yet it is not only a public appearance of acquiescence that the old authoritative men have been forced to display; in addition, they are usually not able to escape moral compromises in the less visible and more private spheres of everyday life where mediation and conflict resolution takes place, and the unequal distribution of power can preclude fair solutions. While in the field, I heard about many such cases.

One story was told to me and my friends by a woman who had decided to seek advice from, or at least get her case recorded by, local human rights activists: One day four men in uniform drove into one of the villages and forced her young niece into their car (despite a couple of the men suggesting that she should be let go as she was so young). It emerged later that the main initiator of the act, a man in his thirties, had bet the others a new car that he would "conquer" a girl by evening. With gun held to her neck, the girl was taken to a place outside the village where she was raped and had her lips torn. Afterwards, the main perpetrator brought the girl to his house, where he had three wives and four children waiting for him (and another child expected soon). When the rapist's father understood what his son had done, he fainted. The son, however, said that he did not want to have the girl as his fourth wife (potentially the most effective measure in saving the reputation of the girl and her extended family). The elders of the rapist's side were immediately summoned in order to take the girl back to her relatives.

Lengthy negotiations followed, in which one of the widely-known religious officials of Chechnya played an important role. The girl's side demanded that the rapist walk with no trousers on in the girl's village as well as in his own, an old Chechen measure of retribution which would compensate for the shame that the girl and her family had been subjected to. This was deemed by the perpetrator's side not to be compliant with sharia (Islamic law). Then a suggestion was made to kill the wrongdoer, which would in principle be acceptable under Islamic law, but was ruled out by the other side, who said that "only Allah can take someone's life." President Kadyrov, who had been involved after the rape victim's aunt had managed to use her contacts, himself suggested "doing away with all of them" (the four men). However, the suggested method of punishment was changed to throwing the wrongdoers into the basement and beating them up once Kadyrov became aware that the man who had initiated the crime was related to him.

A beating did indeed happen but it was of no consolation to the girl's family. "What's the point of it?" asked her aunt, the woman who shared this story with us. "It doesn't make me feel better." The girl's life was ruined: her honor was smeared, and as a rape victim she now had almost no chance of getting married.[17] She was heavily traumatized, alternately laughing and crying, afraid of leaving her room and, most of all, of encountering men in uniform.

One of the elders of the girl's family considered having the girl marry the rapist to be the best option. That would at least save her honor, he said. This opinion was also shared by her aunt, who told us: "Well, she would live there a bit and then return home."[18] Such a marriage, however, did not happen. Instead, the perpetrator's side offered one million rubles (around $50,000 (U.S.)) to the victim's family. Men on the girl's side initially refused to accept the money, which they considered to be dirty. They told the other family: "Look, there is a new mosque under construction. If you don't consider this money dirty, donate it to the building of the mosque." Later, however, they accepted the money.

The case may be far from over. The raped girl's family did not even consider bringing a criminal action against the main perpetrator. "Forget it," the victim's aunt remarked bitterly. "He is their guy. He would be detained and sentenced, and then he would leave the prison through the back door." What lingered on was a sense of lacking justice and pending resolution: the beating of the wrongdoers remained a futile violent act and the considerable money compensation was a corrupt offering, restoring neither the dignity of the rape victim, nor the reputation of her kin group. One of the local human right activists was sure that the girl's relatives, some of them ordinary policemen, would wait for their time to come and achieve retribution through blood revenge.

This account is indicative of some pernicious tendencies in Chechen society which bear directly on Chechen morality. In the rape incident two significant Chechen moral ideals were degraded: female chastity, and compassion and support for the weak. By crippling a defenseless and innocent young girl, President Kadyrov's men were undermining what the President claims to be one of his main priorities, and one for which his government has been a major proponent: the spiritual-moral[19] revival of Chechens, especially the restoration of the "proper status and behavior of women" and the spiritual-moral education of youth. The power elite may be just as disturbed about the widely-perceived "loss of tradition" in Chechen society as ordinary Chechens are. The remedies they have sought through a series of presidential decrees include: requiring all women employed in the public sector to wear headscarves, banning European wedding dresses and the sales of hard liquor, advocating "the right version of Islam," and implementing other crude media campaigns in the Soviet tradition of instructing citizens how to be and what to think. However, the rape committed by Kadyrov's security men shows how those in the circles of power are destroying precisely what they believe or pretend to be advancing, by committing transgressions that are considered unacceptable by the majority of Chechens.

This story also demonstrates the inequality and the lack of access to justice for the powerless compared to the powerful. The unsatisfactory compensation (no matter how big in financial terms) that was forced upon the elders of the raped girl's family would have never been accepted by those in power, had they experienced the same type of injustice. Had the victim been from a more powerful family closely linked to the leadership, the wrongdoers would likely have been executed with no negotiations, further questions, or trials, in the manner of the *carte blanche* killing of enemies widely practiced by Kadyrov's government and its law enforcement structures in today's Chechnya.

There is another kind of powerlessness involved in the story—the powerlessness of elders. Conventionally elders have been the main source of knowledge and authoritative decision making, the main mediators in conflicts, the pronouncers of verdicts and advisors on paths to be taken by individuals, families and village communities—in other words, the bearers of moral tradition. However, elders today often have no sway over those who engage in the violent practices of abduction, torture, and extra-judicial killings, as well as the embezzlement of riches from the federal center, and the heavy corruption and racketeering within the bureaucratic state system where the political merges with the legal, and the law allows for creative yet systematized production and accommodation of violence.[20] All of these practices encroach on the Chechen ideals (virtues) of justice, equality, respect for human dignity, modesty, and compassion, to which I will return shortly. But this is not to say that elders stand totally apart. Even if their authority tends to lie outside the field of state power, they—just like any other members of society—remain a part of the system and are corrupted by it, for example, through the entangled practices of blood feud, which are now frequently carried out through the state structures, with a novel application of torture as part of revenge. The complex multilayered notion of the Soviet-Russian-Chechen state deserves a study on its own which cannot be provided here. For now it suffices to note that elders still retain their important roles in the maintenance of community life—for example, by resolving conflicts between families, approving and organizing marriages, and setting the standard amounts of bride price—so long as they do not substantially interfere with the struggles for and assertions of power perpetrated by state agents. This "division of labor" surfaces in the efforts of men employed by the law enforcement structures (one of the few job options in Chechnya where unemployment is said to reach around 45 percent)[21] to hide or rather not share any details about their work tasks with their parents, supposedly to spare them from worry and moral indignation.[22]

Thus elders remain symbols of authority when their authority has been considerably depleted. As noted by MacIntyre, "the language and the appearances of morality persist even though the integral substance of morality has to a large degree been fragmented and then in part destroyed" ([1981] 2007: 5). Respectful claims that "elders see further" and "elders decide everything" are overturned in situations when the decisions of elders appear inconvenient to the current power holders, or the former even dare to oppose the latter. In such cases, elders can be abducted, tortured, or killed no matter how old or revered they are. In 2003, unidentified military men detained Said-Magomed-Khadzhi Isakov, a widely respected 77-year-old man, in the mountainous village of Dyshne-Vedeno (Politkovskaya 2003a). His family wrote hundreds of letters and paid many visits to different law enforcement offices, searching for him to no avail. Said-Magomed-Khadzhi was one of the few pious learned men who refused to follow the dictates of the then pro-Moscow leader and soon-to-be President Akhmat-Khadzhi Kadyrov Senior. For example, he refused to urge village people to vote in favor of the new Chechen constitution which reinstated Chechnya as inseparable part of federal Russia.[23] More recently, Kadyrov Sr.'s son and successor Ramzan Kadyrov has taken to personally torturing the elderly fathers of his fugitive enemies in his private illegal prisons (see, for example, *Novaya Gazeta* 2009; Chivers 2009).

What is at risk here is not just the maintenance of patriarchal authority (although it is also threatened) but the more general prescription to respect elders, to revere one's parents, to be thankful to them, and to hold their experience and the work they have done during their long lives in high esteem. One rule that follows from this ethical principle is that parents have to be taken care of—sheltered and provided for—until the end of their days. Putting an older man into a torture chamber is perceived by Chechens as an extremely immoral act.

Such neglect of virtues stands in direct relation to the widespread concern about "losing tradition(s)" in Chechen society: the diminishing reverence for elders, to use the current example, indicates the diminution of tradition. Talk of the "loss of tradition" can be interpreted as a statement about the loss of virtues, expressed through worries about the disruption of previous modes of life and the disintegration of previous social rules, that is, the disintegration of the space (tradition) where virtues were learned and enacted. Yet the dissolution of tradition cannot be considered final, and the process of loss cannot be seen as an unambiguous one-way movement. Such a perspective would ignore the desperate collective and public attempts to revive the "spiritual-moral culture" as well as individual efforts to lead a virtuous life despite the overwhelming sense of public moral corruption. In other words, part of tradition has disintegrated and part of it still lingers on, not least because of moral sensibilities "ingrained" and surviving within some individuals. In what follows, I discuss the difficult task of remaining moral in immoral circumstances. I focus mainly on how virtues such as respect for human dignity and justice have been, and are presently, understood and practiced, as well as how they are violated.

(Dis)respect for Human Dignity and Attempts to Achieve Justice

Earlier in this chapter, I evoked the concept of moral confusion. By confusion I mean the state of disorientation and uncertainty ensuing from the massive defiling of moral ideals during the prolonged Chechen-Russian conflict and its aftermath. In the last fifteen years, the Chechen people have witnessed numerous scenes of astonishing cruelty, of human beings bombed, killed, and tortured. As noted earlier, the perpetration of violence within the state system has been transferred from the Russian federal military to the predominantly local Chechen state structures[24] which continue what they call their "fight against shaitans/Wahhabis"—in other words, attempts to quell the armed resistance that are increasingly phrased in Islamic terms.

Many former members of the resistance have now "laid down arms"— that is, they were forced to switch sides and take up the arms in the service of their former enemies, the pro-Moscow Chechen forces. For many, this appeared to be the only way to "descend from the mountains," "get out of the woods," or receive an amnesty (the alternative being continued resistance or an escape to the west) and also save their family members from further persecution. In the last five to six years of the post-war period, a considerable part of the Chechen male population, in their capacity as law enforcers, have engaged in the abductions, torture, and killings of fellow Chechens who are framed as enemies, thus perpetuating, even if in a somewhat different form, the unrestricted violence set off and confirmed during the wars. The overall condition of Chechen society is one of confusion about the reversal of morals that these Chechen men as state agents have contributed to producing, and of incomprehensible suffering and unmanageable feelings of injustice. This state, I would suggest, is related to the concept of moral breakdown proposed by Jarrett Zigon in this volume. There has been so much devastation that ideas of right and wrong, of how one should live, and what kind of person one should be, have been seriously questioned and at times overturned. Recuperation takes time, and the first response is often silence, denial, apathy, and grief. "War is not yet over in our souls. We all are just trying to pretend that everything is fine," says Chechen poet Lula Kuni (Isaeva 2007: 28). Yet nothing is fine when a longer conversation erupts and memories of the war inevitably reappear. It is in these stories that the earlier unresolved moral contradictions and negations surface, overrunning at times the more hushed comments on the current moral condition.

For lack of space I cannot engage here in a study of the diverse forms of remembering and narrating past traumas in Chechen society, which might provide rich insights into how people coped with these moral dilemmas. My intention here is to focus on some experiences of the war years, as well as the current post-war phase, in order to examine the perceptions of, and reactions to, moral violations.

It is impossible to talk about the war without immediately stumbling upon grisly episodes of disrespect for human dignity. I have heard stories about village men, including elders, detained by Russian *federaly* (the nickname for soldiers and officers of the Russian federal army) and kept in large petrol tanks half-full of water for several days, with some of them later killed and some still missing. In one village my host showed me a house from which a woman, her brothers, and her father were kidnapped and taken to an open field where the woman was raped by the troops in front of her male relatives, and then all of them were blown up with a grenade. In another village I was told that grenades were thrown into the cellars where villagers were known to be hiding from bombings.

The omnipresent violent destruction of human dignity—be it the massive killings of civilians, the mutilation of human bodies, or the refusal to return the remains of the dead to families for a prompt Muslim burial without payment of a bribe—has remained impossible for Chechens to comprehend and accept as having happened. As unacceptable are the arbitrary killings and torture of suspected "shaitans/Wahhabis," the mocking of their remains, demands placed on their relatives to disavow them, and refusal to give their bodies to their parents for burial, currently practiced by President Kadyrov and his law enforcers. In the Chechen moral outlook, respect for human dignity occupies a central place. Dignity implies a certain moral self-sufficiency, in other words, the freedom to be virtuous: to subscribe to and enact such fundamental virtues such as justice, equality, courage, compassion, generosity, and modesty, which, taken together, yield an image of the ideal moral person.[25] It is a condition of a person who is both respectful and respectable.

Chechens' idea of freedom, in contrast to the Western idea of an autonomous responsible individual, exists within the confines of the acceptable and unacceptable, the allowed and the forbidden, which are conveyed through the strict social rules of behavior regulating the interaction between people of different genders and ages through disciplinary techniques of the body. These techniques attest to the physicality of morality, of virtues enacted within and through the body while exercising the *habitus,* which in Talal Asad's words, "is not something one *accepts* or *rejects*; it is *part of what one essentially is and must do*" (2000: 38, emphasis in original). One example of such embodied moral sensibility is the Chechen habit of always standing up at least slightly from one's chair to show respect to someone who has just arrived in the room, especially elders. In the same way, sons do not sit down in the presence of their father, younger brothers do not smoke or drink in the presence of older brothers, and sons-in-law do not leave their vehicles right in front of the house of their in-laws to show respect for them. These techniques indicate restraint and distance between bodies; they also connect to the general ideas of respect for the human body, human life and, ultimately, for human dignity. Likewise, they hint at how shocked Chechen society was by the unjustified death of civilians, large-scale atrocities, and why Chechens have not been able to make sense of the overall disregard for human dignity during the war and in its aftermath.

Aishat has not been able to understand why one of her sons was mocked and killed by Russian federal troops and another abducted by unidentified armed men in camouflage uniforms. "For us to kill a person is a very serious matter. ... If it comes to killing, it is very, very serious," she told me during one of our discussions in her kitchen. She was referring to the complex institution of blood feud, which, however transformed and contested, is still very much in force in Chechnya. Some of my acquaintances have claimed that blood feud among Chechens has retained its original indigenous form, rooted in *adat*,[26] where the unintentional or intentional killing of someone is resolved through the reconciliation of the families involved, or by killing the guilty one or another member of his or her family. Others have pointed out the existence of an alternative process of reconciliation through material compensation based on Islamic law. Still others have criticized the ways the blood feud has recently entered the totally different and novel plane of the state system where it is performed or avoided through joining one of the numerous law enforcement structures, thereby engaging in state violence. Often it has been asserted that blood feud triggered by a willful murder or other crime of similar gravity allows for nothing else but exactly the same act done to the wrongdoer.

Whatever the interpretive differences may be, the ubiquitous statements, contemplations, and hints at a possible blood revenge at the right time in the future by those who have suffered abuses from state agents confirm the idea that the loss of a human life, or an assault on human dignity such as rape or torture, has to be compensated for. Even if the war and post-war statistics of around 70,000 thousand civilians killed, 5,000 disappeared, and thousands tortured (often made to confess to invented crimes and sentenced for longs terms in prison)[27] point to the impossibility of attaining appropriate moral compensation, the blood feud remains the principal means for asserting justice. To perform the blood feud is to fulfill an embodied moral necessity and exercise the virtue of justice, whereby an undeserved assault on one's body, and therefore a violation of one's dignity, is counterbalanced with what is perceived to be a similar act, whether performed within the discursive register in rhetorical terms, or within the practical register through concrete physical acts. Blood feud thus tends to prevail over the two other modes of retribution: reliance on divine justice and appeal to secular law.

The ordeal of my friend Khussein's family provides a somber illustration here. Movladi, Khussein's young son, was detained by law enforcement agents a couple of years ago in his home village. He was tortured and then convicted of killing a policeman, a crime which he had no relation to. The innocent youth spent more than a year in prison until his family managed to achieve his release through a complicated and costly appeals process. Movladi's health had deteriorated seriously as a result of torture and his prolonged stay in prison; likewise, his parents had suffered from health problems caused by constant worries about their son's well-being and stress during the long court process. Moreover, Khussein himself was later brutally summoned to the police office and threatened, which made him withdraw the complaint he had launched with the appeals court. The case had been complicated by the fact that the man of whose murder Movladi was convicted had been closely affiliated with the current power elite. Eventually, a somewhat forced reconciliation between Khussein and the people behind the detention of his son was reached. Also, Khussein, an active *murid* (member) of one of the Sufi *wirds*,[28] had enjoyed a strong support and respect from the members of his group, who had advised him "not to go against the state" and explicitly shown that the actions of state agents meant nothing to them and that they still trusted Khussein and his family. The Sufi *murid* circle does not formally support blood revenge. Yet, despite the disapproval of his fellow believers and reconciliation with the offenders, Khussein still nurtures the idea of blood feud as the final settling of accounts. He has found out the names of all the people who were involved in denouncing and torturing his son and has hinted to me that he might revenge the offense when the time is ripe.

Thus, even if a person leaves the problem of justice in the hands of Allah, or attempts to bring a legal action against the wrongdoers (often the commanders or soldiers of the Russian army and nowadays also the members of local Chechen law enforcement units) at a local or international court, and even if the court sentences the wrongdoers (or in the case of European Court of Human Rights, decides that the Russian Federation should pay out the compensation to the victims[29]), he or she might still entertain ideas about performing the blood feud. One of my acquaintances in Chechnya once shared a story about a woman who considered spending the compensation she had received from the Russian government after a positive ECHR decision to hire assassins to carry out a blood feud revenge against the people she had filed a case against at the European Court. To stress once more, when it comes to crimes infringing on human dignity, especially those perpetrated in the last several years under the local Chechen rule, blood feud—even if it cannot be carried out immediately—is often seen as the final step in achieving justice. As summed up by one of my informants: "A lot of blood is unrevenged here."

Conclusion

In this chapter I have tried to show the current fragility of the Chechen moral universe, marked by a pronounced tension between the partial destruction of moral ideals and the concurrent persistence of fragmentary moral notions, discourses, and interpretations. Enhancing moral confusion, this tension spills out on several major planes and in several distinct ways. First, it is evident in the discourse about the "loss of tradition," which implies concern about the partial disintegration and transformation of tradition as a space where virtues are learned and enacted, and a consequent deterioration of virtues. Yet the previous forms and terms of morality have not been discarded, even if their substance has changed and deteriorated, and is still changing considerably. This tendency is vividly exemplified in the ambiguous status of elders, who retain their symbolic status as the bearers of tradition, but who do not possess enough power to reverse the moral corruption and instigate a regeneration of tradition.

Second, this tension is evident in the contradiction between the frantic attempts of the power elite—echoing the widespread collective sentiment about the "loss of tradition(s)"—to set off a revival of spiritual-moral culture through massive public campaigns, while destroying the same revered moral ideals by engaging in unethical acts such as abductions, torture, murders, corruption, and racketeering within the state system.

Third, the tension manifests itself in the continuous individual attempts to counter moral violations through practices stemming from embodied moral sensibilities, such as the necessity of redressing an assault on human dignity through a blood feud. I have argued that the blood feud, in all its diversity, remains the main means to achieve justice, that is, to compensate for the disrespect for human dignity, a breach of a central Chechen virtue.

More generally, I have attempted to comprehend how morality is affected by cataclysms such as prolonged war when human tragedy is brought to an extreme, when pain and suffering cease to be a restricted measure that belong to moral agency in virtue cultivation (Asad 2000), and instead become an overwhelming and all-embracing reality. Amidst massive violence and physical destruction, two types of designs—that of a larger tradition as well as that of a single human life—are crumbling.[30] The disruption of tradition (and the individual lives within it) amounts to the disruption of the moral *habitus*—the embodied sensibilities, the dispositions to feel and act in certain moral ways. What ensues is an agony of the contradictory processes of further moral destruction on the one hand, and attempts at moral renewal on the other. I suggest that it is at this point of tension—where the unclear, partly eroding, partly creatively reworked patterns of the individually embodied moral sensibilities and the fragments of collective moral responsibility are brought together—that the transformation of morality might be best revealed and grasped. A closer look at such tension might provide some clues for answering the important questions of how violence impinges on moral worlds and how moral ideals are redefined in a society.

Notes

I am indebted to Jarrett Zigon for his valuable feedback on the earlier version of this chapter. I am also grateful to Mantas Kvedaravicius and anonymous reviewers for their comments and suggestions in writing and finalizing the current version of this chapter.

1. All personal names and names of locations have been changed in this chapter.
2. In February 1944, Chechens and Ingush were deported *en masse* in from the Chechen-Ingush Autonomous Soviet Socialist Republic (ASSR) to Central Asia, mainly Kazakhstan, but also to Kyrgyzstan and the Vologda, Kostroma, and Ivanovsk regions of Soviet Russia. They were allowed to return in 1957 when the Chechen-Ingush ASSR, which had been abolished in 1944, was restored.
3. *Belkhi* (from Chechen), the practice of communal work, was still alive among Chechens and Ingush in the second half of the twentieth century, especially during the exile to Central Asia, and in the following decades. During *belkhi*, the whole community would gather together to build a house for a family or to provide other help to the weaker and poorer members of the group.
4. In Chechnya, an Islamic prayer done for varied purposes, including for a newborn.
5. Among later journalistic reports, the work of Anna Politkovskaya, murdered in 2006, stands out as a painstakingly revealing and excruciating portrait of Chechnya during the second armed conflict (1999–2001) and after the end of massive warfare in 2001 (Politkovskaya 2001, 2003b, 2007).
6. Gilligan (2009) concentrates particularly on the violations of human rights during the second war and its aftermath, as well as the local, national, and international responses to these violations.
7. A similar point has been raised by Laidlaw (2009).
8. For an insightful joint use of Aristotle's and Foucault's theories, see Faubion (2001) and Mahmood (2005).
9. However, what seems to be the crucial defining feature of MacIntyre's notion of the unity of a single life is not a denial of its possible fragmentation but rather a perception of life as rooted in the past and reaching out to the future: "What I am ... is in key part what I inherit, a specific past that is present to some degree in my present. I find myself part of a history ... and, whether I recognize it or not, one of the bearers of a tradition. ... [I]nsofar as the virtues sustain the relationships required for practices, they have to sustain relationships to the past—and to the future—as well as in the present" (MacIntyre [1981] 2007: 221).
10. According to MacIntyre, a healthy tradition is always partly constituted by argument: "Traditions, when vital, embody continuities of conflict. Indeed when a tradition becomes Burkean [resisting any new reasoning and change] it is dying or dead" (MacIntyre [1981] 2007: 222).
11. A related concept of moral *habitus* has been developed by Saba Mahmood in her work on women's piety in Egypt (2005).

12. Perhaps one indication of such a preference in Chechen society is the priority given to such commendable character traits (or virtues) as generosity, respect, modesty, courage—often grouped together under the general term of "goodness"—in the judgment of people in their daily discourses. In contrast, one's intellectual capacities and one's intelligence are almost never mentioned as attributes and proof of "goodness," without the accompanying virtues of character. I have found a similar contention in a couple of works by Chechen authors Said-Magomed Khasiev (2006) and Musa Akhmadov (2006). Both of them draw an explicit line between virtue and reason, heart and mind, and ethics as virtuous life and philosophy as a process and product of reasoning.

13. Chechen words have been transliterated from Cyrillic according to the transliteration system developed by Nicholas Awde, available at http://ingush.narod.ru/ chech/awde. For the transliteration of Russian words I have used a modified Library of Congress Cyrillic-Latin transliteration system without diacritics as adopted by *Slavonic and East European Review*. The only exception is some personal names where I have adopted the versions used in the media.

14. Among other things, they are said to be unable to dance *lezginka*, a strictly structured dance of Lezgian origin, now widespread across the North Caucasus with different versions in different ethnic communities. *Lezginka* can be performed by males alone or by couples where the man and woman do not touch. Some of my interlocutors have criticized the young people for "not knowing the steps, having the rhythm too fast," and young girls for "looking the guys straight in the eyes and moving their hips."

15. The term "elder"—in Chechen, *vokha stag;* in Russian, *starik*—refers to the elderly learned men and religious authorities and, more generally, to all males and heads of families of the older generation.

16. In addition to the attempts to revive the Chechen spiritual-moral culture, discussed later in the chapter, the government is advancing a particular religious ideology, which rests on a clear-cut divide between the "right" Islam and the "wrong" or "evil" Islam, the former being "traditional" Sufism, the latter so-called Wahhabism. Traditional Sufism emerges as a cluster of arbitrarily chosen religious symbols and practices, such as *mawlid*s—collective prayers, also rites of sacrifice, *dhikr*s, and (trips to) *ziyarat*s—mausoleums of sheikhs and their relatives, most of them forcefully made public. This version of Sufism is presented and promoted by the government as a peacemaking religion and a valid ideational basis for state-building. In its turn, Wahhabism—a vague assembly of various ideas that depart from the "harmless" traditional Islam—is seen as the main source of terrorism. More concretely, the term is reserved for the armed resistance against the current order, with "Wahhabis"/"shaitans" designating the perceived Islamic "radicals" usually equated with "terrorists." Individuals who do not fall within the narrowly defined proper religious framework and prefer "purist" or reformist interpretations of Islam are thus under risk of being defined and persecuted as (potential) terrorists. Wahhabism has indeed been appropriated as an ideological platform by what has become a pan-Caucasus resistance movement under the auspices of the Caucasus Emirate proclaimed in 2007. Yet the reasons, motivations, elucidations on, and justifications for youths joining the ranks of rebels in the mountains and forests present a much more complex interplay between the prolonged experience of so-

cial injustice and state violence, the suffering and hardship of everyday life, and the attempts to conceptualize and oppose them in Islamic terms for the resistance to be straightforwardly attributed to some crude "radical Islamism."

17. In Chechnya, young women live with their parents and their extended family until they get married. They are not allowed to have intimate relationships with their boyfriends or potential husbands before marriage. Dating is strictly regulated and usually takes the form of conversations carried out in public, but away from the eyes of parents and other relatives. A conspicuous transgression can irreversibly smear the family's reputation, and in the worst cases may end with the young woman being killed by her father or brother. There are, however, different and less radical interpretations of this rule.

18. Divorced wives usually return to their parents or to other relatives of their extended family.

19. The terms "spiritual-moral" and "spiritual-moral culture" are somewhat clumsy translations of the Russian terms *dukhovno-nravstvennyi* and *dukhovno-nravstvennaia kul'tura*. In this case, "culture" is used to denote the "inner culture" of a person, the extent to which he or she has managed to cultivate certain virtues or subscribes to certain ideals, and exhibits them in his or her behaviour. Agata Ładykowska (chapter 3, this volume) has found a similar challenge in translating the same terms *moral'no-nravstvennyi* and *dukhovno-nravstvennyi,* which she encountered during her fieldwork in Rostov-on-Don in Southern Russia. The history of these terms—which, as was insightfully noted by Alexander Agadjanian during the workshop on multiple moralities in Russia at the Max Planck Institute of Social Anthropology in September 2008—testifies to the duality of Russian culture and reaches back to Tsarist Russia. The geographical scope of their usage has since spread to the far corners of the Russian state. However, semantic particularities differ from place to place: in Chechnya I did not discern any specific distinction between *moral'* (morals) and *nravstvennost'* (virtuousness), as was discovered by Agata Ładykowska in her research in Rostov-on-Don.

20. I owe this insight to Mantas Kvedaravicius at the University of Cambridge who is currently engaged in an inquiry into the production of confession through systematic practices of torture within the state legal system in Chechnya, and the ways this process is enfolded in and permeated with the local socio-cultural ideas and practices of blood feud, divination, dreams, and conspiracies.

21. This estimate was announced and at the same time doubted as too high by Chechen finance minister Eli Isaev in December 2009 (*Kavkazskii Uzel* 2009).

22. This is not to deny, however, that elders have occasionally been able to influence the actions of their children. One of my acquaintances whose son was unlawfully detained and tortured in prison went to the father of the prison guard-torturer and asked him whether he had done anything wrong to him to deserve such treatment of his son. Stressing the lack of any wrongdoing on his part and the unfairness of the infliction, my acquaintance alluded to possible implications of blood feud. The prison guard later helped him to secretly visit his son, the torture victim, in the prison: No one in the prison management got to know about his visits.

23. Many claimed that both the turnout and the results of the vote in the Republic on 23 March 2003 were heavily falsified. The vote took place while intense clashes between the rebels and the army were still frequent, as were aerial bombardments

and so-called "mop-up operations" in the villages. The referendum on the constitution was supplemented by a separate vote on a new law on the election of president,
which was followed by the presidential elections in October 2003, in which Kadyrov Sr. was elected Chechen president under similar allegations of falsifications.

24. According to authorities, the presence of the various Russian federal military units
in Chechnya was going to be reduced following the revocation of the 10-year-old
status of "counter-terrorist operations" in the Republic in April 2009. The current
number of federal troops in the Republic is, however, not clear; some estimates
point to a total of around 20,000 people (e.g., Agentura 2009); yet private calcula-
tions tend to be two or three times higher. The security and intelligence services of
the Russian federal Ministries of Defence and Interior (some of them staffed with
Chechen employees) and the numerous local law enforcement structures within
the Chechen Ministry of the Interior or under direct control of President Kadyrov
might retain separate spheres of action and influence, and there is a certain friction
between them; yet this does not preclude their occasional cooperation.

25. Here I refer to the qualities which have been brought up or alluded to by my
Chechen interlocutors as well as debated publicly. For example, some Chechen
authors have offered "lists" of fundamental Chechen virtues (Khasiev 2006, 2007;
Akhmadov 2007; Nasukhanov 2008), in which indigenous ideas merge with Islamic
values.

26. Instead of defining *adat* narrowly as "custom" or "customary law," I prefer to see it
as a wider platform of socio-cultural ideas and practices.

27. No precise statistics are available on civilian casualties in Chechnya. The figures
cited here are approximate estimates by the Russian human rights organization
Memorial (Cherkasov 2004, 2005). As regards the disappeared, 5,000 is the approximate number provided by the Chechen Ombudsman while the actual number, according to local human rights activists, might be four to five times higher
(*Kavkazskii Uzel* 2008). Also Memorial, which has been the main registrar of fatali-
ties and disappearances during the Chechen conflict and its aftermath, suspects the
figure to be much higher, as the organization has been able to cover only 25 to 30
percent of the territory of Chechnya. Nor does the official number include the disappearances during the past couple of years under the rule of Kadyrov Jr.'s government, and especially since April 2009, when Chechnya ceased to be a permanent
zone of counter-terrorist operation. The year 2009 saw an increase in abductions
and disappearances that mostly remain unreported and unknown in wider Russia
and abroad, as the work of local human rights organizations has been hampered,
and the victims and their relatives, faced by increasingly arbitrary and extrajudicial
violent measures (e.g., abductions, torture, killings, house-burnings) on the part of
Kadyrov government and the supporting local law enforcement structures in their
fight against "shaitans/Wahhabis," have been afraid to report the abuses.

28. In Chechnya, a section or subgroup of a loose Sufi brotherhood.

29. So far there have been few legal cases in Russia in which army personnel have been
sentenced for crimes committed in Chechnya. Among them is the case of Yuri
Budanov, former colonel of the Russian army, who was sentenced to 10 years in
prison for the abduction and murder of a Chechen girl, Elza Kungaeva, and was
released two years prematurely in January 2009. Some months later a legal action
was again taken against Yuri Budanov involving an alleged abduction and killing of

three other civilians from Elza Kungaeva's village in Chechnya in 2000. At the end of 2007 and after repeated court processes, Sergeant Sergei Lapin was sentenced to 11 years in prison for the torture of a Chechen man, Zelimkhan Murdalov, in Grozny in 2000 (the torture victim has been missing ever since). In the well-known Ulman case, three out of four officers of a special unit of the Russian Counter-Intelligence Department, Captain Eduard Ulman included, managed to escape while on bail in November 2007, shortly before being sentenced to 9 to 14 years in prison for killing six civilians in Chechnya in 2002.

As for the European Court of Human Rights, it had issued 137 rulings on Chechnya by 10 June 2010, holding Russia responsible for the deaths of more than 200 people. The majority of judgments involved forced disappearances, followed by extrajudicial executions, indiscriminate bombings, torture, and property destruction (Russian Justice Initiative 2010).

30. This is not to say, however, that tradition and individual life are perceived, in their original form, as neatly coherent narratives.

References

Agentura, Studies-Research Centre. 2009. "Bor'ba s terrorizmom: Chechnya." http://studies.agentura.ru/tr/russia/sk/chechnya/ (accessed 11 September 2008).

Akhmadov, Musa. 2006. *Chechenskaia Traditsionnaia Kul'tura i Etika.* Grozny: Vainakh.

Asad, Talal. 1993. "The Construction of Religion as an Anthropological Category." In *Genealogies of Religion,* ed. Talal Asad. Baltimore: John Hopkins University Press.

———. 2000. "Agency and Pain: An Exploration." *Culture and Religion* 1, no. 1: 29–60.

———. 2006. "Responses." *Powers of the Secular Modern: Talal Asad and His Interlocutors,* ed. David Scott and Charles Hirschkind. Stanford, CA: Stanford University Press.

Bobrovnikov, Vladimir. 2002. *Musul'mane Severnogo Kavkaza: Obichai, Pravo, Nasilie.* Moscow: RAS, Vostochnaia Literatura.

Carrithers, Michael. 2005. "Anthropology as a Moral Science of Possibilities." *Current Anthropology* 46, no. 3: 433–56.

Cherkasov, Aleksandr. 2004. "Book of Numbers. Book of Losses. Doomsday Book." www.kavkaz.memo.ru (accessed 25 January 2005).

———. 2005. "Zakon Bol'shikh Chisel." *Ezhednevnii Zhurnal,* 17 August. http://ej.ru/?a=note&id=1612 (accessed 18 September 2005).

Chesnov, Ian. 1999. "Byt' Chechentsem: Lichnost' i Etnicheskie Identifikatsii Naroda." In *Chechnia i Rossia: Obshchestva i Gosudarstva,* ed. Dmitry E. Furman. Moscow: Zhurnal Zvezda.

Chivers, C. J. 2009. "Slain Exile Detailed Cruelty of the Ruler of Chechnya." *New York Times,* 1 February. http://www.nytimes.com/2009/02/01/world/europe/01torture.html?scp=1&sq=israilov&st=cse (accessed 17 February 2009).

Dunlop, John. 1998. *Russia Confronts Chechnya: Roots of Separatist Conflict.* Cambridge: Cambridge University Press.

Edel, Abraham, and May Edel. [1959] 1968. *Anthropology and Ethics: the Quest for Moral Understanding.* Cleveland, OH: Press of Case Western Reserve University.

Evangelista, Matthew. 2002. *The Chechen Wars: Will Russia Go the Way of the Soviet Union?* Washington, D.C.: Brookings Institution Press.

Fassin, Didier. 2008. "Beyond Good and Evil? Questioning the Anthropological Discomfort with Morals." *Anthropological Theory* 8, no. 4: 333–44.

Faubion, James. 2001. "Toward an Anthropology of Ethics: Foucault and the Pedagogies of Autopoiesis." *Representations* 74: 83–104.

Fowkes, Ben. 1998. *Russia and Chechnia: The Permanent Crisis: Essays on Russo-Chechen Relations.* London: Macmillan.

Gall, Charlotte, and Thomas de Waal. 1997. *Chechnya: a Small Victorious War.* London: Pan Books.

Gammer, Moshe. 2006. *The Lone Wolf and the Bear: Three Centuries of Chechen Defiance of Russian Rule.* London: C. Hurst & Co. Publishers.

———. 2008. *Ethno-Nationalism, Islam and the State in the Caucasus.* London: Routledge.

Gilligan, Emma. 2009. *Terror in Chechnya: Russia and the Tragedy of Civilians in War.* Princeton, NJ: Princeton University Press.

Grant, Bruce. 2005. "The Good Russian Prisoner: Naturalizing Violence in the Caucasus Mountains." *Cultural Anthropology* 20, no. 1: 30–67.

Hughes, James. 2007. *Chechnya: From Nationalism to Jihad.* Philadelphia, PA: University of Pennsylvania Press.

Isaeva, Taisa. 2007. *Zhenshchiny i Deti: Pravo na Zhizn'.* Grozny: Informatsionnyi Tsentr SNO.

Kavkazskii Uzel. 2008. "Nukhazhiev: v Massovoi Mogile v Chechne Zakhoroneny 300 Chelovek." 2 July. http://www.kavkaz-uzel.ru/articles/138647 (accessed 13 January 2009).

———. 2009. "Ministr Finansov Chechni Usomnilsia v Statisticheskikh Dannykh o Bezrabotitse v Respublike." 8 Dec. http://www.kavkaz-uzel.ru/articles/162869/ (accessed 25 March 2010).

Khasiev, Said-Magomed. 2006. "Dukhovno-nravstvennaia Kul'tura Chechenskogo Naroda kak Faktor Ego Samosokhraneniia v Usloviiakh Deportatsii." Paper presented at the conference "Deportatsiia Chechenskogo Naroda: Posledstviia i Puti Ego Reabilitatsii," 18 February 2006, Grozny, Chechen Republic, Russian Federation.

———. 2007. "Nekotorye Aspekty Pozitivnogo Razvitiia Chechenskogo Naroda. Paper presented at the conference "Vosstanovlenie Checheno-Ingushskoi ASSR—Reshaiushchii Faktor Reabilitatsii Chechenskogo Naroda," January 2007, Grozny, Chechen Republic, Russian Federation.

Laidlaw, James. 2002. "For an Anthropology of Ethics and Freedom." *Journal of the Royal Anthropological Institute* 8, no. 2: 311–32.

———. 2009. "Morality: An Anthropological Perspective." *Ethnos* 74, no. 3: 435–37.

Lambek, Michael. 2000. "The Anthropology of Religion and the Quarrel between Poetry and Philosophy." *Current Anthropology* 41, no. 3: 309–20.

———. 2008. "Value and Virtue." *Anthropological Theory* 8, no. 2: 133–57.

Lieven, Anatol. 1998. *Chechnya: the tombstone of Russian power.* New Haven, CT: Yale University Press.

MacIntyre, Alasdair. 1988. *Whose Justice? Which Rationality?* Notre Dame, IN: University of Notre Dame Press.

———. 1997. "The Virtues, the Unity of Human Life, and the Concept of Tradition." In *Memory, Identity, Community: The Idea of Narrative in the Human Sciences*, ed. L. P. Hinchman and S. K. Hinchman. New York: SUNY Press.

———. [1967] 2000. *A Short History of Ethics*. London: Routledge.

———. [1981] 2007. *After Virtue: A Study in Moral Theory*. London: Duckworth.

Mahmood, Saba. 2005. *Politics of Piety: The Islamic Revival and the Feminist Subject*. Princeton, NJ: Princeton University Press.

Nasukhanov, Magomed-Khadzhi. 2008. *Vird: Nasledie Shaikha Bamatgirii-Khadzhi*. Grozny, Elista: Dzhangar.

Novaya Gazeta. 2009. "Venskoe Ubiistvo." 4 February. http://www.novayagazeta.ru/data/2009/011/00.html (accessed 5 March 2009).

Pandian, Anand. 2008. "Tradition in Fragments: Inherited Forms and Fracture in the Ethics of South India." *American Ethnologist* 35, no. 3: 466–80.

Parkin, David. 1985. Introduction to *The anthropology of Evil*, ed. David Parkin. Oxford: Blackwell.

Politkovskaya, Anna. 2001. *A Dirty War: A Russian Reporter in Chechnya*. London: Harvill Press.

———. 2003a. "Za Chto Kadyrov Nevzliubil Dedushku Balu." *Novaya Gazeta*, 20 November. http://2003.novayagazeta.ru/nomer/2003/87n/n87n-s17.shtml (accessed 5 September 2008).

———. 2003b. *A Small Corner of Hell: Dispatches from Chechnya*. Chicago: University of Chicago Press.

———. 2007. *Za Chto?* Moscow: Novaya Gazeta.

Read, K. E. 1955. "Morality and the Concept of Person among the Gahuku-Gama." *Oceania* 25, no. 4: 233–82.

Rigi, Jakob. 2007. "The War in Chechnya: The Chaotic Mode of Domination, Violence and Bare Life in the Post-Soviet Context." *Critique of Anthropology* 27, no. 1: 37–62.

Robbins, Joel. 2007. "Between Reproduction and Freedom: Morality, Value, and Radical Cultural Change." *Ethnos* 72, no. 3: 293–314.

Russell, John. 2007. *Chechnya—Russia's 'War on Terror'.* London: Routledge.

Russian Justice Initiative. 2010. "ECHR Cases from the North Caucasus." http://www.srji.org/en/legal/cases (accessed 10 June 2010).

Sakwa, Richard, ed. 2005. *Chechnya: From Past to Future*. London: Anthem Press.

Scott, David. 1999. *Refashioning Futures: Criticism after Postcoloniality*. Princeton, NJ: Princeton University Press.

Smith, Sebastian. 2000. *Allah's Mountains: The Battle for Chechnya*. New York: I. B. Tauris Parke.

Sokirianskaia, Ekaterina. 2005. "Families and Clans in Ingushetia and Chechnya: A fieldwork report." *Central Asian Survey* 24, no. 4: 453–67.

———. 2008. "Ideology and Conflict: Chechen Political Nationalism Prior to, and During, Ten Years of War." In *Ethno-Nationalism, Islam and the State in the Caucasus*, ed. Moshe Gammer. London: Routledge.

Tishkov, Valerii. 2001. *Obshchestvo v Vooruzhennom Konflikte: Etnografiia Chechenskoi Voiny*. Moscow: Nauka.

———. 2004. *Chechnya: Life in a War-torn Society*. Berkeley, CA: University of California Press.

Widlok, Thomas. 2004. "Sharing by Default? Outline of an Anthropology of Virtue." *Anthropological Theory* 4, no. 1: 53–70.

Wood, Tony. 2007. *Chechnya: The Case for Independence.* London: Verso.

Zigon, Jarrett. 2006. "'You Should Reform Yourself not Other People': The Ethics of Hope in Contemporary Moscow." Working paper No. 88. Halle/Saale: Max Planck Institute for Social Anthropology.

———. 2007. "Moral Breakdown and the Ethical Demand: A Theoretical Framework for an Anthropology of Moralities." *Anthropological Theory* 7, no. 2: 131–50.

 CHAPTER 7

Morality, Utopia, Discipline
New Religious Movements and Soviet Culture

Alexander A. Panchenko

Anthropologists and sociologists of religion usually do not recognize the study of morality or ethics as a specific subfield within their fields of research. Morality is thought of as part of the wider system of values or set of practices associated with a religious world view or social order. It might be reasonable, to proceed from this point of view because it is usually not easy to determine the boundary between "moral" and "amoral" forms of religious culture within a specific group or community. However, many parts of religious discourse can be interpreted in terms of morality, and morality may not be directly related to the theological or spiritual dogmas shared by group members. It is important to understand the role played by moral codes and forms of ethical reasoning in the everyday life of a given religious community. In this context, it is preferable to understand morality not as a stable system of values or a world view but as a range of moral discourses and ethical practices people use for various purposes within the framework of particular social structures and power relations. Therefore, the production of morality and the ways in which individuals switch between various moral codes is closely related to the discipline of religious groups and movements, and their construction of a meaningful universe. These processes can be described in terms of continuity and change, since moral models are borrowed and elaborated anew according to the particular social and ideological context. Another important issue is the distinction between habitual moral patterns shared by group members, and public discourses or institutions of morality that can occupy a certain place in religious ideologies and sometimes in the everyday practice of contemporary confessions, denominations, and spiritual movements. It would be quite helpful for anthropologists of religion to interrogate how institutional and public discourses of morality correlate with habitual moral choice and what cultural resources are used for their construction (see: Zigon 2009).

In the following chapter I will discuss a post-Soviet religious movement that attends closely to moral issues, both on an institutional and a practical level. Although it is quite common for new religious movements in various parts of the contemporary world to develop and employ specific ethical techniques to support group solidarity and discipline, the case analyzed below seems to be quite peculiar. In this case, both the institutions of morality and the everyday forms of moral reasoning go far beyond basic social needs of solidarity and discipline. I propose that this peculiar moral culture has its origins in Soviet collectivist practices inherited by post-Soviet new religious movements. Thus, I argue that contemporary Russian new religious movements should be discussed in terms of social and cultural continuity rather than change or influence from abroad.

New Religious Movements in Russia: The Last Testament Church

The collapse of the Soviet Union has given rise to a number of indigenous new religious movements which make ample use of both domestic and transcultural patterns of spirituality, dogmatic teachings and moral ideas to create their unique religious worlds. However, many specific features of the movements appear to be related to the late Soviet urban culture with its peculiar mixture of New Age beliefs, utopian expectations, and totalistic forms of social control. This paper explores the genealogy and dynamics of moral utopias and social relations in a new religious movement in Central Siberia known as "the Last Testament Church" or "the community of Vissarion."

To begin with, it is necessary to make some general remarks about the history, dogmatic and social teachings, ritual practice, and everyday life of the movement. The Last Testament Church (LTC) is a religious community founded by amateur artist and former policeman Sergey Torop, born on 14 January 1961 in Krasnodar, in Minusinsk, Krasnoyarskii *krai* (region).[1] After a spiritual awakening in the summer of 1991, he took a new name—Vissarion—and claimed to be the Son of the Lord or the Word of the Lord. His followers venerate him as Christ, call him "the Teacher" and consider his activities to constitute the Second Coming. With the help of a small circle of followers Vissarion began to preach in Minusinsk, and later, in other larger cities in the former USSR. His primary audiences were the clubs and groups of so-called "(spiritual) seekers" oriented toward various versions of late Soviet occultism or "esoteric culture."

While Soviet secular ideology and culture was largely successful in substituting for Orthodox religious praxis, it does not mean, however, that the population of the cities and towns of the USSR were "atheist" in the strict sense of the word. In fact, during the late Soviet decades (especially the 1970s and 1980s) there appeared a number of social and cultural movements that were not satisfied with the goals and rewards (both material and spiritual) offered by communism, "scientific atheism," and so on. It would be interesting to consider, in this context, the religious and symbolic roots of the political resistance of Soviet dissidents, alternative culture and arts, and the very ideology of the intelligentsia, but now I am just referring to the religious tendencies of late Soviet urban culture. In her essay "The Occult Revival in Russia Today and Its Impact on Literature," Birgit Menzel remarks:

> The first and in post-Soviet Russia the most obvious way to be involved in the occult is through what Mikhail Epstein has called "Pop-Religion," which is basically what we see in popular culture: a mixture of the most diverse, even contradictory, religious, spiritual and esoteric ideas, promoted, followed and practiced as an immediate force of salvation. This includes all non-arcane phenomena of popular magic, witchcraft, astrology, cults and sects, Western mixed with Eastern, Oriental mixed with Orthodox heretics, such as the Old Believers. The attraction to random, sometimes extreme, choices and the readiness to support an amazingly wide variety of irrational syncretistic belief systems can be seen as a transitional reaction to compensate for the formerly imposed atheist condition. (2007: 7)

Although the "invisible religion" of late Soviet and post-Soviet Russia (along with a number of other New Independent States (NIS)) that Menzel refers to has not yet been properly studied by anthropologists, historians, or sociologists,[2] it is obvious that "esoteric" beliefs and practices influenced post-Soviet religious culture in general, and new religious movements in particular. The social and organizational framework for the post-Soviet "cults" were provided by a number of spiritual circles or discussion clubs with an interest in UFOlogy and contacts with extraterrestrial civilizations, extrasensory perception, faith-healing, paranormal phenomena, astrology, and meditation. Their members were also interested in spiritual practices such as Yoga and Zen Buddhism, as well as number of more recent occult and spiritual teachings such as books by Elena Blavatskaya, *Agni-ioga* by Elena and Nikolai Roerich, and *Roza Mira* by Daniil Andreev.[3] The discussion clubs collected and discussed evidence of the paranormal and engaged in spiritual and extrasensory exercises. Usually, their members were *technicheskaya intelligentsia,* the educated technical specialists who comprised a large social class of the late Soviet urban population. These people then became the founders and the most active members of the post-Soviet cults. However, supporters of these occult and spiritual practices could also be found outside these organized groups. The unconventional forms of religious expression described above were immensely popular among the educated urban population of Russia. They were especially widespread amongst groups of young people oriented towards alternative or "underground" ideologies, cultures, and social practices.

In the early 1990s, Vissarion and his closest followers founded an isolated community in Western Sayany Mountains in the southwestern part of the Krasnoyarskii *krai* (region). Here, on Sukhaia Mountain, near Lake Tiberkul', they began to build "the Solar City" (also known as "*ecopolis Tiberkul',*" "the Abode of Dawn," or simply "the City"). Some of Vissarion's disciples were to live with him in "the City," while others lived in surrounding settlements of the Kuraginskii district. Until 1995, the majority of the LTC members migrated to the Kuraginskii and neighboring Karatuzskii districts. Today, the approximate number of Vissarion's followers in Kuraginskii and Karatuzskii districts is about 4,000. This territory is generally divided by the movement's elite into three areas: (1) "the Mountain and the City," where Vissarion and about 60 LTC members live; (2) "the villages of taiga zone," or *derevni taezhnoj zony* (which include Petropavlovka, Cheremshanka, Guliaevka, and Zharovsk—villages about 35 to 45 kilometers from "the Mountain"), where about 1,200 followers live; and (3) all other settlements of the two districts including their centers, Kuragino and Karatuz. There are about 30 LTC communities in this part of Krasnoyarskii *krai*. There also exist more than a dozen urban communities and centers of the movement situated in various cities of Russia, Ukraine, Byelorussia, Kazakhstan, and other NIS countries. I have no statistical information about "urban" members of the movement, but it is likely that there are several thousands of them. Although the majority of the LTC members come from former Soviet republics, there are a number of followers from Bulgaria, Germany, Belgium, and other European countries. The followers of Vissarion tend to be former city dwellers with a medium or high level of education. The movement grew rapidly in the early 1990s, but since the middle of the decade and up to today, the quantity of its members seems to be quite stable. It might be said that the majority of the LTC members represent the last Soviet generation.

Although Russian society was rapidly changing during the two decades of the history of the LTC, the movement itself has not changed greatly either socially or ideologically. The radical eschatology of the early years has gone, but the LTC members still think that they are the only people able to survive the planetary catastrophe when it happens. The movement has become more "worldly" in terms of dietary prescriptions, use of technical devices, and economic relations with the outer society. Today, the LTC has its own representatives in the district council and maintains good relations with the regional authorities and local populations. At the same time, it still preserves its key ideas and rituals due, at least partially, to its geographic and social isolation in a remote taiga corner of Central Siberia. It is not easy to decide whether the LTC has already established its particular religious and social tradition to become a "church" in Weberian terms, but at least some young men and women that were brought up in its communities seem to be devoted believers who do not want to break up their ties with the movement and return to secular life in big cities.

The theology of the LTC as described in its spiritual literature tends to present a holistic cosmological conception of the universe. Although complicated and sometimes contradictory, it is important to note that some basic concepts play an important role in the religious ideology and practices of the movement. These include the idea of Vissarion's divine mission, the cult of "Mother Earth" (or "Mother Nature"), and the concept of "external consciousness" (or "galactic mind"), which usually implies the existence of extraterrestrial civilizations (which may be either friendly or hostile to humanity). Despite claims by LTC members, their veneration of "Mother Earth" bears no relation to Slavic popular culture or folk religion. Ideas of reincarnation and special energies that connect every person with the cosmic environment are very popular among the followers of Vissarion. The cosmology of the LTC does not presume any personified evil. Rather, evil is considered to be "the negative energy" of humankind. All LTC members are vegetarians, and smoking and consuming alcohol are strictly prohibited for those who consider themselves true believers. Both the dogmatic teachings and the history of the movement are represented in the multi-volume Holy Writ known as the Last Testament (LT).[4] It includes records of the early sermons by Vissarion, the continued history of the Second Coming titled "The Narrative by Vadim" (since it is being written by Vadim Red'kin, one of the closest disciples of Vissarion) and two cosmological books written by Vissarion in the late 1990s.

Apart from its theological and cosmological dogmas and ideas, the religious culture of the movement has inherited a broad range of beliefs and practices related to contemporary urban and New Age spirituality. These include: the notion of "bio-energies," "thin force fields," and "vibrations," which influence and determine the whole universe; alternative healing beliefs and practices; "extra-sensory" powers and perception; and UFOlogy and spiritual contacts with extraterrestrial civilizations. Although the teachings of the LTC include elements of Christianity and other world religions along with various forms of the New Age spirituality, many of the ritual, social, and spiritual patterns of the movement's culture are represented and discussed by its followers as quasi- or para-scientific.

Although the ideology of the LTC has undergone some changes during its more than 15-year history, its main goal was always the creation of a new society free from violence and aggression and living in harmony with nature. In the 1990s, this ideology was supported by more or less explicit eschatological expectations. For example, LTC members declared that future social and natural cataclysms would lead to the destruction of the majority of humankind (with the exception of LTC members). During the past decade, however, this eschatology has gradually evanesced. Today, they believe the formation of a new society is supposed to occur after a number of generations have elapsed.

The practical steps to achieve the future new society are, as declared by the LTC leaders: (1) moral and spiritual perfection of the movement's members; (2) establishment of new social and economic relations within the community; and (3) attempts to give up modern technology and all activities leading to "pollution" of the natural environment and human body. These activities involve a number of projects that affect both the private and public everyday life of the LTC community. The most ambitious project, started in the late 1990s, relates to the social and economic organization of the LTC communities. It is called "the program of unity" and requires the organization of communes with collectivized property and labor. The members of the communes, known as "united families" (as opposed to "natural families"), are supposed to work together and share the products of their labor. It is generally assumed that in time all the followers of Vissarion will be united in a great commune independent of the external world. Although today LTC members have to purchase a lot of goods in shops, they suppose that eventually they will be able to produce all the goods they require by themselves and "to go away" from traditional economic relations (including trade or even commutation).

Moral Discourses and Ethical Techniques of the LTC

LTC members declare that the future society they create should avoid any "negative" (or "unfavorable") forms of human behavior and social life including selfishness and pride, aggression, and social inequality. This moral discourse of the LTC is based upon a number of key ideas and concepts borrowed from Vissarion's sermons and elaborated on in discussions of moral issues by ordinary LTC members. These concepts include:

> *egoism* ("selfishness"): sometimes imagined and represented in
> accordance to the binary oppositions of "human/inhuman"
> and "culture/nature," as "the beast" (*zverek*), or "the shaggy"
> (*lokhmatyi*);
>
> *gordynya* ("pride"): designated as "the medusa" (*meduza*) in one
> of the most famous Vissarion's sermons on 24 October 1998;[5]

mudrost' ("wisdom"): includes not only abstract knowledge but also a method for solving a particular moral problem. One can "ask for wisdom" (*prosit' mudrosti*) or "give wisdom" (*dat' mudrost*) in certain circumstances;

gorenie ("burning") which designates various states of agitation and excitement but most often is used to describe the emotional and physical state of a person trying to overcome his or her selfishness and pride;[6]

polianka smireniia ("the glade of humility") is another image introduced initially in Vissarion's sermon of 24 October 1998.[7] It symbolizes the difficult pathway of a person struggling against his or her pride and selfishness.

In addition to these specific moral ideas, concepts and symbols, the movement has elaborated forms of ethical communication and techniques that provide stable types of social interaction and means of mutual control within LTC communities. These practices include "suggestions" (*podkazki*), "the chair of wisdom" (*stul'chik mudrosti*), "moral meetings" (*moral'no-eticheskie sobraniia*), and "meetings for common understanding" (*edinoe ponimanie*).

On of the most common forms of everyday communication about ethical issues is the "suggestion" (*podskazka*), which comprises critical but friendly advice about one's behavior, words, ideas, habits, and so on. The term comes from Vissarion's idiolect in the earliest parts of the LT including *The Book of Appeals* (33:74, 35:29, etc.), *The Book of Fundamentals* (3:10, 12:70), and the second part of the *Narrative* by Vadim (13:49). As with many other aspects of LTC discourse, "suggestion" connotes unequal power relations between teacher and student since the most common meaning of the word in colloquial Russian is related to daily school life. Since at least the mid 1990s, the word has become one of the key concepts within the moral discourse of LTC members. In the whole text of the LT, the word is used more than 1,200 times. A member of the movement joked in 2001 that, "Here 'in the Church' they can give you a suggestion even during a funeral."[8] A *podskazka* is not simply an abstract moral term; it also refers to a more or less formalized mode of social interaction which can prevent or produce conflict between two or more LTC followers. This practice was described by our informant as follows:

Suggestion helps a person see what he does not see. Sometimes he does not want to see either. But here you have to approach this very gently, because you must not hurt the person. Human beings, in fact, are very vulnerable, and, just now, at least among us, people are becoming more open, and we are trying to open ourselves completely to each other, having nothing left to hide. And when everything negative begins to come out from a person ... Now, we've got a sort of milieu created to help us to get rid of everything negative, as far as we can. And it comes out, and people become very vulnerable. And in order to make them less vulnerable, it had been said to us, at first, that we should give suggestions to other people. Then, generally speaking, it has become clear that people were getting more closed instead. And now, it has been suggested to us that we should be very careful and tender with each other and that we should not give suggestions immediately. When a person has splashed out, yes, something from himself, something has come out from him, you should try and let him calm himself, so he can settle down and you yourself can be completely calm without any negative bursts inside you. Only after that you may drop a hint, and since the person does not understand it, you may "give him a suggestion," but it must be given gently and fondly. ...

I am a very peremptory person, and it is not easy for me, for example, to give a good suggestion. And suggestions must be always helpful. They are given only to help people, so that a person would see what he needs, what he needs to work on. They are given for this purpose only, not for disparagement or abasement.[9]

A more regular and organized technique of collective criticism, moral discussion, and discipline is "the chair of wisdom" (*stul'chik mudrosti*), which emerged in the late 1990s (the first record of this practice in the LT is in December 1999).[10] It was first introduced among those living in "the City" but soon "the chair of wisdom" became popular in the majority of LTC communities. Although it was not obligatory, normally every male member of a community would go through the chair of wisdom once a year in early January. The person in the chair of wisdom must listen to all criticism from the members of his community, and has no right to argue with the criticism or justify his behavior. At the same time he may tell community members about his misdeeds and moral problems and ask for suggestions. In recent years this technique has lost some of its popularity, but it is still practiced in both Siberian and urban communities of the LTC. As one community member explains:

We've got the timeless days (*dni bezvremen'ya*), from the first to the fourteenth of January, when the Teacher invites everybody to sit in the chair of wisdom. One could sit in this chair of wisdom anytime though. If one wants to change something in himself, to see all what others see in him, he would sit on this chair and listen to everybody; he does not justify himself, he only makes all more exact: where and how, well, sort of facts of the matter. It is, you know, it is a beautiful thing indeed! You are sitting there, you are burning! But then after that ... I don't know, you are so glad to see how people look after you. They don't try to find out any negative traits, but they just want to help each other to see.[11]

The website of Samara LTC community described the chair of wisdom in 2004 as follows:

Today Misha Vashurov passed the sacrament of the chair of wisdom. The brother has told openly about his foibles, he has told that he often could not handle various accidents in his family and at his work. Brothers and sisters suggested to Misha that he overestimated his vigors and that it led him to unnecessary self-reproach. Misha was advised that, in order to have the right relationship with his son, he should not be too exacting, that he was to show more concern about his son, and that he should change himself, first of all, and not his child.[12]

"Asking for wisdom" (*prosit' mudrosti*) is a technique similar to the "chair of wisdom," although it is less formalized. It is performed in various circumstances and requires a number of people who are expected to "give wisdom" to the person who asks for opinions and suggestions related to his or her thoughts and deeds. As one church member related:

For example, I wanted today to ask girls to give me ... just tonight, if it would be possible, to give me wisdom regarding some of my thoughts that are not related to reality. ... I will ask for wisdom. I will say: "Girls, what do you see in me that leads me to these or those thoughts?" I've got these or those misunderstandings, they accumulate in my mind. So, the girls would talk to me in order to take all this out, to make me pure. And after that I will look and see that, yes, it is right indeed, yes, it is so, I need to work with this, and I am working with that. Perhaps I would not even understand something, and I would say: "Well, it does not have any relation to me. Why do they speak so?" But maybe I don't know it. Or I don't see it yet. I have not realized something, but it is already in me. Then, I will realize that with time.[13]

Another common technique of discipline, for a period, consisted of "moral meetings" (*moral'no-eticheskie sobraniia*), which were stopped by an order of Vissarion in 2004. Usually, such a meeting was called in a community (or in a "united family") in order to discuss a particular situation, for example, improper behavior of one of its members, disorder in a "natural family," or a conflict between two or more followers of Vissarion. I never had the opportunity to attend such a meeting, but it seems that in some cases they led to an increase of conflicts within the LTC communities. Since these moral meetings were stopped, some of their functions have gone to the centralized "council on moral and ethical issues" (see below) and others to "meetings for common understanding" (*edinoe ponimanie*).

At first, "meetings for common understanding of the Truth" (i.e., of Vissarion's words) functioned as discussion clubs for the study of the LT and recent and unpublished sermons by Vissarion. Changes have occurred since the practice of holding moral meetings was ended, and now "meetings for common understanding" have begun to combine abstract theological or ideological discussions with an analysis of everyday moral dilemmas. A person who wants to discuss a particular ethical situation asks the members of the community to prepare for the discussion by looking at relevant passages in the LT. In the communities I worked in, meetings for common understanding happened daily, started early in the morning, and lasted for about an hour. Although attendance at these meetings was not obligatory, the most active community members always attended.

In order to regulate this complicated set of practices, the leaders of the LTC movement have recently tried to develop a routine related to the discussion of moral issues known as "the sacred algorithm for the analysis of a situation." The term "sacred algorithm" might be borrowed from the science fiction story "Men and Moulds" (first published in 1974) by the Russian writer Zinovii Yuriev (Z. Yu. Grinman), where it referred to the program of behavior prescribed by a super-computer to the members of a Universal Church. In the LTC, however, the algorithm is an ethical prescription for a sequence of actions to be undertaken by every LTC follower in case of any "misunderstanding" or "confusion" related to another person's words or conduct. If the contracting parties cannot agree on the problem, they may discuss it at a local meeting or appeal to the "council on moral and ethical issues" situated in Petropavlovka. Today the council includes the church organizer Vladimir Vedernikov (*ustroitel' tserkvi*, the leader of the LTC in charge of various practical and secular matters), the priest Sergei Chevalkov, and a small number of competent members of the local "united family." If the judgment of the council does not stop the conflict, it is necessary to apply to Vissarion himself either in writing or personally. His word, of course, is the ultimate authority in any case. The algorithm was formulated a few years ago by Vedernikov and Chevalkov in order to regulate the flow of appeals to Vissarion and the LTC leaders from ordinary church members.

It might seem from the preceding discussion that both formulation and transmission of moral codes and forms of ethical reasoning in the LTC are totally controlled by the leaders of the movement and Vissarion himself. This is only partly true. The oral culture of the movement also plays an important role in the transmission and maintenance of social and moral norms (see Panchenko 2006), and practices include personal experience narratives, discussion and interpretation of the LT and various printed texts and, last but not least, pieces of information "from the beyond" distributed by those who say they are in contact with extraterrestrial civilizations and with the dead. The overall structure of the "ethical narratives" by the LTC members can be presented as follows:

Table 7.1. Ethical narratives of LTC members.

Sign of disorder	Reason	Cure	Result and confirmation
Negative thoughts, words, or misconduct	Selfishness Pride	Self perfection; suggestion(s), discussion at the chair of wisdom, moral meeting(s) or common understanding meetings; questioning the Teacher	Moral reinforcement and improvement; approval by the voices of the dead
Conflict	Selfishness Pride	Suggestion(s), discussion at the chair of wisdom, moral meeting(s) or common understanding meetings; questioning the moral council; questioning the Teacher	Individual and/or collective moral improvement; approval by the voices of the dead or of the external consciousness
Disease(s)	Negative thoughts, words, or misconduct	Individual or collective repentance	Recovery
Accident(s)	Negative thoughts, words, or misconduct	Individual or collective repentance or prayer	No more accidents

The stories told by the LTC members are usually about "life accidents" and support the beliefs and social practices of the movement. Stories tell, for example, about successful spiritual healing in the course of which illness is revealed to be caused by "resentments against neighbors":

> Once I was with my granddaughter when doctors said that she had tuberculosis. She was six years old. And I just … talked with my son; I said: "Well, sonny … All pulmonary diseases, bronchitis and so on, are caused by resentments. Resentments against neighbors.

Against life ... By and large ... Well, resentments." He recalled his life, we talked about those resentments; in case we had forgotten something, we helped each other to recollect. And then, literally, medical inspection showed no tuberculosis. She did have a predisposition, yes, but no tuberculosis.[14]

Although the structure of these narratives is quite typical of didactic stories from the oral cultures of various Christian churches, they omit the categories of sin and miracle which play an important role in the Orthodox tradition. Instead, both physical and moral disorders are explained in a pseudo-scientific manner as the results of "energy imbalance," either within the human body or in the environment. This explanatory model is widely used by the LTC members for moral reasoning. Morality is often thought to be a part of or a representation of universal physical laws that cannot be changed or doubted.

The LTC and the Soviet Past: Genealogy of Ethical Techniques

Although special attention to moral issues is common among new religious movements in both Russia and the West, it may be useful to think about the genealogy of this peculiar regime of "moral production." Of course, it could be determined by some practical reasons. It is notable that both the project of united families and the majority of the moral models and ideas described above were articulated by Vissarion in the autumn of 1998, after the well-known Russian financial crisis which also seriously undermined the weak economics of the LTC. Thus, "the collectivization" of 1998 (in social, economic, and moral domains) can be viewed as an attempt to survive through a severe economic crisis. Yet, it does not explain what particular sources were used for the ethical practices developed by the LTC in the late 1990s.

The majority of the LTC followers are thus far former citizens of the USSR and therefore inherit some practices and ideological patterns of the Soviet period. It would be reasonable to assume that their collectivistic ethical practices are in some way related to aspects of the Soviet ethos of the 1960s–1980s with its discussions of "personal cases" at Party and Komsomol[15] meetings, "comradely courts," the "Moral Code of the Builder of Communism," and so on. However, even here we face a variety of patterns and tendencies. The "Soviet ethos" of the Khrushchev and Brezhnev periods should not be viewed as monolithic, as it included multiple moralities. Moreover, some contemporary scholars insist that the late Soviet moral culture paradoxically combined socio-centric and individualistic goals, ideals, and methods of discipline (Kharkhordin 2002: 10; Zigon 2006: 5). It is necessary then to look for particular aspects of the "Soviet ethos" that could be viewed as a source or a model for the forms of moral reasoning and social control appropriated and elaborated by the LTC.

Although the reign of Nikita Khrushchev (1953–1964) is described as "the Thaw," and known as a period of liberalization and "de-Stalinization," the changes in public life introduced by the elite of the Communist Party and the Soviet government during this decade should not be overstated. As Oleg Kharkhordin points out, "if one considers the increase of mutual surveillance in everyday life from a long-term perspective, the year 1957 would be direct continuation of the tendencies of 1937" (2002: 392). Indeed, the revival of "comradely courts," the establishment of the DND (*dobrovol'naia narodnaia druzhina*, volunteer auxiliary police), and the Komsomol patrols can be viewed as an attempt to create a total system of mutual control on the grass-roots level of Soviet society. According to Kharkhordin, the Khrushchev projects of collectivization of private life led to the creation "of a system of mutual surveillance and mutual control, a system which was more accurate and reliable in practice than the preceding openly repressive Stalinist system" (389).

However, unlike the hierarchic state system created by Stalin and based on the rule of specialized bureaucrats (primarily Party officials and officers of special services), the practice of "partial democracy" introduced by Khrushchev closely resembled Italian fascism since it resulted in the creation of groups of lay activists who aspired to control aspects of everyday and private life. Joseph Brodsky made this suggestion when talking with Solomon Volkov about his memories of the DND of the Dzerzhinskii district of Leningrad and its leader Iakov Lerner, who did so much to prepare the poet's trial:

> At that moment, his work was to manage a *narodnaia druzhina*. Do you know what is *narodnaia druzhina*? That was a petty form of fascisation of people, especially young men. ... First of all, they kept an eye on the "Europeiskaia" hotel where a lot of foreigners stayed. ... They hunted, for the most part, for *fartsy* [illegal small traders with foreigners]. And, by the way, when these *druzhinniki* conducted a search of *fartsovschiki* they reserved a lot to themselves, both money and icons. (Volkov 1998: 63–64)

It is also important that Kharkhordin is not quite right in talking about these pseudo-democratic changes in the USSR in the late 1950s as repressive government initiatives. It is well known that the massive rehabilitation of political prisoners in 1955–1956, Khrushchev's report at the 20th Communist Party of the Soviet Union (CPSU) Congress, and other actions aimed at the "de-Stalinization" of the USSR were interpreted by parts of society (and, particularly, by many intellectuals) as a sign of the real democratization of the state. At the same time, the repudiation of Stalinist discourse was often interpreted as a return to a more or less imaginary heritage of Lenin, and the ideas, values and moral norms of the early 1920s that he was associated with. It is indicative that images of the October revolution and the civil war played an important role in the ideological project of the Khrushchev period, along with ideas of the "Bolshevik heroic spirit" and "the creation of the new man." Bulat Okudzhava, a cult figure of the Soviet intelligentsia, wrote a song titled "Sentimental March" in 1957, two years after he had joined the CPSU. The song finished with the following verse:

> But if ever at once I would not protect myself,
> And whatever new battle would shake the globe,
> I will perish at that only Civil war,
> And commissars in dusty helmets will bend silently over me.
> (Okudzhava 2001: 135)[16]

It is not easy to decide to what extent both Soviet society and its leaders believed in the twenty-year program of building communism proclaimed at the 22nd CPSU Congress, but the idea that the "moral standards" of the average Soviet person standing on the threshold of communist society should be transformed met with a certain amount of support from the liberal intelligentsia. In this context, the notorious "Moral Code of the Builder of Communism" included in the 3rd CPSU program was taken quite seriously by many, the more so since it was the only part of the broader program oriented towards the formation of a new communist morality. In 1959, "the first scientific conference on aspects of Marxist-Leninist ethics" was held in Leningrad (see *Voprosy marksistsko-leninskoj etiki* 1960), and a year later departments of ethics and aesthetics were set up in Moscow and Leningrad state universities (Nazarov 2003: 183–84). In 1961, the first university textbook and the first reader on Marxist ethics were published (Shishkin 1961; Shishkin, ed. 1961). There is a strong analogy between this new moral culture and journalistic campaigns of the late 1920s against *meschanstvo* and the "petty bourgeoisie" (see Vihavainen 2004: 161–232).

The social and ideological context of the 1950s and 1960s gave rise to the "communard movement" (*kommunarskoe dvizhenie*), which seems to have had a strong influence on the LTC. This movement started as a local pedagogical experiment but later had considerable influence upon behavioral practices of the Soviet intelligentsia in the last decades of the twentieth century.[17] In the mid 1950s, Igor' Ivanov (1923–1992), a Komsomol official, education specialist, and the future professor of the Leningrad State Pedagogical Institute, established a pedagogical group known as "the Union of enthusiasts" (*Sojuz entuziastov*) in the Leningrad Research Institute of Pedagogy. The group was oriented towards the search for new methods of "collective organization of work with the Young Pioneers." Initially, it included the employees of the Institute and Young Pioneer leaders from a number of Leningrad secondary schools (Ivanov 1990: 82–85). In 1959, Ivanov and his followers established a district school for Young Pioneer activists at the Frunzensky House of Pioneers in Leningrad. The school assumed the name "Commune of Young Frunzentsy" (*Kommuna Yunykh Frunzentsev*), or the CYF. According to Ivanov, he was inspired, first of all, by the pedagogical ideas and methods of Anton Makarenko (1888–1939). Makarenko's methods included the arrangement of Poltava and Khar'kov (Kuriazh) labor colonies for juvenile delinquents along with the "Dzerzhinsky commune." He described his pedagogy in *Pedagogicheskaia poema, Flagi na bashniakh* and other writings, and was regarded as the "classic expert in Soviet pedagogy" (Ivanov 1990: 5–16).[18] Additionally, the organization of the CYF was influenced by stories written by Arkadii Gaidar and the practice of the "Timur movement."

The CYF was not aimed at juvenile delinquents but instead at activists of public work. Thus Ivanov's project generally conformed to the state policy of establishing grassroots networks and groups of activists oriented towards the new moral imperative of the "builder of communism" described earlier. The founder of the CYF most likely thought of it as a pedagogical experiment that, if successful, could be extended over the whole system of secondary education. The CYF, however, was accepted neither by school educational specialists nor by the communards themselves. It seems that the difficulties on this point between Ivanov and the communards were the reason behind him leaving the CYF in 1962 (see Solovejchik 1972: 79–83; Ivanov 1990: 114).

The main principle of the CYF organization was the collectivization of all activities of members that, as a rule, included work at *subbotniki* (*volunteer work on holidays in the Soviet Union*) in the city, and summer farm work during annual camps (*sbory*) in the Efimovskii district of the Leningrad region (which was under the patronage of the CYF), along with various forms of art activities, role-playing games and discussion clubs. An important feature of the CYF was an orientation towards self-government and egalitarianism. The governing body of the Commune was elected by the communards themselves. The adult leaders often did not have the deciding vote, although in practice they did have a great deal of influence. The basis for "communard upbringing," according to Ivanov, was the organization of "collective creative deeds," which included labor, educational or entertainment projects discussed at all stages by the whole commune (or its separate groups) and managed by elected "deed councils" (see Ivanov

1989). Everyday life of a communard inevitably involved participation in one or more of these projects and a lack of private time during the *sbory;* the idea of "collective creative deeds" implied both methods of performing labor tasks and overall forms of organized recreation and leisure.

It is important to stress that according to Ivanov, collectivization involved not only collective activities but all possible interpersonal relations in the Commune (which united teenagers from 11–12 to 16–17 years old) during *sbor,* either in the countryside or in the city. The main tool for totalistic mutual control was the *ogoniok* ("small light"), an everyday evening meeting of the whole Commune (or of its single "detachment") that combined collective singing and detailed discussion of all daily occurrences. The communards themselves described the *ogoniok* in the following manner:

> Our ogoniok, what is it?
>
> Every evening, the whole commune gathers around the fire. We sit in a circle to see the faces of comrades.
>
> The fire is small, a couple of logs burn there. It is comfortably. At first they are singing, in low voice, for a proper mood. Then they begin to discuss how the day passed. Three questions they ask at ogoniok:
>
> "What was right today?"
>
> "What was wrong?"
>
> "What else is to be done?"
>
> Think, use your brains, appreciate, talk! ...
>
> On the day after the first ogoniok we became a tiny bit more thoughtful about the life in the commune.
>
> What was right? What was wrong? We would have to talk in the evening. And if you were lazy or sluggish during the day the lads would carp at your behavior at ogoniok ...
>
> The ogoniok is very simple but very intricate at the same time. Now we are used to every deed being looked into and discussed at ogoniok. And if we are put out to a *trudovoi desant,* to work at a kolkhoz field, and do not discuss it together in the evening, we feel a sort of dissatisfaction, as if the work has not been finished.
>
> After all, we are used to work, to doing something, this is not new experience. But do all of us think about what is done, how it is done, how to do this? Ogoniok is the beginning of meaningful life. Should not every person have his own ogoniok in the evening discussing his day and his life? (Solovejchik 1972: 22–23)

Among various types of *ogoniok* differing by forms and goals of discussion, special attention should be paid to the "frank talk" (*otkrovennyi razgovor*) *ogoniok* which Ivanov borrowed from the pedagogical practice of Makarenko. "Frank talk" was introduced to the CYF in the summer of 1959.[19] A "frank talk" was described as follows: "All the members of a collective talk by turn (in a circle) about one of the comrades ... or about everybody. The law for participation in such a talk is: to speak the truth boldly, both good and bad, and nobody resents what is said" (Ivanov 1989: 182). One of the communards recollected a "frank talk" as follows:

> At the "frank talk" I got a lot of criticism, first of all, because I did not like manual labor. ... I had not been used to it at home. In the field, at my ridge, I became tired after several meters. I was sick of these beets that I had to save from weeds. I did my work in a slapdash manner, and I did not take the weeds at the roots. (Solovejchik 1972: 134)

However, such discussions of personal merits and failings could also take place without the formalized context of "frank talks." Another passage from the collection cited above reads in this connection:

> It is not frightful at *ogoniok*. It does not look like an ordinary *prorabotka*. When they discuss you at school, for some reason, everybody turns into your enemy, and it is not easy for you to look into eyes of your comrades long after that. Its quite different here: everybody tells what does he think about you and that is it. After a moment you discuss the next deed with the other. (24)

All these forms of collective control not only correspond with the projects of revival of public life and the development of mutual surveillance during the Khrushchev reign, but have visible analogies in the social practice of the LTC. Thus, "frank talk" can be directly compared with the "chair of wisdom." Additionally, a number of other customs and rituals of the LTC correspond with forms of everyday culture of the 1950s and 1960s communards. The latter sometimes arranged their meetings with direct allusions to Christian symbolism. For example, the game designated by Ivanov as "the evening of discovered and undiscovered secrets"[20] but known by his charges as *tainaia vecheria* (the Last Supper) is described as follows:

> In the evening we met in the hall. There were 12 candles burning on a big dish.
>
> 'Oh the wisest of the wise! Let me, by your consent, open our first *tainaia vecheria*. However powerful the light of knowledge might be, the man has barely lifted the veil of surrounding darkness. The world around us is full of great and small undiscovered secrets. Let everybody tell the high assembly about the secrets of heaven and earth. Who, oh the wisest, will blow out the first candle?'

Fluctuating flame highlights figures, faces, someone's hand lying on a comrade's shoulder. ...

It might be that no secrets would be discovered tonight. But still we will blow out all the 12 candles. And somebody will know something that he was not aware of, and the world will be closer and more interesting when the electric light is turned on in the hall. (Solovejchik 1972: 32–33)

Thus the links between social practices, forms of mutual control and some ritual traditions of the CYF and the LTC are at least analogous, if not directly derived. If one nevertheless assumes the existence of a certain historical continuity, it is necessary to find out how the communard traditions of the late 1950s and early 1960s could influence the culture of a post-Soviet NRM, and what social and ideological factors might underlie the influence.

Although Ivanov resigned his leadership of the CYF in 1962, his advocation for the "communard upbringing" was not at all finished. As early as 1963, he established "the Makarenko Commune" in the Leningrad State Pedagogical Institute. The new network united students of the Institute and educational specialists interested in the methods of "upbringing by Ivanov." The CYF continued to exist, but now it was managed by Faina Shapiro, an educational methodologist of the Frunzensky House of Pioneers. Moreover, in these very years, the CYF and its pedagogical practices became immensely popular outside Leningrad. In the early 1960s Simon Soloveichik, a correspondent of the newspaper *Komsomol'skaia Pravda* who was extremely interested in the experience of the CYF, began to popularize "the new forms of upbringing" in his articles, and also organized an extramural "Club of young communards" attached to the newspaper (Ivanov 1990: 114). In 1962, the CYF was mentioned with a laudatory tone on the pages of the *Communist,* the principal journal of the CPSU Central Committee:

As a protest, in a way, against routine and formalism, along with excessive wardship from the side of the adults, there has appeared a new form of work among the Young Pioneer activists in Leningrad. ... Here boys and girls learn how to place private interests under public ones. This organization is for creative work, for living activities, for interesting pioneer games, for self-governing and collectivism, against dullness and boredom, against formalism. Their principal commandment is: "Let you, the communard, be the creator of a new life, the brave soldier of the army of Lenin." (Dmitrevskii 1962: 75)

In the same year, the representatives of the CYF and the members of regional sections of the "Club of Young Communards" visited "Orlionok," the All-Russian camp of the Komsomol Central Committee established recently on the Black Sea coast of the Caucasus. Here they served as the "commanders" and "commissars" of pioneer detachments that gathered teenagers from all parts of the country. The "communard season" along with the "All-Union camp of the young communards" that took place in "Orlionok" the next year promoted the dissemination of social practices and rituals originating in the CYF throughout various towns and cities of the USSR (Solovejchik 1989: 124–25). Although in the mid 1960s the Komsomol officials changed their attitude toward communard clubs and tried, as far as possible, to hamper their activities,[21] the forms of social organization, behavior and ritual practice developed in the CYF still continued to be popular amongst young men and some educational specialists. Apparently, many communards of the late 1960s thought the practices of mutual denunciation and control to be the most important part of "Ivanov's method." A report from the CYF published in *Komsomol'skaia Pravda* in 1965 reads:

> And, of course, there were traditional events of the commune: daily *ogoniok* in the evening and "frank talks"—everybody tells what they thinks about everyone else, and, in addition, a serious war against various "prominent" personages. In one of the camps there was the "bench of rare specimens" for those who violated discipline. They put a bench near a tree with a mirror hanging from it—one had to sit there and to think about his life. They gave him a lot of food but did not allow him to work. The person endured that for only a day. He then repented and promised to obey all the rules. (Nikolaev1966: 186–87)

The elite pioneer camps played a special role in the transmission of the communard tradition. Apart from "Orlionok," "Artek," the All-Union camp of the Komsomol Central Committee, was the most famous Soviet camp, along with "Zerkal'nyi," the camp of the Pioneer and Komsomol activists of the Leningrad and Leningrad region (established in 1969). Other camps of this kind existed in many regions of the USSR. A number of communard rituals and practices were also adopted by various educational and travelling clubs that existed in the 1970s and 1980s within state offices of extracurricular education, for example, the "palaces" and "houses" of the Young Pioneers, the "teenage clubs" and so on. It seems that these clubs were the medium for the transmission of the specific forms of communard culture that were then used by the LTC. A large number of LTC movement followers were previously members of the various formal and informal social networks mentioned above. Both collectivistic social practices and mystical teachings were quite popular in the Soviet underground culture of the 1980s that influenced the LTC in many respects.

The central ritual of the LTC known as the "spiritual circle" probably goes back to the tradition of elite pioneer camps and to the practices of the CYF.[22] The image or form of "communard circle" (or "singing circle") constituted by human bodies (each person taking the hand of their neighbor or putting their own hands over their neighbor's shoulders) and symbolizing group unity was widely used in the rituals, social events and role games of the CYF (for example, the description of *tainaia vecheria* cited above and in Solovejchik (1972: 32–33)). It could be also said that the two symbolic units that played the central role in the CYF rituals, the images of a circle and a small light (either of a candle or of a camp fire), are both related to the idea of collectivistic discipline, and allude to the categories of group unity and visibility/invisibility within a certain social body. Both categories were already used in the social practice of Makarenko who suggested standing a delinquent in a spotlit place surrounded by all other members of the commune discussing his undesirable behavior. In his discussion of this disciplinary method, Kharkhordin argues that it could be viewed as "double inversion" of the famous idea of "panopticism" introduced by Michael Foucault in *Discipline and Punish* (Kharkhordin 2002: 126–28). However, in the case of the "circle rituals," the ideas of discipline and punishment were and are less important than the idea of group unity represented by the image of collective body. Since at least the mid 1960s, singing of songs in a "communard circle" became very popular in the "Orlionok" and "Artek" camps, and the ritual practice soon became known as *orliatskii krug* or *artekovskii krug*. However, it was not usually associated with "frank talk" and other disciplinary practices of the CYF. A participant in the "Zerkal'nyi" camp in the 1990s describes the practice as follows:

> All the boys and girls and the leaders stand in a big circle; everyone puts his right hand on the shoulder of his neighbor to the right, and his left hand on the waist of his neighbor to the left; and the favorite songs are sung in this tight and indivisible circle. The main thing is that the *orliatskii krug* unites the group and symbolizes its unity. (Chinyakova 2000: 341)

The "spiritual circle" of the LTC, in which people stand in a circle and hold each other's hands, is very similar to the camp ritual described above. The spiritual circle is often accompanied by a burning candle or a camp fire, and can also include the singing of spiritual songs. Although the meaning of the ritual is expressed in religious (or quasi-religious) terms, it still preserves the symbolism of group unity: According to LTC members, those standing in the spiritual circle unite their personal energies, allowing them to master all problems collectively and to accomplish every goal successfully. Therefore, all social events in the LTC communities are started and finished with

Illustration 7.1. LTC. Spiritual circle. Krasnoyarskii *krai*. Photo by Sergei Shtyrkov (2001).

Illustration 7.2. LTC. Discussion of daily events with a priest. Krasnoyarskii *krai*. Photo by Sergei Shtyrkov (2001).

Illustration 7.3. LTC. Spiritual circle at a funeral. Krasnoyarskii *krai.* Photo by Alexander Panchenko (2001).

a spiritual circle. It is also an important part of more complicated rituals such as weddings, funerals, and so on.

Conclusion

Although the religious and social practices of the LTC can probably be derived from various cultural sources, it seems then that one should not underestimate the role of Soviet heritage in formation of social practices and specific ideas of morality constructed by the movement. It could be said, of course, that the forms of social control practiced in LTC communities are more or less similar to those being observed within various new religious movements all over the world and known to sociologists of religion as "brainwashing" or, in more accurate terms, as "ideological resocialization" (see Zablocki 2001: 159–214). I would argue, however, that practices of ideological resocialization can be observed in nearly all stable social groups that possess a more or less explicit collective identity and a need to socialize newcomers. However, the case of social control in the LTC is quite different from more common types of ideological resocialization. The

LTC's peculiar "machine of ethics" conceals all habitual forms of individual moral choice and social hierarchy in favor of egalitarian and collectivistic representations.

One might say that similarities like those between communard practices and moral techniques of the LTC can and will be found elsewhere in various social and cultural contexts. It is true, at least partly, but the particular case I am dealing with seems to be important indeed in historical perspective. In fact, the late Soviet society was more or less atomistic and individualistic, so the disciplinary practices and moral norms elaborated by communards and inherited by the LTC were not quite typical for the period. I tried to demonstrate in this chapter that particular moral words and techniques of discipline in a given society do not depend directly on a political regime or official ideology and can be reproduced and cultivated independently, in accordance with their own rules and functions.

Thus, this chapter is more about continuity than changes. Vernacular ethical practices developed and practiced during the late Soviet period are used as meaningful cultural resources by even the most innovative and exotic religious movements. Therefore, the division between "Soviet" and "post-Soviet" in the history of religion and morality might not be as solid as it seems to be. It is quite common for both scholars and the general public to think about contemporary Russian new religious movements as "eclectic" or even "entropic" (Filatov 2002: 447) religious culture grounded partly or totally in ideas and teachings borrowed from abroad. I would argue, on the contrary, that these movements should be considered some of the last remnants or survivals of late Soviet culture, and that their seemingly foreign appearance does not contradict their domestic heritage.

Notes

The research for this chapter was carried out within NEWREL, a project of the European Science Foundation's EUROCORES Programme BOREAS—"Histories from the North: Environments, Movements, Narratives." The ESF EUROCORES Programme BOREAS is a European Science Foundation (ESF) initiative supported by the European Commission, FP6 Conract No. ERAS-CT-2003-980409. The discussion of the history, religious culture, and social practices of the Last Testament Church presented below is based upon field research done by the author of this paper in collaboration with Sergei Shtyrkov in 2001, 2007, and 2008 in the Kuraginskii and Karatuzskii districts of Krasnoyarskii krai, Russia. The field research was supported by the National Science Foundation of the USA (2007–2008) and the John D. and Catherine T. MacArthur Foundation (2001)

 1. There exist a number of sociological publications about the LTC, but the movement has not yet been properly analyzed from an anthropological perspective. For the details of the history of the LTC and other post-Soviet new religious movements

in Russia, see Balagushkin (1999); Grigor'eva (2002); Panchenko (2004, 2006); and Kanterov (2006).

2. Lingquist (2006) is an example, but is dedicated to only one aspect of contemporary Russian occultism, namely, healing magic and fortune-telling in urban environments.

3. For example, a memorandum titled "On the problem of establishment of research and cultural center based on ideas by N. K. and E. I. Roerich" was submitted to the CPSU regional committee in 1979 by a group of researchers from various institutes of the Russian Academy of Sciences located in Novosibirsk. The text claimed that the occult teaching of the "Living Ethics" elaborated by the Roerichs should be interpreted and used as an important development of Leninism and the communist ideology (see Kuznetsov (2003)).

4. The quotations from the LT given below are from an electronic version prepared by the LT members using the computer program BibleQuote 5.0.

5. As seen in the video record of the sermon produced by the LTC video studio: Slovo 24 oktyabrya 38 g. E. R. (1998) v Petropavlovke. "Polyanka smireniya." Petropavlovskaya videostudiya. DVD-17.

6. The concept was introduced by Vissarion in 1999 as an interpretation of the well-known passage from Matthew 3: 11 ("He will baptize you with the Holy Spirit and with fire"). The "baptism with fire" is understood as spiritual victory over selfishness (LT, Narrative by Vadim, Pt. 9, 72: 53–65; Pt. 10, 3: 202–244)

7. Slovo 24 oktyabrya 38 g. E. R. (1998) v Petropavlovke. "Polyanka smireniya." Petropavlovskaya videostudiya. DVD-17.

8. Interview, Mikhail, 36 years old, 19 September 2001, Cheremshanka (Kuraginskii district, Krasnoyarskii *krai*).

9. Interview, Svetlana, 50 years old, 28 September 2001, Kuragino (Kuraginskii district, Krasnoyarskii *krai*).

10. "Then the days of wisdom have begun for those living in the City and they called them 'the chair of wisdom' or 'the bench of wisdom.' And this undertaking spread rapidly amongst the believers of the community. ... Such a day was carried out as follows: the person who embraced wisdom sat on a chair or a bench in front of brothers and sisters living with him in the Abode and was ready to listen with gratitude every suggestion about his negative deeds. ... The person who embraced wisdom was able to specify details that were unclear but could not in any case do anything to justify his deeds" (LTC, Narrative by Vadim, Pt. 9, 72: 2–11).

11. Interview, Svetlana, 50 years old, 28 September 2001, Kuragino (Kuraginskii district, Krasnoyarskii *krai*).

12. Novosti Samarskoj Tserkvi Poslednego Zaveta 1.01.04. Informatsiya ob obschem sobranii 25.12.03. http://samvis.narod.ru/news.files/news11-12.2003.html.

13. Interview, Azaria, 45 years old, 28 September 2001, Kuragino (Kuraginskii district, Krasnoyarskii *krai*).

14. Interview, Valentina, about 50 years old, September 2001, Cheremshanka (Kuraginskii district, Krasnoyarskii *krai*).

15. The Communist Union of Youth, usually called Komsomol (a syllabic abbreviation from the Russian *Kommunisticheskiy Soyuz Molodyozhi*), was the communist organization for young men and women in the Soviet Union.

16. Original as follows: No esli vdrug kogda-nibud' mne uberech'sya ne udastsya, / ka-koe b novoe srazhen'e ni pokachnulo shar zemnoj, / ya vse ravno padu na toj, na toj edinstvennoj Grazhdanskoj, / i komissary v pyl'nykh shlemakh sklonyatsya molcha nado mnoj.

17. The communards movement has not yet been studied either by historians or anthropologists. There are some papers about the movement published by educational specialists, which tend to be more apologetic than analytic. The only publication in English I am aware of is by Alexander Sidorkin (1995). For works in Russian, see Solovejchik (1972, 1989); and Ivanov (1982, 1989, 1990). There is also a website dedicated to the history of the communards at http://www.kommunarstvo.ru.

18. For Makarenko's impact upon Soviet ideology and everyday culture see Bowen (1962) and Kharkhordin (2002: 93–103, 125–32, 249–65). A passion for Makarenko's pedagogy was quite appropriate to the official ideology of "collectivistic upbringing of the masses." Thus the proceedings of the "conference on the Marxist-Leninist ethics" mentions Makarenko more than once. See *Voprosy marksistsko-leninskoj etiki* (1960: 46, 69, 100, 209).

19. Ivanov describes the "frank talk" as follows:

    The camp was concluded by a carnival (with a surprise from each detachment) and a deed which was new for us. There were detachment meetings where everybody was discussed in the circle, their merits and failings being discussed, and friendly advice for self-improvement being pronounced. This experience has been borrowed from the practice of the commune named after F. E. Dzerzhinsky described by A. S. Makarenko. . . . All detachments had really frankly and friendly talk, everything about everyone was discussed without separation of "superiors" and "privates," old communards and newcomers, senior and junior. Everyone soon understood that it was necessary not only to point out the failings of a person, but also to point out their merits and abilities, they corrected those who overemphasised criticism and used an unfriendly tone, they shamed those who spoke about things in the past, and they consoled nicely the girls who were crying. (1990: 107)

20. Ivanov describes the "evening of discovered and undiscovered secrets" as follows: "This fascinating game allows knowledge exchange, opinions, and hypotheses. It teaches people to put questions, to argue and to disprove, and to look for the truth collectively on the basis of information from various sources including books, journals, newspapers, cinema, radio and television" (1989).

21. The CYF was officially disbanded in 1972 (Solovejchik 1989: 160).

22. This idea was suggested for the first time by Liudmila Grigor'eva (1999: 15).

References

Balagushkin, Evgenij G. 1999. *Netraditsionnye religii v sovremennoj Rossii.* Morfo-logicheskij analiz. M.: Institut filosofii RAN.

Bowen, James. 1962. *Soviet Education: Anton Makarenko and the Years of Experiment.* Madison, WI: University of Wisconsin Press.

Chinyakova, Milena. E. 2000. "Traditsii 'Zerkal'nogo'." In *Tradiciya v fol'klore i litera-ture*, 332–67. SPb.: AG SPbGU.

Dmitrevskii, V. 1962. "Shkola vospitaniya yunykh lenintsev (k 40-letiyu pionerskoi organizatsii imeni V. I. Lenina)." *Kommunist*, no .7: 73–75.

Grigor'eva, Liudmila I. 1999. "Ushedshie v 'Gorod Solntsa.'" *Nauka i religiya*, no. 2: 14–16.

———. 2002. *Religii "Novogo veka" i sovremennoe gosudarstvo.* Krasnoyarsk: SibGTU.

Ivanov, Igor' P. 1982. *Vospityvat' kollektivistov.* Moscow: Pedagogika.

———. 1989. *Entsiklopediya kollektivnykh tvorcheskikh del.* Moscow: Pedagogika. http://orlyonok-c.narod.ru/ektd.html (accessed 13 May 2011).

———. 1990. *Metodika kommunarskogo vospitaniya: Kniga dlya uchitelya.* Moscow: Prosveschenie.

Kanterov, Igor' Ya. 2006. *Novye religioznye dvizheniya v Rossii. Religiovedcheskij analiz.* Moscow: MGU im. M. V. Lomonosova.

Kharkhordin, Oleg V. 2002. *Oblichat' i litsemerit': genealogiya rossijskoj lichnosti.* SPb., Moscow: Izd-vo Evropejskogo un-ta v SPb, Letnij Sad.

Kuznetsov, Ivan S. 2003. *"Eretiki" Akademgorodka: delo "initsiativnoj gruppy": Dokumental'naya khronika.* Novosibirsk: NGU.

Lingquist, Galina. 2006. *Conjuring Hope: Healing and Magic in Contemporary Russia.* Epistomologies of Healing series, vol. 1. Oxford: Berghahn Books.

Menzel, Birgit. "The Occult Revival in Russia Today and Its Impact on Literature." *The Harriman Review* 16, no. 1 (Spring 2007): 1–14.

Nazarov, Vladimir N. 2003. "Opyt khronologii russkoj etiki XX v.: tretij period (1960–1990)." *Eticheskaya mysl'.* Vyp. 4. Moscow: IF RAN. http://iph.ras.ru/uplfile/root/biblio/em/em4/11.pdf (accessed 13 May 2011).

Nikolaev, S. 1966. "Kommuna, god pyatyj." *Alyj parus* Moscow: Molodaya gvardiya. 186–187.

Okudzhava, Bulat Sh. 2001. *Stikhotvoreniya.* SPb.: Akademicheskij proekt.

Panchenko, Alexander A. 2004. "New Religious Movements and the Study of Folklore: The Russian Case." *Folklore* 28: 111–28.

———. 2006. "Novye religioznye dvizheniya i rabota fol'klorista." In *Sny Bogoroditsy. Issledovaniya po antropologii religii,* ed. Zh. V. Kormina, Alexander A. Panchenko, and S. A. Shtyrkov, 119–30. SPb.: Izd-vo Evropejskogo un-ta v SPb.

Shishkin, Aleksandr F. 1961. *Osnovy marksistskoj etiki.* Moscow: Izdatel'stvo instituta mezhdunarodnykh otnoshenij.

Shishkin Aleksandr F., ed. 1961. *Marksistskaya etika. Khrestomatiya.* Moscow: Izdatel'stvo instituta mezhdunarodnykh otnoshenij.

Sidorkin, Alexander. 1995. "The Communard Movement in Russia." *East-West Education* 16, no. 2 (Fall 1995): 148–59. http://sidorkin.net/pdf/communard.pdf (accessed 13 May 2011).

Solovejchik, Simon. 1989. *Vospitanie po Ivanovu.* Moscow: Pedagogika.

Solovejchik, Simon, ed. 1972. *Frunzenskaya kommuna. Kniga o neobychnoj zhizni obyknovennykh rebyat, napisannaya imi samimi,* 2nd ed. Moscow: Detskaya literature.

Vihavainen, Timo. 2004. *Vnutrennij vrag: bor'ba s meschanstvom kak moral'naya missiya russkoj intelligentsii.* SPb.: Kolo.

Volkov, Solomon. 1998. *Dialogi s Iosifom Brodskim.* Moscow: Nezavisimaya Gazeta.

Voprosy marksistsko-leninskoj etiki: Materialy nauchnogo soveschaniya. 1960. Moscow: Gospolitizdat.

Zablocki, Benjamin. 2001. "Scientific Theory of Brainwashing." In *Misunderstanding Cults: Searching for Objectivity in a Controversial Field,* ed. Benjamin Zablocki and Thomas Robbins, 159–214. Toronto: University of Toronto Press.

Zigon, Jarrett. 2006. "'You Should Reform Yourself Not Other People': The Ethics of Hope in Contemporary Moscow." Halle/Saale: Max Planck Institute for Social Anthropology Working Papers, no. 88.

———. 2009. "Morality Within a Range of Possibilities: A Dialogue with Joel Robbins." *Ethnos* 74, no. 2: 251–76.

 CHAPTER 8

Constructing Moralities around the Tsarist Family

Kathy Rousselet

In the early 1990s the Russian Orthodox Church was reproached for its lack of morality during the Soviet period and its appeasement of Soviet power. Fifteen years later, this aspect of the Church's history is no longer mentioned. On the contrary, more and more martyrs who were killed in the early years of the Bolshevik regime, and who managed to maintain their faith at the time of the Great Terror, are being discovered and canonized. The last Tsar himself and his family were glorified. These canonizations, which were one of the conditions for reconciliation with the Russian Orthodox Church Abroad,[1] seem to restore the Church's moral standing. It has been asserted that there were more canonizations in the Russian Orthodox Church during the twentieth century than all nine preceding centuries combined, with this Church canonizing the greatest number of saints.[2]

These new saints are mainly presented as moral figures—examples for Russian people today. Among them, the Tsarist family is particularly revered, especially in the Yekaterinburg region where Nicholas II, his wife, and his children were arrested, killed, and buried. The glorified family no doubt increases the religious status of the region. In Yekaterinburg, every year on 16–17 July, the vigil at the Church on Blood in Honor of All Saints Resplendent in the Russian Land—which is built where the Royal Family was murdered—and the procession from Yekaterinburg to Ganina Yama—where, according to the Church, the family was buried—gather several thousands of believers. According to some sources, about 35,000 people took part in the procession in 2008, on the ninetieth anniversary of the event.[3] Moreover, a festival of Orthodox Culture is held every year in July in the Urals' capital. But the worship of Nicholas II is not limited to Yekaterinburg. It is spreading throughout the country. Parishioners from not only Saint Petersburg but also the Kaluga region organize pilgrimages to imperial residences. Icons of the family are more and more numerous.

In the patriotic context of post-Soviet Russia, the Tsar and his family who were disgraced during the Soviet period are honored. New moralities are constructed through the growing publication of hagiographies. A patriotic and conservative discourse on culpability and shame draws new boundaries between good and evil. Rewriting and rereading the past inevitably leads to its reevaluation. Past and present are remoralized through repentance, rehabilitation, and canonization.

This new morality which is created by some elites and that stands as a breakdown with the past has not yet a wide impact on Russian believers. Nevertheless it echoes with the moral demands of some Christian patriots.

This chapter will elucidate the transformation in the official representation of the Tsarist family from the "bloody Nicholas" (*Nikolai krovavy*)—a Soviet cliché that was taught in all schools—to the passion-bearer (*strastoterpets*). It will identify and examine the political as well as the religious entrepreneurs of this moral perestroika. Furthermore it will analyze the insertion of new saints, especially the Tsarist family, into the new official morality. But this chapter will also explore some logics from below: the believer's yearning for tradition and his reaction to post-Soviet moral disorder.

The research presented in this chapter is primarily based on fieldwork in Yekaterinburg in July 2006 and 2007, where I met believers, priests, nuns and lay people during the "Tsarist Days" at the vigil and the procession on 16–17 July. Attendees came from the Urals and other regions of Russia. They were mainly adults over 45 and belonged to all social classes. However a lot of them were members of the intelligentsia taking part in an Orthodox film festival, organized during the "Tsarist Days." There were some Cossacks as well. The research is also based on interviews conducted in 2008–2009 with priests and believers from other regions of Russia, especially Saint Petersburg and the Kaluga region.

The Entrepreneurs of Moral Perestroika and the Rereading of Russia's Past

A lot of corpses were reburied in the post-socialist countries in order to mark political change (Verdery 1999). In 1998 Boris Yeltsin decided to ceremonially rebury the Tsarist family. Ten years later Dmitri Medvedev accepted the Romanovs' request for rehabilitation. Moreover, Nicholas II, his wife, and his children were canonized in 2000 by the Russian Orthodox Church, under the pressure of the Russian Orthodox Church Abroad. All these acts, which were performed by the elites, symbolize a rereading of the Soviet period and imply some moral changes.

The history of the discovery of the burial of the Tsarist family goes back to the mid 1970s. In 1976, Muscovite film producer G. T. Riabov went to the town of Sverdlovsk to show his film *Born from Revolution* (*Rozhden-*

naia Revoliutsiei) to the local policemen. This event sparked an interest in Ipatiev House, where the family was murdered, as well as in the town's history. In Sverdlovsk, he met A. N. Avdonin, a geologist who had been conducting a long investigation into the murder of the Tsar and his burial. From 1976 until 1979, the two secretly searched for the corpses using all the historical documents at their disposal. In 1979, skulls were found at Porosenkov Log but in the absence of proper identification they were subsequently reburied. Investigations officially recommenced in 1991. The remains were declared as belonging to the Tsarist family by several scientific commissions, and on 17 July 1998 Nicholas II and other members of his family were reburied in St. Petersburg with much pomp and circumstance. But the Orthodox hierarchy expressed its doubts about the expertise of the scientific commissions which examined the remains that were found. At the last moment, the Patriarch refused to take part in the reburial of the Tsarist family in St. Petersburg. As for the remains of two of Nicholas II's children, Alexei and Maria, they were discovered in 2007, and their identity was confirmed by American and European experts.

According to the liberal elites, these reburials "put an end to Terror" and helped Russia "pay its moral debts." They helped it move forward towards "normality" (*Pokaianie* 2003). For the elites in the 1990s, normality meant democracy, a free market, and prosperity. Boris Nemtsov, the first deputy prime minister who also headed the Identification Commission, explained that this murder represented all Soviet crimes. He said he personally repented for his indifference and tolerance towards the Terror and hoped that everybody would do the same. Beyond the crimes committed by the Bolsheviks, it was believed that all Russians should shoulder a certain degree of guilt. Last but not least, the reburial of the remains of the Tsarist Family was expected to become an act of reconciliation.[4] As we will soon see, these arguments were not so different from those of the Church. The murder was considered by these elites as a sin, as a "transgression of the moral order," and not a crime.[5] Viktor Aksiuchits, adviser to Boris Nemtsov and head of the Christian Democrat Party at the beginning of the 1990s (a period in which the party became more and more nationalist), argued that the reburial was a "civic [*grazhdanski*], moral, and spiritual duty."[6] He added a symbolic justification: "The living have one duty: as long as the dead are not buried their souls are not in peace. The consciences of the living are not in peace either. In other words the spiritual trouble in Russia will not stop as long as the remains of the Tsar and his family are not buried" (*Pokaianie* 2003: 9).

The law was also used to reaffirm the culpability of Bolshevik power. As a matter of fact, the 1998 repentance of the Yelstin regime was not considered sufficient. The Grand Duchess Maria Vladimirovna had long requested the rehabilitation of the Tsarist family but the Prosecutor-General's Office had refused. What happened in Yekaterinburg on 17 July 1918 could actually not be covered by the 1991 Law called "On the Rehabilitation of the Victims of Political Repressions": "A premeditated murder, even with a political tinge, was perpetrated by persons not vested with the relevant judicial or administrative powers. No charges, if only formal, have been brought against the Emperor and members of his family. On the strength of that, the perpetrated murder is a general crime from the legal point of view."[7] Russian authorities also feared that the descendants of the Romanov family would ask for compensation, and the Prosecutor-General's Office's position may also have been financially motivated.

The Tsar and his immediate family were finally rehabilitated on 1 October 2008 by the Presidium of the Supreme Court of Russia. According to a survey of the Russian Centre for Public Opinion Research (VTsIOM), 69 percent of the population approved of the decision. It was considered by lawyers to be a breach of Russian legal practices as the rehabilitation took place without any formal judgment. For the Department for External Church Relations of the Moscow Patriarchate,[8] it meant the "restoration of the historical continuity of the Russian State with a millennial tradition." The rehabilitation was also painted by the barrister representing the Royal house, German Lukyanov, as a civic act showing the emergence of the state of law in Russia.[9] On 8 June 2009 six other members of the Imperial family were rehabilitated: Mikhail Aleksandrovich Romanov, Elizaveta Fedorovna Romanova, Sergei Mikhailovich Romanov, Ioann Konstantinovich Romanov, Konstantin Konstantinovich Romanov and Igor Konstantinovich Romanov.[10]

The Russian Orthodox Church: Repentance and the Canonization of the Tsarist Family

In 1993, 75 years after the Tsarist family's murder, Patriarch Alexei II called Russian people to repent for the deaths, regardless of their ethnic or religious background, political point of view, or attitude towards the monarchy:

> With augmented prayer and great pain in our hearts we commemorate this sad Anniversary ... The sin of regicide, which took place amid the indifference of the citizens of Russia, has not been repented of by our people. Being a transgression of both the law of God and civil law, this sin weighs extremely heavily upon the souls of our people, upon its moral conscience. And today, on behalf of the whole Church, on behalf of her children, both reposed and liv-

ing, we proclaim repentance before God and the people for this sin. Forgive us, O Lord! We call to repentance all of our people, all of our children, regardless of their political views and opinions about history, regardless of their ethnic or religious background, regardless of their attitude toward the idea of Monarchy and the personality of the last Russian Tsar. Repentance of the sin committed by our forefathers should become for us a banner of unity. May today's sad date unite us in prayer with the Russian Orthodox Church Abroad, with whom we so sincerely desire restoration of spiritual unity in faithfulness to the Spirit of Christ. ... ("Poslanie" 1993)

In 1998 Alexei II was even more explicit. Repentance was to become a banner of the unity of Russian people "which can be achieved not through indifferent approval but only by reflexive understanding of what happened to the country and the people."[11] He argued that the Russian people were guilty not only because they took part in the murder, but because they accepted it or were simply indifferent to the event. In some ways, he simply repeated the same arguments as the patriarch Tikhon (*Akty Sviateishego Tikhona* 1994: 142–43) or the archbishop Ioann Maksimovich, at the Second General Council of the Russian Church Abroad in 1938. A new moral judgment had to be made on Soviet history. The understanding of the spiritual dimension of the Soviet tragedy and the subsequent repentance were considered to be grounds for reconciliation of all Russian people.

All believers do not share the official position of the Church. As a matter of fact, literature by fundamentalists opposed to Patriarchy's official views has been spreading for some ten years, first on leaflets and notice boards, and now more and more on the Internet. Leaflets were distributed during the procession from the Church on Blood in Honor of All Saints Resplendent in the Russian Land in Yekaterinburg to Ganina Yama in 2006 and 2007. This literature virulently disapproves of the West and of globalization, denounces all identification numbers such as tax numbers (*INN*) and insurance policies, attempts to evoke unique Russian traditions, and urges the Russian people to repent for the Tsar's murder. A new rite of collective repentance of the Russian people (*chin vsenarodnogo pokaiania russkogo naroda*)[12] is becoming more and more visible. It has been performed every year in Taininskoe, a village in the suburbs of Moscow, and now in some eparchies of the Church. According to these fundamentalists, malediction has fallen upon the Russian people for its "betrayal" and murder of the Tsarist family: the Russian people have broken the oath taken in 1613 at the advent of the Romanov dynasty. According to these authors, this oath was taken not only by the members of the Zemsky Sobor (the Russian assembly at that time) but it also included the whole Russian people, the future as well as the past generations. The malediction will also be passed down from generation to generation as long as the people do not repent. Thus Orthodox believers must repent for a sin they did not personally commit and a new notion of "collective person" (*sobornaia lichnost'*) has appeared. This rite was denounced by the Holy Synod in April 2005 for its non-conformity to the forms of repentance in the Orthodox Church's tradition.[13] At the Moscow Assembly of bishops in December 2007 Alexei II deemed it to be an unauthentic religious act which purpose was only to "agitate" the Orthodox flock. Moreover its instigators are firmly criticized, as they believe that the Tsar expiated, similar to Jesus Christ, the Russian people's sins, which the Russian Orthodox Church categorically denies. Patriarch Kirill, on his part, seems to be more radically opposed to repentance for the regicide. In April 19 2010, in Yekaterinburg, responding to "certain appeals to national repentance inciting people," he said that Russia redeemed sins of fighting against God and regicide by blood. "Much was given to our nation and the Lord asked from us sternly," he said.

The Place of Nicholas II and the Tsarist Family in the Construction of a New Official Morality

In a social context that has been described as "demoralized," the Russian Orthodox Church is largely endorsed by the State due to its capacity to define new official norms in a national spirit. As a matter of fact the Church points out the new moral failings of post-Soviet society. Perestroika brought religious sects, immorality on television, alcoholism and drug addiction among the young generation, and all kind of "false" values from the West. The increase in divorces as well as abortions are also considered to be a sign of moral decline, even if numbers had already been rising during the Soviet period. In such a context, religious elites consider that saints, as moral examples, should play a major role in children's upbringing. According to Foucault (1984), every morality comprises codes of behavior and forms of subjectivation; in post-Soviet Russia moral examples are to play an even larger role than the codes themselves. These considerations show a striking continuity with Soviet hero-identification practices. Indeed, during the Soviet period (Kharkhordin 1999: 247), individuals, responsible for their own acts, had to work continuously on themselves and to attempt self-improvement by matching their conduct to Communist principles and by imitating Soviet heroes.[14]

The relationship with the saint is seen by the religious elites as a *personal* one. It is the reason why the temporal and the social proximity to a given saint are considered so important; it is also why the new martyrs (*novo-*

muchenniki), the ones who suffered for Christ in the twentieth century, and the glorified Tsarist family occupy a special place among the saints. According to the hegumen Damaskin Orlovsky who heads the Synodal Commission on the Canonization of the saints:

> The martyrs' and confessors' experience is much closer to our own life than that of the ancient saints. … The saints who were glorified in 2000, lived during the same period as we do. We can live through their experience (*voiti v ikh opyt*). Among them there are all sorts of saints. They reflect the vast diversity of human beings. Each of us will find the saint to whom he feels the closest. (2003)

In patriotic discourses, these new saints should embody some specific *collective* values. The morality of the saint and the revelation of his heroic individuality (*lichnost'*), embedded in the Russian cultural tradition, are weighed in opposition to liberal values and also to those of consumer society. The saint is an example of modesty, patience, tirelessness, courage and fidelity. He is also a model of success, but the proper kind of success, achieved in the "right way":

> Contemporary youth have to understand correctly what success in life means. Spiritually speaking, we can say that Russian Orthodox saints were highly successful. They acquired intellectual and physical qualities they did not have from birth. They were able to challenge the world they were living in. … In the conscience of our nation Russian Orthodox saints are considered as the best people in Russia. … Love of Motherland, respect for older people, care for the neighbor, solicitude towards surrounding people, ability to sacrifice oneself for higher aims, respect for the ancestral religion—these are the virtues which can be found in the Orthodox saint's life, in the life of the ones who lived in the past as well as in the life of the newly glorified ones. (Pogorelov 2006)

The *novomuchennik* is presented as a hero who is able to resist the pressures of the secular world and die for his people (*narod*). The significance of martyrdom depends on the interpretation one makes of the Soviet period. For many religious elites, sovietization is the consequence of the Europeanization of Russia and the loss of its national roots; in that sense, the new martyrs represent the figure of the victim sacrificed for the nation who now intercedes for Russia.[15] According to the hegumen Damaskin Orlovsky:

> [they] are national heroes. They are not heroes of war nor heroes of work. They are heroes of the spirit who will stay heroes in all regimes and governments. They are similar to a rock around which

the national life can be built, however profound it is. The publication of books on this question and the glorification of the martyrs are in some way the first significant steps towards the revival of Russian life. If the Russian people will catch the opportunity to live in a national and religious way, the martyrs will be the basis of Russia's revival. ... If not ... the martyrs will only be the last monument of our Russian civilization's XXth century.[16]

The new saints' religious achievement (*podvig*) is definitely seen as patriotic by the religious elites: They have all stood in defense of Holy Russia.

After long discussions about the possible political consequences of their glorification, the Tsarist family members were canonized in August 2000 not as new martyrs, but as passion-bearers. As was the case with the first saints of the Kievan Rus', Boris and Gleb, who were regarded as political rivals by their brother and killed during the wars of 1015–1019, they are considered to be saints who followed Christ courageously, with Christian humility and patience, endured suffering, and faced death in a Christ-like manner.[17] The Canonization Commission did not formulate any political judgment on Nicholas II's reign. It referred to the facts that Nicholas II allowed the preparation of the All-Russian Local Council of 1917–1918—which addressed many important reforms in the Church—and that the number of canonizations under his reign exceeded the number of canonizations during the two former centuries. Referring to "Bloody Sunday" (9 January 1905)—when striking workers and their families, led by Father Gapon, marching to deliver a petition to the Tsar, were shot down by the Imperial Guard—the Commission specified that the Tsar didn't take any decision to repress the workers, as no document could prove that he gave the order to shoot. Moreover, his renunciation of the throne was not against the Church's laws. The enigmatic figure of Nicholas II (Podbolotov 2004: 193) as well as the popular representations of the *tsar-batiushka*—at least until Bloody Sunday, which definitely "broke the 'sacred bond' which tied the Russian people to the Tsar" (Ferro 1991: 115)—contributed to the present mythification of the Tsar and his family. In keeping with Orthodox tradition, the canonization was preceded by the publication of a series of religious miracles, gathered in the 1990s,[18] in which believers testified to the glorification of the Tsarist Family.

Nicholas II occupies a special place among new saints. The moral values conveyed by the hagiographic books and booklets about him largely repeat the same *doxa*. Nicholas II is spiritually and historically linked to some of the more venerated Russian saints such as Ioann of Kronstadt (1829–1908) and Seraphim of Sarov (1759–1833), who would have predicted the fatal destiny of the Tsarist family. Much more, as he was born on the feast day of St. Job, Nicholas II would have said: "I am fated to suffer."[19] The Tsar's moral profile is well defined and resonates in the sociopolitical and cultural context of post-Soviet Russia: He had a sense of compassion towards his subjects ("he continually strove to reduce his people's sufferings"), he was well and highly educated, and he managed to make his wife convert to Orthodoxy through his prayers. In politics, he followed the example of his father who insisted on Russia's own path, as opposed to Western liberalism. In a context where public opinion still blames those who are keen on distinguishing themselves socially, and where the elites are criticized for their haughty distance, the booklets insist on the fact that Nicholas II had a modest way of life ("he did not like squandering or luxury") and felt a real closeness toward his subjects, which was not understood at his time ("A lot of people did not understand the Tsar's Christian virtues, his meekness, the goodness of his heart, his modesty and simplicity. His virtues were considered to be a sign of weakness"). The morality being promoted here reflects not so much an aspiration to pre-revolutionary nineteenth-century Russia, but rather a reaction to today's situation. It is also close to some aspects of Soviet morality.

The hagiographies, all of which reproduce the same standard discourse, dwell on the figure of the Tsarist family as a role model for every believer. The story of the Tsarist family is the example people are expected to follow in coping with familial strife. A booklet called *Saint Royal Martyrs, Pray to God for Us* is sold with some words of Alexandra Fedorovna, Nicholas II's wife, on family life and marriage, and includes the famous words of Alexander III in his testament to his son: "Strengthen family. It is the basis of any State. ... Good and solid families are the condition of Russia's salvation." The Tsarist family is presented as the Holy Family and thus as a model for the believers in their everyday life. It also becomes the basis of the nation.

Yearning for Tradition

One can consider with Boris Dubin that religion is a "light burden" (Dubin 2005) for Russian Orthodox Christians. The impact of the Church's moral discourse is quite weak among them. Moreover the Tsarist family is not a role model for all believers faithfully attending Church. Some priests are quite critical about the canonization of the last Tsar, although they can't oppose the presence of an icon of Nicholas II in their church when it is offered by a believer. Nevertheless we can distinguish among Orthodox church-going believers who intensively worship the Tsarist family. The believers reveal some specific motives for their commitment, especially a yearning for tradition.

Some of the zealots who worship the Tsarist family are former opponents of the Soviet regime. Father Petr[20] is one of them. He was born in the Perm oblast in 1949; he studied philology and entered the prestigious institute of theatrical studies GITIS. After working in several Soviet theatres, he attended Anatoly Zhigulin's[21] courses in Leningrad. Baptized in 1978, Petr lived in Moscow and then in the Urals, where he served in a parish church as a cantor (*psalomshchik*). He discovered religion through the conservative Father Dmitri Dudko and didn't like the liberal views of Father Alexander Men. Petr learned about the Tsar through Western publications and the Russian Orthodox Church Abroad. In the early 1980s, he took part in an underground editing unit dedicated to religious publications, which was subsequently shut down by the KGB. This is probably the reason why he couldn't become a priest before 1988, and why his service has been restricted to the countryside in the Yekaterinburg eparchy.

In the eyes of the Church, Father Petr would not be considered mainstream due to his radical monarchist position and his attitude towards Nicholas II, whom he considers as a new martyr and not a passion-bearer. He maintains the dissident position he had during the Soviet period, and still criticizes all political and religious powers. Father Petr contributed to the veneration of the Tsarist family before its official canonization. In the early 1990s he started spiritually accompanying the Brotherhood of the new Tsarist martyrs formed by the Yekaterinburg monarchists and members of the right-wing nationalist movement *Pamiat*. This was a period of active commitment ("*boevoe vremia*"); supported by Bishop Melchisedech, the group pursued investigations into the death of the Tsarist family in Ganina Yama, set up a new cross there, and organized *molebny* (prayers) for the Tsarist family. After asking renowned elders (*startsy*)[22] for advice, in 1996, Father Petr convened a community of women in the village where he served as a priest. This community of thirty persons, which achieved the status of monastery in 2000, has been intensively worshipping the Tsarist family, commemorating the name days of its members (*dni angela*), their birthdays, and the day that Nicholas II renounced the throne. Following the Father's dissident spirit, they have been praying for the Russian people to love the *tsar-martyr* and to repent for the regicide. They have also been venerating an icon with the head of Nicholas II on a platter, as some testimonies suggest that the Tsar and his son were beheaded and their heads were then offered to the Bolsheviks just as John the Baptist's head was given to Herod's stepdaughter, Salome. Moreover, Father Petr urges them, as well as all his followers, to worship Grigori Rasputin, friend of the Royal Family, who was not canonized, and whose martyrdom they commemorate in December.

Father Petr would like to see a greater commitment to society on the part of the Church. He explains that the Church hierarchy lacks the real involvement the new martyrs had in Soviet times (*dukh ispovednichestva*). One of his spiritual sons echoes this sentiment by saying that the Church suffers from a lack of true freedom (*tserkovnaia nesvoboda, pridavlennost'*). Generally speaking, Father Petr's life is marked by an ethic of conviction and asceticism, which is undoubtedly linked to his veneration of new martyrs. As in many other fundamentalist-oriented parishes, the religious discipline is severe: Liturgy is very long and fasting is extremely strict. *Blagoslovenie* ("blessing") and *poslushanie* ("obedience") play a decisive role in the lives of believers.[23] Father Petr, as their spiritual father (*dukhovnik*), is the one who knows what should be done, he is the competent and definitive authority in all aspects of his "children's" spiritual and moral life.[24]

Another example of religious commitment may be given by Tania, 52 years old, who says she is of noble descent, both on her father's and her mother's side. She says she comes from a priest's family. In her case, the worship of the Tsarist family is linked to a transmitted heritage. She insists on the fact that her values differ completely from those of people surrounding her, both now in the post-Soviet period as in the Soviet one, and among believers as well as non-believers. These values require a particular behavior that cannot be taught or learned, she says. It is in one's genes; people of noble descent recognize each other:

> The education I received from my parents was specific. When I argue, I cannot shout, I restrain, I cannot speak loudly. I saw in my family how to sit, how to speak, how to talk, when to keep silent ...
>
> Everything goes through genes. ... You should not do this. You should do that. Yes, that's what you think, but you should keep silent. Your opinion is not the main thing. ... Few people understand this. Basically people usually shout to achieve what they want.

Tania's narrative seems characteristic of people of her class (Tchouikina 2006). She adapted to the Soviet context; she worked as a senior researcher at the department of economy of the Party Committee of the Region (*Obkom*) without being bothered by the Party in spite of her religious affiliation (although she was denied the possibility of traveling abroad). She explains this favorable treatment by her high level of competence: "I don't want to boast, but they needed me," she says. Her entire narrative aims to explain that while other Soviet citizens looked for a high position in the Party for material reasons (*pozicia cherez zhivot*), her whole life, by contrast, was moved by spiritual goals. Religion was part of the family's life: There were icons at home, and her family celebrated religious feasts and even painted eggs at a time when there was a deficit of special painting materials. Her four children were baptized and she used to go to church. After the death of her husband in 1990, Tania vowed not to remarry, and she now wishes to enter a monastery.

Her close interest in the Tsarist family is also justified by her personal identification with their condition. In 1982, her mother revealed to her before she died that her father had been repressed as a so-called "enemy of the people." Since perestroika she has been working in the political archives and discovered a lot about the eparchy's history, the monasteries, the new martyrs, and the assassination of the Tsarist family. Boasting about her scientific skills, she looks for historical truth.

But Father Petr and Tania are exceptions. The great majority of the people who worship Nicholas II and his family are ordinary post-Soviet people who converted in the 1990s or in the beginning of the 2000s, and who are rediscovering Russian history. Indeed, the Church's official position stresses the link between the Church and Russian history, between the Church and the Fatherland it has been defending for centuries. Thus, for the committed believer, worshipping the Tsar means studying Russian history in greater depth. By the end of the 1980s, religion was being rediscovered at the same time as Russian history. Then in the 1990s the debate surrounding the canonization of the Tsarist family was linked to the debate over the authenticity of the corpses, which were found at Porosenkov Log and reburied in 1998.

Committed believers are not only concerned about the history and memory of their Fatherland. They are also concerned about the memory of their family, in order to reproduce the religious beliefs and practices of their believing ancestors. Many pilgrims have asserted that they discovered the Tsar through the tales of another member of their family and now they wish to retell the stories that have been imparted to them. One believer explains that religion means finding a vivid link with her parents:

> The Church is history. In the atheist period I used to go sometimes into a church. Yes, I did… I wanted to meet my forefathers. For example, when there was a religious feast. My grandmother, my great-grandmother, my great-great-grandmother listened to the same prayer as I did. I met with them. The Church is living history.

Learning about history and practicing religion are very much interconnected. In the small memorial rooms of the last house-prison of the Grand Duchess Elizaveta Fedorovna in Alapayevsk, near Yekaterinburg, people can learn about her life as well as venerate her icons; the believer/tourist prays either before or after reading documents about her past affixed to big stalls. Both activities are unified in the same quest for proximity with the saint. In the same way, parishioners from the Kaluga region visit all Tsarist residences to feel closer to the Royal family. They go and pray in Tobolsk, Yekaterinburg, Ganina Yama, and Alapayevsk, "to better understand what the Tsar and his family could feel when they met death."

The strong link between history and religious worship explains why believers strive to pass down traditions, including those that are not explicitly religious as well as so-called traditional values, to the younger generations. The interest for traditions explains also why the Tsarist days in Yekaterinburg are a "festival of Orthodox culture"—Orthodox meaning Russian. Ira, the head of a folk group, sees her activity in the club as a way of safeguarding and transmitting traditional folk songs and dances, as well as the values of her own family. She expresses a strong sense of responsibility towards others and feels that the transmission of traditions and the revelation of historical truth is her duty:

> I wanted to transmit to my own husband and children my parents' experience, for they built a traditional family. I fervently wanted to save people around me. They didn't know what the traditions are. ... Everything will be forgotten. If *we* don't do anything, who will do it?

Worshipping the Tsarist Family as a Reaction to Post-Soviet Disorder

In Russian Orthodox thought, a true believer must endure suffering. Prayer and suffering are indeed "performances of moral self-analysis and improvement" (Zigon 2006: 2). In Yekaterinburg, penance remains the leitmotif and reveals the transformation of the moral conceptions of the believer. But the form of penance expected by the Church may not be exactly the same as the one that is lived by the individual. The believer may experience and reveal sufferings and values which are very different from those expected by the church. Penance may cover past and present, personal and social suffering. Olga, a 50-year-old woman who works as an oncologist, explains:

> I lived without God. When my son died in Afghanistan, I started to have completely different feelings. It was in 1988. The Lord has put me on my place. I am grateful to Him for it. ... And there is so much felicity here ... the place is so quiet although I felt so much grief at the Liturgy [she starts to cry].
>
> It is our history ... what else can we say? We have so much offended the Tsar, his children. We have committed so many sins. We have done so many abortions. All Russia is getting dirty through our sins and we are receiving what we deserve. ... The State is in disorder. ... We have moved away from God.

The assassination of the Tsar's family is considered by some residents of Yekaterinburg to be *their* sin, a stigma of the disgrace (*kleimo*) that they felt during the Soviet period and which they continue to bear now (Agadjanian and Rousselet 2010). In an informant's narrative, repentance is the duty of all Yekaterinburg inhabitants:

> Living in this city, we are somehow marked (*nesem pechat'*) by the inhabitants' participation in this tragic event. If we shall begin, in Yekaterinburg, to repent, the whole Russia may hear our voice, it may hear the sound of this bell. Maybe even our authorities will hear it. And the whole Orthodox world will surely hear us, and the Christian one, too.

Guilt can be also considered to be a familial burden. Suffering is carried and shared by the parents of the one who committed the sin. Religious literature gives many examples of this collective guilt. Before he died, a man who had guarded the Imperial family and who felt extremely guilty for not reacting when the Tsar was arrested asked his grand-daughter to pray for him and to order prayers wherever she went. His grand-daughter had five children; the youngest was very ill and did not learn to talk before the age of fourteen. According to the stories, the grand-daughter's prayers "washed away the grandfather's sin" and her child was cured (*Po molitvam sviatogo Tsaria* 2000). One young informant told also a story about her father, who had been a member of the team that had demolished the Ipatiev house. She believed this guilt had provoked the disease of both her father and her grandmother; all members of the family repented to purify themselves.

Worshipping the Tsarist family expresses a breakdown, a radical change with the Soviet ideology. But, as shown by the example of Olga who points out the problems of post-Soviet Russia and who repents for them, the worship of the Tsarist Family also contains a negative reaction to what is often called the moral disorder of the 1990s. People yearn for order, and in some way the believers met in Yekaterinburg often felt nostalgic for some aspects of the former Soviet moral code, especially what concerns education. Some of them said they had completely transformed their way of life and their moral dispositions. Some had changed their employment under the influence of their *dukhovnik,* and started working for their parish or entered a monastery. But beyond the discourse of a radical break, for many others there was a strong sense of continuity between some new and old values.

Elena was born in 1939. After she lost her husband in 1993, she says she experienced both psychological and financial hardship; she understood at that time that God was helping her and she started believing in God (she adds that she always believed in Him, in a way). The roots of Elena's moral inclinations are based in her Soviet experiences. In her narrative, one does not actually notice any great difference between her former moral dispositions, as she describes them, and the ones she professes today. After working in a factory belonging to the military-industrial complex, she became the head of the factory's museum and then the director of a small monastery's museum which is dedicated to the memory of the Tsarist family. She started developing an interest in the Tsar in the 1990s, when the official discourse was already rehabilitating him. Yet in her narrative, she justifies her attitude to the Tsar through her entire life history. She was marked by people who demonstrated to her proper values and who became moral role models. The few allusions to Nicholas II and to the Ipatiev House made by these people, the moral values they transmitted (honesty, rectitude, humanity, kindness, truth-seeking, disciplined work-ethic, etc.), their way of speaking about the Tsarist period, her love for history and the many history books she read (even if they related some false evidence), some objects such as a 1913 sewing machine given to her by the spouse of a head constructor of the factory: All these elements moved her towards the worship of the Tsarist family. The values she strengthened by worshipping Nicholas II and his family are rooted in her Soviet experience.

Indeed, the Soviet morality (presented by the Soviet films which Elena considers "nice" and "pure"—*dobrye, krasivye, chistye*), and the morality of the first Christians and that of the Tsarist family overlap with her own interest in child rearing. In the small museum she exhibits some materials of the Royal Family which help her inculcate in others the educational ideas she always had. For example, regarding the diaries the Tsar's daughters had to keep, she says she asked the same from the girls of her village, for it helped them to self-improve. The museum illustrates the everyday life of the Royal Family in a way familiar to believers. This Soviet-educated woman insists that the Tsar and his wife used to live and raise their children like ordinary people. Children of this family were remarkably well educated, and, most importantly, they were brought up with great humility despite their social standing.

In addition to the importance she gives to education, Elena has a negative opinion about consumerism. Here again, her thinking coincides with Nicholas II's modest way of life and the Church's position. But she describes it rather as a moral disposition she always had. She says she definitely criticized the *veshchizm* ("materialism") that developed in the 1960s when people's standard of living began to improve. She argues that at that time she didn't like this superficial focus on material goods and preferred to buy books instead of fashionable clothes. And this moral disposition, she adds, can be seen in the museum where she doesn't keep any precious objects: The aim is not to have a rich collection but to fill the soul (*napolnit' dushu*) and to educate. Elena definitely does not express any radical moral breakdown.

Believers' commitment is justified by the concern toward the other, by *agapè* in the definition given by Boltanski: disinterested love and compassion towards others, which is not moved by a quest of reciprocity and interest (1990). *Agapè* has religious roots (Nygren 1962) but the post-Soviet concern toward others may have also some connections with some Soviet values and the so-called *zabota* (Bogdanova 2006). This moral category, which is at the core of social relations in the Soviet Union and socialist paternalism, is mentioned in the 1977 Constitution of the USSR: "[Soviet society] is a society in which the law of life is concern (*zabota*) of all for the good of each and concern of each for the good of all." During the Soviet period, Ira, the head of the folk group mentioned above, used to be a nurse and also had a voluntary job in the House of Culture. She sees her activity in the club as a social work ("I am a social worker," she says.) and longs for social utility for her people (*narod*) in terms that echo Soviet ideology ("I saw my friends' mistakes," she says. "I just wanted to show them how they should interact with their husband and children in order to strengthen their family and avoid divorce."). She yearns to strengthen the social bonds with the people around her (*obshchenie, splochenie*) through feasts, but also through shared religious and domestic practices.

Mutual aid and charity are the leitmotif of many of the narratives I collected. The figure of the grand-duchess Elizaveta Fedorovna, who opened a hospital and an orphanage in the Convent of Sts. Martha and Mary, and who devoted the last years of her life to the poorest, is also a role model in this regard. The community of believers aspires to be like a big family in which people help each other by giving money or other goods, or simply by praying. This is, for example, the way a woman (a film producer who took part in the Orthodox Film Festival in Yekaterinburg) expresses this widespread idea: "Pray, work and share. ... If we are Orthodox people, we should help each other. Collective prayer [*obshchaia sobornaia molitva*] may sometimes heal. ... If not, it will warm the soul."[25] More than *agapè*, this insistence on the community, religious or not, seems specific to Russian Orthodox moralities. These values of mutual aid, which are linked to a longing for communality, are said to be in complete opposition to the present dominant morality of success ("One has to be successful; one has to be strong.") where children, the poor and the elderly have no place. Some believers also say these communal values are in opposition to Soviet egoism, which in some way led to post-Soviet liberal values. These values are the grounds for the patriotic identity of these believers and Russia is seen as a family. Lena, a young lady whose parents are divorced, decided to build an Orthodox family, which guarantees, she says, genuine relations: "For me the Fatherland is like a big house, an Orthodox family, earth, everyone helps each other."[26]

The commitment of the worshippers to the Tsarist family doesn't specifically express a desire to return to a pre-revolutionary way of life. It means a return to a better life and it is linked to a nostalgia for some aspects of the Soviet past and for a sense of order.

Most of the patriot-worshippers of Nicholas II do not long for the monarchy even if the monarchist flag floats in the processions. The majority of the believers interviewed shared a common indifference towards Russian politics, as attested by all-Russian surveys.[27] Many of them expressed the idea that Russia is not ready for monarchy and supported the present political leaders. Inspired by fundamentalists, some saw political parties as linked to money, which is considered the sign of the Antichrist. Among the believers who attended the procession in Yekaterinburg, the Cossacks expressed their yearning for political order and efficiency. As the police fails to inspire confidence, they contributed to maintaining order during the religious demonstrations in the streets. The ones who agreed to be interviewed said that the Cossack organization compensates for the State's negligence and corruption; according to them, it is a form of patriotic commitment to Russia and can be seen as the continuation of the Communist organizations of the pioneers and the Komsomol.

Conclusion

In order to facilitate reconciliation of all Russian people, political elites as well as the Russian Orthodox Church have called for moral perestroika and have asked Russian citizens to repent—even if the position of the newly elected Patriarch Kirill seems to indicate a different way. The assassination of the Tsarist family is not only defined as a crime; it is also considered a sin. Other moral entrepreneurs even assert that the Tsar's death expiates the Russian people's sins. In a demoralized social context where family values are seen by the believers to be discredited, the Church presents the Tsarist family as a Holy family. The imitation of newly canonized saints is considered by the Church to be central in the process of moral transformation of the believers.

But we may question the Church's efficiency in inculcating a new morality. The Church plays a lesser role in the process of worshipping the Tsarist family than personal contexts and interpersonal relations. The ordinary people who gathered in Yekaterinburg engaged the official morality in the contexts of their everyday lives. Repentance may get a new significance.

Moreover, believers often understand the exemplary values of the saints and the official morality they represent in resonance with examples given by people whom the believers know much more intimately, as well as with the social context in which they themselves have grown up. Moralities of the small group echo collective ones. Some elements of continuity with the Soviet moral code paradoxically appear.

These faithful worshippers of the Tsarist family, whom we have named "Christian patriots," reveal some specific motives of commitment: a special interest in the past and tradition, *agapè* (which may have connections with the Soviet "concern") and the yearning for order (a very multi-semantic notion). The worship of the Tsarist family exemplifies "religion as a chain of memory" in the practice of believers (Hervieu-Léger 2000). It helps to grasp the Tsarist but also the Soviet past of the believer. The patriotic worship of the Tsar offers the believer a means of continuity in a universe marked by ruptures in moral values, and it also offers them a way of analyzing the past. These faithful worshippers of the Tsarist family cope with the post-Soviet moral disorder by reasserting some Soviet principles, but they also comply with the dominant values of the current sociopolitical order: the attitude towards the Fatherland and the Russian nation, as well as the desire for order.

Notes

1. The two churches officially signed the act of canonical communion on 17 May 2007.
2. See http://www.pravoslavie.ru/guest/igumendamaskin.htm.
3. "Approximately 35,000 Pilgrims took part in an Evening Religious Procession in Yekaterinburg in Honour of the Royal Martyrs," according to one news release, 17 July 2008, http://www.interfax-religion.ru/?act=news&div=25513.
4. Boris Nemtsov spoke about the reburial as follows:

   We put an end to the history of the Terror. ... Russia is still in a period of transition but it has already paid its moral debts. It repents of its terrible sins. ... Attitudes towards Nicholas II as an historical figure are diverse. But his murder without any judgement is undoubtedly a crime, as well as the murder of clearly innocent people: his family and the faithful servants who did not want to leave the Monarch in misfortune. Our longstanding tolerant attitude towards the Terror is also a sin for which we have to repent. I feel guilty myself for my former indifference to this period of our history. And I hope you feel guilty too.

   The miraculous discovery of the remains of the last Emperor of Russia gave us the opportunity to reconcile on his grave. But we have not done it yet. The killers' heirs are still powerful. We still endure political games. They slow down those transformations which could help the country develop normally and solidly. People suffer from long-standing depression. ...

Today we can say that science overcame speculation. ... By paying our debts we shall move more steadily forward towards the future. (Pokaianie 2003: preface) See also Boris Yeltsin's speech to the funeral ceremony.

5. For a theoretical distinction between a sin and a crime see Hertz (1922: 50). Moreover he argues that in a modern context where civil society and the religious society have separate attributes, a sin, defined as a "transgression of the moral order," applies only to religious society. The discourse of the political elites shows that this is definitely not the case in post-Soviet Russia.

6. According to Viktor Aksiuchits: "It helps all citizens remember the history of their country, the significance of monarchy and the tragedy of the revolution. It is an act of national reconciliation; in spiritual terms, it is the conclusion of the tragic twentieth century" (Pokaianie 2003: 9).

7. See Romanov (2007).

8. "V RPTs MP rady reabilitatsii sem'i Romanovykh," See http://www.religare.ru/2_58058.html

9. "Verkhovnyi sud RF reabilitiroval chlenov Tsarskoj sem'i," See http://www.rian.ru/society/20081001/151756122.html.

10. "Top Russian Law Office Rehabilitates the Saint Great Duchess Yelizaveta Fyodorovna Romanova." *Interfax* 8 June 2009, http://www.interfax-religion.com/?act=news&div=6104 (accessed 15 May 2011).

11. "Poslanie Patriarkha Moskovskogo i vseia Rusi Alekseia II i Sviaschennogo Sinoda Russkoi Pravoslavnoi Tserkvi k 80-letiiu ubienia Imperatora Nikolaia II i ego Sem'i," http://patriarch.voskres.ru/090698.htm.

12. See http://chin-pokayaniya.ru/files/documents/chin_pokayaniya.pdf.

13. In the Orthodox tradition, one cannot repent for the sins of the dead; one can only pray for them. The believer must repent for his or her own sins during his or her own life. The figure of repentance which is present in the *chin vsemnirnogo pokaiania russkogo naroda v grekhe careubiistva* is considered to be a magic one. In its judgment, the Russian Orthodox Church referred to *Psalm* 48: 8 and *Ezekiel* 18: 14–20 in the Bible.

14. These practices are themselves rooted in the pre-Soviet religious tradition.

15. See Orlovsky (2000).

16. From the introduction by the hegumen Damaskin Orlovsky at the session on new martyrs at the XI Rozhdestvenskie chtenia. 29 January 2003, http://www.fond.ru/zvuk/damask_xi.htm.

17. "Osnovania dlia kanonizatsii Tsarskoi sem'i. Iz doklada Mitropolita Krutitskogo i Kolomenskogo Iuvenalia, predsedatelia Sinodal'noi Komissii po kanonizatsii sviatykh." http://www.pravoslavie.ru/sobytia/sobor/juvenalij.htm.

18. Among the people who have gathered the stories of miracles is a Moscow priest, Alexander Shargunov.

19. All the following quotes are from the *Zhizneopisanie sviatykh tsarstvennykh strastoterptsev* 2003.

20. All names have been changed.

21. This poet and prose writer survived the Kolyma camps in the early 1950s.

22. Those elders included Archimandrit Kirill Pavlov, Hieromonk Rafail Berestov, Archimandrit Vlasi Peregontsev, and Archimandrit Kirill Borodin.

23. The significance of these acts is under debate: Actually some priests and laypersons consider that the believer should enjoy some moral autonomy.
24. A lot of new believers who are actively committed to the Church actually refrain from choosing and deliberating in the main aspects of their lives. These behaviors can in part be explained by their absence of religious knowledge but also by the persistence of Soviet habits marked by a lack of freedom of expression, and by the charisma of the *dukhovnik*. In Father's Petr's case, the fact that he studied in Moscow may be a cause of his charisma; his "sincere faith" (*chuvstvo iskrennee*) and his "deep sense of the liturgy" are also praised by the followers.
25. Interview, 15 July 2006.
26. Interview, 20 July 2006.
27. See, for example, the results of the VTsIOM's surveys ("Interes k politike: rastet ili padaet?" 2011).

References

Agadjanian, Alexander, and Kathy Rousselet. 2010. "Individual and Collective Identities in Russian Orthodoxy." In *Eastern Christians in Anthropological Perspective*, ed. C. Hann and H. Goltz. Berkeley, CA: University of California Press.

Akty Sviateishego Tikhona, Patriarkha Moskovskogo i vseia Rossii. 1994. Moskva: Pravoslavny Sviato-Tikhonovski Bogoslovski Institut.

Bateman, Patricia. 2004. "L'Expérience Morale Comme Objet Sociologique." *Année Sociologique* 54, no. 2: 389–412.

Bennett, W. Lance. 1979. "Imitation, Ambiguity, and Drama in Political Life: Civil Religion and the Dilemmas of Public Morality." *The Journal of Politics* 41, no. 1: 106–33.

Bogdanova, Elena. 2006. "Sovetski Opyt Regulirovania Pravovykh Otnoshenij, ili 'v Ozhidanii Zaboty'." *Zhurnal Sociologii i Socialnoj Antropologii* 9, no. 1: 77–90.

Boltanski, Luc. 1990. *L'Amour et la Justice comme Compétences: Trois Essais de Sociologie de l'Action.* Paris: Editions Métailié.

Boltanski, Luc, and Laurent Thévenot. 2006. *On Justification: Economies of Worth.* Princeton, NJ: Princeton University Press.

Dubin, Boris. 2005. "Un 'Fardeau Léger': Les Orthodoxes dans la Russie des Années 1990–2000." *Revue d'Etudes Comparatives Est-Ouest* 36, no. 4: 19–42.

Ferro, Marc. 1991. *Nicolas II.* Paris: Payot.

Fond. N.D. "Pamiat' muchenikov i ispovednikov Russkoj Pravoslavnoj Cerkvi." http://www.fond.ru/index.shtml (accessed 15 May 2011).

Foucault, Michel. 1984. *L'Usage des Plaisirs*, vol. 2 of *L'Histoire de la Sexualité.* Paris: Gallimard.

Fox, Jon E., and Cynthia Miller-Idriss. 2008. "Everyday Nationhood," *Ethnicities*, 8: 536–63.

Hertz, Robert. 1922. *Le Péché et l'Expiation dans les Sociétés Primitives.* http://classiques.uqac.ca/classiques/hertz_robert/peche_expiation/peche_expiation.html (accessed 15 May 2011).

Hervieu-Léger, Danièle. 2000. *Religion as a Chain of Memory*, trans. Simon Lee. New Brunswick, NJ: Rutgers University Press.

Humphrey, Caroline. 1997. "Exemplars and Rules: Aspects of the Discourse of Moralities in Mongolia." In *The Ethnography of Moralities*, ed. Signe Howell, 25–47. London: Routledge.

"Interes k politike: rastet ili padaet?" http://wciom.ru/inde.php?=268&uid=111495 (accessed 15 June 2011).

Kharkhordin, Oleg. 1999. *The Collective and the Individual in Russia: A Study of Practices.* Berkeley, CA: University of California Press.

"L'Amour des Autres: Care, Compassion et Humanitarisme." 2008. *Revue du Mauss* 32, no. 2: 1-618.

Menchtchérinov, Piotr. 2007. "En nous souvenant de 1937." http://www.orthodoxie.com/2007/09/en-nous-souvena.html (accessed 15 May 2011).

Nygren, Anders. 1962. *Éros et Agapè: La Notion Chrétienne de l'Amour et ses Transformations*, trans. Pierre Jundt, 3 vols. Paris: Aubier.

Orlovsky, Damaskin. 2000. Interview by Sergei Kotkalo. http://www.fond.ru/zvuk/kotkalo.htm (accessed 15 May 2011).

———. 2003. "Svidetel'stvo o zhizni": Interview by Anastasia Verina, 5 July. http://www.pravoslavie.ru/guest/igumendamaskin.htm (accessed 15 May 2011).

"Osnovania dlia kanonizatsii Tsarskoi sem'i. Iz doklada Mitropolita Krutitskogo i Kolomenskogo Iuvenalia, predsedatelia Sinodal'noi Komissii po kanonizatsii sviatykh." 2000. http://www.pravoslavie.ru/sobytia/sobor/juvenalij.htm (accessed 15 May 2011).

Pharo, Patrick. ed. 2004. "Éthique et Sociologie, Perspectives Actuelles de la Sociologie Morale." *Année Sociologique* (direction) 54, no. 2: 321-629 .

Podbolotov, Sergei. 2004. "'… And the entire mass of loyal people leapt up': The Attitude of Nicholas II towards the Pogroms." *Cahiers du Monde Russe* 45, nos. 1–2: 193–208.

Pogorelov, Stanislav. 2006. "Obrazy sviatykh v dukhovno-nravstvennom vospitanii sovremennykh shkolnikov." *III Simeonovskie obrazovatel'nye Chtenia*, Yekaterinburg. http://www.prosvetcentr.ru/1/30.html (accessed 15 May 2011).

Pokoianie. 2003. *Materialy pravitel'stvennoi Komissii po izucheniu voprosov, sviazannykh s issledovaniem i perezakhoroneniem ostankov Rossiiskogo Imperatora Nikolaia II i chlenov ego sem'i.* Moscow: OOO Bost-K.

Po molitvam sviatogo Tsaria. 2000. Moskva: Novaya Kniga, Kovcheg.

"Poslanie Patriarkha Moskovskogo i vseia Rusi Alekseia II i Sviaschennogo Sinoda Russkoi Pravoslavnoi Tserkvi k 75-letiiu ubienia Imperatora Nikolaia II i ego Sem'i." 1993. *Zhurnal Moskovskoi Patriarkhii* 6.

"Poslanie Patriarkha Moskovskogo i vseia Rusi Alekseia II i Sviashchennogo Sinoda Russkoi Pravoslavnoi Tserkvi k 80-letiiu ubienia Imperatora Nikolaia II i ego Sem'i." 1998. http://patriarch.voskres.ru/090698.htm (accessed 15 May 2011).

Romanov, Pyotr. 2007. "Rehabilitation of the Tsar's Family: The Labyrinth of the Russian Penal Code, History and Faith." http://en.rian.ru/analysis/20071109/87355104.html (accessed 15 May 2011).

Rousselet, Kathy. 2010. "Le Religieux dans la Construction du Patriotisme: L'Exemple des Vénérateurs de Nicolas II et de la Famille Impériale de Russie." In *L'Identité en Jeux—Pouvoirs, Identifications, Mobilizations*, ed. Denis-Constant Martin, 291–310. Paris: Karthala.

Séguy, Jean. 1980. "La Socialisation Utopique aux Valeurs." *Archives de Sciences Sociales des Religions* 50, no 1: 7–21.

———. 1999. *Conflit et Utopie, ou Réformer l'Église: Parcours Wébérien en Douze Essais.* Paris: Cerf.

Slater, Wendy. 2007. *The Many Deaths of Tsar Nicholas II: Relics, Remains and the Romanovs.* London: Routledge.

Tchouikina, Sofia. 2006. "Le 'Grand Compromis' et la Mémoire Familiale. Les Ex-nobles Russes à l'Epoque Stalinienne." *Revue d'Etudes Comparatives Est-Ouest* 37, no. 3: 165–97.

Verdery, Katherine. 1999. *The Political Lives of Dead Bodies: Reburial and Postsocialist Change.* New York: Columbia University Press.

"Verkhovnyi sud RF reabilitiroval chlenov Tsarskoi sem'i." 2008. http://www.rian.ru/society/20081001/151756122.html (accessed 15 May 2011).

Veyne, Paul. 1996. "L'interprétation et l'interprète." *Enquête, Interpréter, Surinterpréter.* http://enquete.revues.org/document623.html, 21 January 2008 (accessed 27 March 2009).

"V RPTs MP rady reabilitatsii sem'i Romanovykh." 1 October 2008. http://www.religare.ru/2_58058.html (accessed 15 May 2011).

Weber, Max. 1978. *Economy and Society: An Outline of Interpretive Sociology,* ed. Guenther Roth and Claus Wittich and trans. Ephraim Fischoff et al. Berkeley, CA: University of California Press.

Zigon, Jarrett. 2006. "'You Should Reform Yourself Not Other People': The Ethics of Hope in Contemporary Moscow." Halle/Saale: Max Planck Institute for Social Anthropology Working Papers, no. 88.

———. 2007. "Moral Breakdown and the Ethical Demand: A Theoretical Framework for an Anthropology of Moralities." *Anthropological Theory* 7, no. 2: 131–50.

Zhizneopisanie sviatykh tsarstvennykh strastoterptsev. 2003. Yekaterinburg: Informatsionno-izdatel'skii otdel Yekaterinburgskoi Eparkhii.

 CHAPTER 9

St. Xenia as a Patron of Female Social Suffering
An Essay on Anthropological Hagiology

Jeanne Kormina and Sergey Shtyrkov

The first post-Soviet canonization took place during perestroika, a period of very fast and dramatic transition in the Soviet political and ideological system. This was the very beginning of religious revivalism in Russia, which coincided with the 1988 celebration of the 1,000[th] anniversary of the baptism of Russia.[1] At that time the Moscow Patriarchate realized that Russian Orthodoxy was transforming quickly and drastically from the ideological enemy of Communism into the main guardian of Russian national cultural heritage. The canonization conducted at the 1988 Church Council reflected this transformation very clearly: the Council's list of new saints started with the names of well-known figures who are associated with Russian cultural and historical greatness.[2]

Among the nine saints canonized on that day only one was a woman, St. Xenia of St. Petersburg (also known as Xenia the Blessed), glorified as a "Holy Fool" (or a "Fool for Christ," *yurodivaya*) (Kanonizatsia 1988: 109–17).[3] She differed from the other canonized saints not only in her gender, but also in her social status. Other canonized persons were either monks (including three bishops) or famous rulers like Prince Dimitri Donskoi. Xenia was a lay woman of (allegedly) non-noble origins. She also was the only one who had already been an object of popular veneration amongst the common people. Xenia's sepulcher in a shrine at the Smolensk Cemetery in St. Petersburg/Leningrad had been revered since at least the middle of the nineteenth century (Toporov 1995; Filicheva 2006; Kizenko 2003). Active pilgrimage to the shrine continued during the Soviet period.[4] Her canonization sent a message to Soviet authorities about the continuity of religious tradition represented by this pilgrimage. It stressed that despite all the antireligious campaigns of the Soviet state, there were many Orthodox believers in the country who still needed church shrines, and were waiting for the reestablishment of the Church. But if we examine the message sent by Xenia's canonization to the Russian public, we see that its primary purpose was to institutionalize Xenia's veneration, as well as to create and popularize a female image that would be understandable and attractive to the majority of actual and potential believers—lay women.

Indeed, Xenia the Blessed has become a very popular saint in post-Soviet Russia. Many churches and chapels dedicated to St. Xenia have been built throughout Russia; her icon can be bought in most church shops in the country. Every time we went to her shrine in the Smolensk Cemetery in St. Petersburg to do our field observations, we saw both men and women (mostly women) praying to St. Xenia.

Illustration 9.1. Pilgrims at St. Xenia shrine. Photo by Sergey Shtyrkov (2009).

We observed people writing notes or even long letters to the saint, which were put into the walls of the chapel—a custom that has survived all attempts of the local parish priests to stop it (Filicheva 2006). Many read a special akathist[5] to St. Xenia or prayed to her in their own words, circling around her chapel three times or standing for several minutes by the wall of the chapel with their palms and forehead touching the chapel wall. When the chapel was open, there were also people queuing at the chapel door to buy church oil from the shrine or to participate in the service conducted by a local priest.

Participant observation was conducted at the shrine in different seasons, both on weekdays and church feasts, and including the day annually dedicated to her memory on 6 February, which is usually incredibly cold and windy. We interviewed religious activists and average believers, and studied letters to the shrine of St. Xenia printed in different publications, from the local parish newspaper to special books, usually edited by lay women.[6] One more important and revealing source for our research has been the Internet, which contains official information provided and controlled by the Church (including variants of the life of Xenia and akathists) and, at the same time, provides space for believers to express their religious feelings and ideas freely while remaining anonymous and outside of church authority. Usually, those believers (or religious "seekers") who are active in Orthodox internet chat rooms are not churchgoers. Finally, we examined popular images of Xenia the Blessed in contemporary Russian literature and mass media, which provide many examples of what we call the "lay life" of Xenia. In 2007 the play *St. Xenia of St. Petersburg in her Life,* by Vadim Levanov, won a prestigious prize in Russia; in 2009 under the title *Xenia: The Love Story,* this play is being performed in St. Petersburg's Alexandrinski Theatre.

In our research we were especially interested in popular perceptions of the saint, reflected in oral and written narratives about the life of Xenia, her apparitions, and the miraculous help she provided. However, we were faced with a rich variety of images of the saint, not only in the sphere of "popular" religion, but in "official" religion as well. The very fact that someone is canonized means that there must be official (or canonical) texts of her or his life and akathists approved by the Church (either by the Church authorities or by certain institutions, such as the Synodal Canonization Commission). But in fact there are at least three variants of akathists for Xenia. All of them appear in church publications (including Internet materials), and it is hard to say which one is canonical.[7] As for the life of St. Xenia, one can find a dozen versions that claim to be canonical. In other words some church authors and most readers of those texts take it for granted that this is the official version of the life although the texts have important differences, and one could say that some canonical life with unified ideological meaning just does not exist.

In this chapter we consider why Xenia the Blessed has become so popular among contemporary Orthodox believers. To answer this question we first seek to understand the "target audience" of this saint, and the specific features of these contemporary believers. Second, we analyze the image of Xenia, how she is depicted in various narratives and visual representations, and how she is depicted by the Church and perceived by believers in their written and oral reflections.

An Over-age Contemporary Believer: The Genesis

There is a clear tendency in public discourse about the Russian Orthodox Church to compare contemporary religious life with the pre-revolutionary situation and to draw conclusions about continuities between them. The Soviet period in these speculations is either silently skipped or represented as a hard time for the Church and faith, which were both preserved uncorrupted by the zealots of faith. On the basis of our field research, we tend to stress the discontinuities, and to insist upon the "invention" of the religious tradition, especially in the realm of lay religiosity. A religious tradition can be transmitted via personal participation in routine (church services, icon veneration, etc.) and through a special system of education. As is well known, in the USSR both of these means of transmitting religion were closed to the average Soviet citizen. Soviet atheistic propaganda, which mocked religion as an old-fashioned, rural phenomena, and simple superstition, was rather effective in the age of rapid Soviet modernization. Village immigrants to the cities and their children, some of whom received a good professional education, became teachers, engineers or physicians, and eventually composed the so-called Soviet intelligentsia,[8] who tried their best to distance themselves from their rural low-status heritage, including religion.

In contemporary Russia there is a widespread belief that religious tradition was preserved in the Soviet period by village grandmothers: those women who did not migrate from the countryside to the city. These women allegedly transmitted religious faith and practices to their urban grandchildren. The idea is inspired by little more than today's conception of the continuity of national traditions which were able to survive the Soviet period. The fact that a significant number of Soviet children were baptized, sometimes secretly by their grandmothers or other older female relatives (often parents pretended that they did not know about these baptisms because they could lose their jobs), does not automatically mean that those children were raised as religious persons. Some of them did not even know about their baptism until they became adults; for others their religious education was restricted to some knowledge about special foods their elder relatives prepared for Easter (painted eggs) and for burial ceremonies (*kutia*, a sweet meal made of rice or wheat with honey or raisins). In some senses, atheism has won.

The image of a pious grandmother as a keeper of religious tradition is willingly used by the converted. Martha,[9] born in 1930, and the daughter of an eminent Soviet civil engineer and official who was a committed atheist, converted to Russian Orthodoxy at the beginning of the 1990s at the age of 60. She did not know whether she had been baptized in her childhood, and she addressed this question to a priest whom she respected very much and whose church she started visiting in St. Petersburg. According to Martha, "The priest looked at me and said: 'You have been baptized already; you don't need to be baptized again.'" From that expert's words she concluded that her grandmother, with whom Martha lived in a village in her childhood, did baptize her. As with many other converts who did not have even elementary religious knowledge, Martha started her self-education by reading books from church shops and communicating with other people who had converted during outdoor religious activities such as pilgrimages. In the mid 1990s she organized her own pilgrimage service which she continues to lead to this day.[10] The method of conversion and the religious career of Martha proves our assumption of discontinuity between traditional and new religiosity. The post-Soviet urbanized believers live in a different social and economical environment than their (mostly village-based) grandparents. In creating suitable new forms of religious life, these children of the Soviet system reuse their Soviet social habits. Thus, the genealogy of Russian organized pilgrimages shows that post-Soviet religious travelers draw directly on their Soviet experience of domestic heritage tourism (see Kormina 2010).

It is not just the contemporary believers who have Soviet roots; many traits of contemporary Russian religious culture originate in the USSR and have evident traces of Soviet heritage. One of the characteristic features of a certain segment of Orthodox believers is their suspicion of the public demonstration of someone's religiosity. Some people contend that they avoid going to church because in their mind, religious life must be a private matter. This prejudice against the display of private matters in public space is perhaps related to Alexey Yurchak's observation that the "last Soviet generation" learned to live in two separated worlds simultaneously—the false world of communication with the state, full of simulacra of different sorts, as opposed to the intimate world of sincere friendship and true feelings (2006). It is very possible that the representatives of the last Soviet generation reject the prospect of becoming regular churchgoers because of their antipathy towards the institutional control of their lives. Although they feel that it is necessary to be affiliated with the Russian Orthodox Church, they are not enthusiastic about participation either in parish community life or in the liturgical life of the Church. They prefer to consider themselves Orthodox believers (or even just Orthodox people, meaning belonging to Russian culture). They are sure that their inner faith and infrequent visits to the church, or a little pilgrimage to a local shrine like St. Xenia's chapel for an individual prayer, is a perfectly adequate form of Orthodox worship. Thus, they remain believers outside the Church, who use the concept of Orthodoxy or, rather, the concept of Orthodox identity, for their own purposes. The Church is increasingly trying to control such irregular Orthodox believers, although not always successfully and consistently.

It might seem to be a paradox, but the Church, which must encourage regular institutional practices, has good reason to represent irregular religiosity as legitimate and Orthodox (with some reservations, and by certain rhetorical methods, such as assuming the sincere but childlike and unsophisticated faith of common believers). We suggest that in doing so, the Church pursues two goals. First, if one counts irregular believers as observant, then most citizens of Russia will fall within the purview of the Russian Orthodox Church, and it would have a right to represent itself as a majority institution. This political outcome could be described as the inclusive strategy of Orthodox identity. Second, the Church considers irregular believers to be Orthodox by their nature, and just one step from entering the Church. Thus, these two goals can be seen as important aspects of an "inner" missionary program. Consequently, the church must sometimes create and promote lay figures to be saints in order to have an avenue of contact with people who try to escape from the control of religious institutions. In this sense, the "promotion" of St. Xenia seems to be a very successful missionary project.

St. Xenia and Irregular Religiosity

The image of St. Xenia must look very sympathetic to the irregular believer. An important feature of the image presented in official accounts of her life is her alienation from the regular life of the official church. We do not know whether she was raised by pious parents or was herself a pious person (a typical motif in such official accounts). In the earlier official account of her life, one cannot find any mention of clerics, or even her confessor. As a saint, Xenia did not need them. Some versions of the lay accounts of her life even tell us about Xenia's anticlerical actions. For example, Vadim Levanov, in his play *St. Xenia of St. Petersburg in her Life*, portrays a scene in which

Xenia exposes the local ecclesiastics' secret sins. The reader of the official biographical accounts of her life does not encounter Xenia praying in a church or monastery.[11] Both official and lay variants of her biography say that the religious life of Xenia, after she had become a *yurodivaya*, or "Fool for Christ," occurred secretly and outside the church walls.

There are two stories replicated in almost every life narrative of the saint. The first story says that in the daytime, Xenia roamed the neighborhood where she used to live before her husband's death, visiting her acquaintances and having tea with her fellow women. But every night, in all seasons, she used to go to a field outside the city and pray, alone, the whole night through. As one Orthodox writer puts it in an article published in the weekly tabloid *My Family*, "She never prayed in public. At night she went out of the city. There, in the fields, barefoot, she prayed kneeling before daybreak, bowed down to all four sides of the horizon" (Basha 2001). The second well-known story about Xenia that celebrates her hidden religious deeds—what we call her "night religiosity"—tells of the saint's secretive help to the builders of the church at the Smolensk Cemetery. At night Xenia lifted bricks up onto the scaffolding around the church to speed up the construction work. The workers did not know who helped them. "Finally," as another writer put it in her book about Xenia for children, "they decided to find out who the invisible helper was. Everyone learned that this onerous work had been done by Xenia, the Fool for Christ, who was known all over the neighborhood" (Kundysheva 1995: 9).[12]

The idea that proper spiritual and devotional work can and must be done secretively is well-known among all Christian traditions. This conception is based on Jesus' words in the Sermon on the Mount about secret alms (Matt. 6:1–4), fasting (Matt. 6:16–18), and prayer (Matt. 6:5–6). However, in the post-Soviet variant of Orthodoxy, such a practice of secret religious deeds has an additional implication: Those secret deeds of faith cannot be under the control of any institution. One who does not attend church services and cannot remember when and where her last confession was can still pray in her heart, and from time to time she can light a candle at an icon in a church she has never visited before and to which she will not return. This "light" variant of religious activity is usually accepted by the Church. As Metropolitan (now Patriarch) Kirill said in an interview on the Internet portal "Interfax-Religia" in January 2009, "Every day, let each of us—either those who visit church regularly or those who go to church infrequently, or even those who do not remember the last time they crossed the threshold of the church—begin with a prayer to God."[13] In an earlier interview, Kirill explains that "us"—the Orthodox people—includes all his baptized Orthodox compatriots who are not convinced atheists (Metropolitan Kirill 2002). According to this tolerant discourse, irregular believers are given legitimate rights to be considered truly Orthodox. This corresponds with the previously discussed inclusive strategy for defining believers that is promoted by the Russian Orthodox Church.

As we have written elsewhere (Kormina and Shtyrkov 2008), in the situation of a post-Soviet and post-atheist country, the Russian Orthodox Church cannot enjoy total domination in the ideological sphere. In many social contexts the Church cannot simply provide direct instructions to believers without any explanations (and wait for their obedience) just because of its institutional authority. In new circumstances the Church needs to represent publicly the source of the legitimacy of its power, such as the support of common believers. To achieve this legitimacy, the Church has to create new grounds and a new language for communicating with its actual, and especially, with its potential followers. It also has to elaborate and promote a new image of the ideal Orthodox person suitable for this particular social and historic situation. This ideal, translated through the cults of saints in particular, is embodied in an image of the saint herself and in the images of ordinary believers who became the recipients of miracles. In the case of St. Xenia, these two images—of the saint and of her followers—obviously overlap. Her alienation from the church and her hidden private religiosity might look very attractive for people used to an irregular religious life.

Female Saint Needed

In his well-known work, *The Saints of Old Russia,* George Fedotov considered the phenomena of female sanctity in pre-revolutionary Russia and wrote, not without some sadness, "The number of women saints in the Russian Church is not large; the Church seams to have canonized only 12 of them" (2000: 176). One can find slightly different numbers,[14] but nevertheless, some things are quite clear. First, the number of canonized female saints was and still is much lower than the number of males: Trofimov asserts that the total number of Russian saints is about 400, so only three percent are women.[15] Second, most of the female saints are princesses and often simultaneously nuns. Third, all of them lived several centuries ago. The "newest" female saint, Yuliania Lasarevskaya of Murom, was accepted for all-Church veneration in 1903, almost 300 years after her death.[16]

It should be mentioned that according to Orthodox Christianity, many female saints lived in the first centuries of Christianity. So one can suppose that there would be no shortage of female saints in the Russian Orthodox tradition. Indeed, some holy women of the Ancient Church were well-known in Russia. And perhaps the most venerated female saint in the Russian religious tradition has been St. Paraskeva (Piatnitsa), whose cult spread to Russia from the Balkans in the process of Christianization. In Russian popular religion, St. Paraskeva has been a protector of women, especially married women, and a patron of women's activities, such as spinning. Some ritual restrictions were connected with her, and there were also associated folk legends about the punishment of those who transgressed them (Afanas'ev 1990: 84–85; Levkievskaya 2001: 414). In her study of the veneration of St. Paraskeva, Eve Levin points out that her popularity declined in Russia after the revolution and has almost disappeared today (2006: 126).[17] Was this cult, rooted in traditional peasant society, wiped out because of modernization and the mass migration of village dwellers to the cities? Or was the decline in the veneration of St. Paraskeva caused by the emancipation of women, whose sphere of competence changed so radically? In the twentieth century, women became involved in Soviet industrialization as workers and professionals, instead of (or rather, in addition to) the activities that St. Paraskeva was patron to, such as housekeeping, child rearing, and spinning.

The decline of the old objects of devotion should not be explained solely in reference to the Soviet social transformation, for one can see changes in social processes taking place in pre-revolution mass religiosity. From the second half of the nineteenth century, the presence of women in Church public life became more and more visible.[18] Some Orthodox authorities began to think that women's religious activism (both lay and monastic) was a real foundation and support for the Church in times of rapid social change (Wagner 2007: 130). In the 1900s, some activists, inspired by the canonization of a popular saint—Serafim of Sarov in 1903—started looking for an ideal female saint. Yuliania Lasarevskaya, mentioned earlier, could have been such a person, as she was not a nun or a princess. But her image was too special and, in some respects, outmoded. According to official accounts of her life, Yuliania was a noblewoman famous for her self-sacrificing philanthropy and who had a special concern for her serfs. That role was attractive to some women from the intelligentsia who wanted to devote themselves to social service; but it was not attractive for the common urban or rural female believer (Fedotov 2000: 182). There was no Orthodox saint whose life would resonate with the average female believer. To put it another way, female sainthood was located outside of real contemporary religious life.

A twelve-volume collection of biographies of unglorified Russian Orthodox devotees was complied and published between 1906 and 1912 (Zhizneopisaniya 1906–1912). It was a sort of program for future canonizations. The volumes include several biographies of pious Imperial Russian women who could become saints (including Xenia the Blessed) and who came from a variety of backgrounds. If this collection is correlated with the Church's internal discussion on the religious role of women,[19] one can conclude that there was a good chance that a prominent Abbess would become a saint—one whose convent was well-known because of its prominent social welfare program. But as we know, the new official female saint didn't appear until 1988, when most potential or actual Orthodox people had no idea what nuns looked like. Then the Church needed a person of another type—St. Xenia.

From the beginning of the nineteenth century, Xenia was venerated as a saint for common city-dwellers. According to the official account of her life, she lived in the capital of the Russian Empire and was involved in the everyday routine of the big city. Characters in the official and lay narratives of her life (and the recipients of her miracle help) are people with small businesses, such as shopkeepers or carriers, or average urban dwellers (such as the widow of a noncommissioned officer who rents a room in her house, or builders erecting a church). Xenia herself is a typical city-dweller of her time. The *Life of St. Xenia* tells a story of an ordinary lay urban woman. As a young girl she was married to Andrei Fedorovich Petrov and lived in her husband's house in the neighborhood of Peterburgskaya storona, St. Petersburg. At the age of 26 she lost her husband, who died suddenly. After his death the young widow gave her house to her former tenant and her possessions to the needy, and started living on the street in the same part of the city where she had previously lived, begging for food. Local city-dwellers supported the "Holy Fool" by giving her food and clothes. She lived a long life and was buried in the Smolensk Cemetery in St. Petersburg, where her much venerated chapel is now located.

Xenia's life story sounds as if it happened very recently, not in the eighteenth century. An abundance of geographical details put the narrative in the context of contemporary St. Petersburg. For example, the reader is informed about the current name of the street where Xenia's house was once located. On her icons, Xenia is put into the actual, not the imagined, landscape. Painters create icons with the recognizable landscapes of the Smolensk Cemetery, with crosses on the graves, and the chapel of Xenia and the Church of Smolensk Icon of the Mother of God. Not surprisingly, in their narratives about "meetings" with Xenia, visionaries see her at the bus stop, in the market, in the church, or by the chapel of Xenia at the Smolensk cemetery. Here is a typical story about meeting with Xenia, published on the web site for Russian amateur poets (stikhi.ru) in response to the poem "To Matushka Xenia," which was posted by a female poet:

> I met Xenia the Blessed in the underground two years ago. She came into the carriage at Lesnaya station and alighted at Finland rail station. In the carriage she blessed people loudly, asking only for one ruble.[20] She wore a faded pink coat and green skirt. I had

the luck to talk to her! She said to me, "Don't rely upon mind, but the God's will only. Say always: God is up and down, on your right and on your left, in front of you and behind you." This was like in the dream. I asked her, "Are you Xenia?" And she laughed with a thin little voice. People in the carriage got excited. "This is Xenia! This is Xenia!" and started opening their wallets. And she said something to everybody, very distinctly and loudly![21]

The holy icons of Xenia quickly inform us of her age. She is pictured grey-haired; on some images we can see wrinkles on her forehead. Interestingly, those visionaries who saw the Mother of God usually describe her appearance as bright but uncertain, as a woman shining in the divine light. In contrast, descriptions of Xenia are precise and realistic. In their narratives about miraculous Xenia meetings, dreams and visions, Xenia believers also often describe her appearance as an aged woman (*starushechka* or *pozhilaya zhenshchina*) dressed in an outmoded long skirt and jacket, with a headscarf on her head, as the following two examples illustrate. The first is from a popular collection of apparitions and miracles of the saints: "Her garment was common—a skirt, a cardigan, a warm plain handkerchief of deep purple color put on her head and wrapped around her neck. She held a stick and leaned on it. I remember very well her tired, reddened eyes" (Svidetel'stva 2006). A second example is from the book for children mentioned earlier: "They say that she wanders about St. Petersburg's streets today. She looks like an older, threadbare woman, like a typical pensioner" (Kundysheva 1995: 21). So St. Xenia resembles an archetypal representative of the majority of the contemporary Russian Orthodox flock—an aged lay woman.

"The Holy Fool" Versus "A Typical Pensioner"

The images of the female saint as they are offered in the official accounts of Xenia's life and in holy icons are altogether contradictory and uncertain. As a Fool for Christ, she appears strange and dangerous, whereas as a typical compatriot and neighbor, she appears as normal as common urban people. As we shall see later in this article, the images of St. Xenia are evolving in two separate directions that were silently proposed in earlier Church accounts of her life. In fact at least two different versions of Xenia's life and religious deeds existed, each with its own moral message.[22]

The Xenia as "Holy Fool" variant has been developing in the lay narratives written by professional or semi-professional writers in literature, movies, and drama. According to the official narratives, after her husband's death, Xenia took his name (Andrei Feodorovich) and wore his uniform (he had a rank of colonel). At her husband's funeral ceremony, she claimed that Andrei Feodorovich was alive and that it was his spouse, Xenia, who had died. The story about changing her name and changing her clothes expresses the quite traditional idea that a woman who is widowed changes gender. She symbolically dies as a woman, at least for the period of mourning. Xenia had no children and did not perform the traditional female role of mother. Hence, her female gender was weak and, consequently, a radical gender change was possible. However this fascinating story of gender change as a sign of becoming a *yurodivaya* is not stressed or even used by contemporary believers. This part of the story perhaps seems too exotic and extravagant for them; it makes their saint a strange and odd person. Although the holy icon with the transvestite image of Xenia does exist, it has not become popular. On the icons of Xenia which can be found literally in every church shop in Russia, one sees an elderly woman, clothed modestly and neatly in the female Orthodox style.

Among more than 70 holy images of St. Xenia collected by worshippers of the saint on the web site www.xenia-spb.narod.ru,[23] only one icon depicts Xenia in her husband's military uniform.[24] The Church (if one can

Illustration 9.2. Icons in a church shop at the Smolensk Cemetery. Photo by Jeanne Kormina.

talk about it as a unified actor) is not active in promoting this strange image of Xenia. It seems that the believers prefer to see their popular saint as a pensioner in a headscarf and long skirt rather than as a transvestite wearing a male military uniform.

In the lay narratives of Xenia, however, the very fact of her husband's death has become one of the key aspects of creating her image. Much attention has been paid to the fact that it is because of his death she has become a saint. The official narratives of the life of St. Xenia leave the figure of her husband vague and unclear. They mention that he was a chorister and a high-ranking officer, which must be very confusing for the contemporary reader.[25] Those readers who have some general knowledge about Russian history of the eighteenth century can draw a parallel with the famous favorite of Empress Elisabeth, Count Andrei Razumovskii, who started as a chorister in the court choir and then had a meteoric career.[26] This line of associations leads to an image of an unfaithful, empty-headed husband, as Xenia's husband is indeed depicted in the play by Levanov mentioned earlier. Included in the play is a scene of an accidental meeting between Xenia and her husband's former lover. Similarly, in folk narratives about Xenia recorded by Victor Toporov in Leningrad in the 1980s, Andrei Petrov is represented as a thoughtless officer: "Xenia was of princely birth and fell in love with an officer. But he was unfaithful to her. Then she gave away all her wealth and started to wander" (Toporov 1995). Other lay accounts of her life turn Xenia's spouse into "a dashing cavalry officer" (McLees 2000) and even "an army colonel who drank himself to death and who may have been an abusive, violent husband" (Forest 1997: 140). This narrative is one way to make St. Xenia seem unhappy and thus able to understand the suffering of other women. In contrast, other lay accounts of her life stress that Xenia and her husband loved each other very much. In these versions, when her husband died, she lost the closest person to her, and was forced to live alone in poverty. It is a critical point of transformation of the official image of the saint when her freely chosen asceticism turns into a forced disaster. Her suffering becomes her virtue. Here we see an easily recognizable portrait of a woman who can become a saint because of her pain and patience.

The circumstances of the death of Xenia's husband have also been subject to creative interpretation in latter accounts of the life of Xenia. According to pre-revolutionary narratives of her life, he died unexpectedly, and Xenia's religious life began after and because of his death.[27] The Church councilor document on Xenia's canonization and almost every lay version of the life of Xenia gives an explanation of how these two facts are connected. Generally, it is stated that in her grief Xenia took a vow to become a Fool for Christ to expiate the sins of her husband, who passed away without confessing (Kanonizatsia 1988: 107). In one of the recent versions of Xenia's life (an Orthodox educational project which appeared as a book, a 4-part DVD, and on a special Internet site approved by Patriarch Alexy titled *Scripture Lessons for Family and School*), the relationship is explained as follows: "Understanding that her husband's death was far from the ideal of the Christian decease, Saint Xenia decided to please God on behalf of her spouse who had passed away."[28] Some texts go so far as to blame her husband's drunkenness and even suicide as causes for his "less-than-ideal Christian death."[29] Traditionally, those who died of drunkenness (*opoitsy*) or committed suicide were buried out of a cemetery, and thus were symbolically excluded from the local community of Christians (Zelenin 1995). People were prohibited from praying for these deceased in the Church. However, in contemporary Russia there is a practice of petitions to diocesans from relatives of suicide victims asking to allow a church funeral and church prayer. These requests are often granted.[30]

The councilor versions of the official life of Xenia and some lay biographies of this saint tried to articulate an important and, in some respects, novel moral message addressed to female believers. They said that Xenia was a religious virtuoso who felt responsible for her husband's salvation and spent all her life trying to achieve it: "[T]o save her husband's soul Xenia repudiated herself (*otkazalas' ot sebia samoi*), she rejected her own name and took the name of her husband to live with it the rest of her life" (Kanonizatsia 1988: 107). The message is that contemporary female believers have to take care of the souls of their spouses. Indeed, in contemporary Russia, there are wives and mothers who represent their families in the church and who, in particular, have to organize a proper church burial ceremony for their deceased husbands, usually non-believers who perhaps were not even baptized. In these cases, a woman appears as the head of her family in the face of God. Her responsibility for the religious well-being of the family perhaps originates in her duty, during the Soviet period of shortages, to supply the household with food, clothes, and everything needed for its welfare. However, the majority of those who venerate Xenia the Blessed do not accept this message of responsibility for the salvation of a husband or the idea of a personal religious life composed of altruistic deeds of devotion. Most believers see the death of St. Xenia's husband as causing personal distress that led her to faith, as happens to many other people (since one who has lost everything becomes closer to God as a result ("vsio poteriali—blizhe k Bogu stali")).[31] They do not see her husband's death as the reason she became a "Holy Fool." Later Church versions of her life also omit the idea that she became *yurodivaya* as a voluntary penance for her husband's sins, leaving the story to lay artists who are very enthusiastic about that unusual idea (see, for example, the play by Levanov; the documentary by Plugatyreva; and others).[32] In the eyes of common believers, Xenia appears not as a religious virtuoso but as a lonely elderly woman whose faith helps her to get through the suffering of everyday earthly life. This popular image of her has become a model of religious life for the contemporary believer.

The Saint of Female Suffering

As we have already seen, St. Xenia is perceived by believers as a compatriot, a contemporary, and a neighbor. She is also a wise, experienced, female friend who can give good advice and support in complicated circumstances. The sphere of her competence includes experiences of suffering:

> Oh, Xenia Blazhennaya, you had so much patience!
> You suffered privations, and misfortune, you suffered for us.
> Mother [*Matushka*] Xenia, strengthen me in my patience,
> Help me to withstand my terrible grief.

> Oh, Xenia Blazhennaya, you are so tired!
> You are tired of suffering and crying for everyone.
> Mother [*Matushka*] Xenia, I am absolutely exhausted,
> And I won't withstand without your prayerful help.[33]

These are strophes from a song about *matushka Xenia* that is quite popular among female believers. We heard it many times near Xenia's shrine: women pilgrims singing this song together with the akathist, or instead of it. Anthropologist Detelina Tocheva (see chapter 5, this volume) told us that her church-going female informants in the village of Maloe Zamostie, located about 40 kilometers from St. Petersburg, performed this song in chorus at somebody's birthday party together with secular lyrical songs of Soviet origin. Both the melody and poetry of the song are similar to pseudo-folk Soviet lyric songs that focused a great deal on feelings. In this particular song, the singer addresses Xenia Blazhennaya, comparing their life experiences and asking for moral support. The singer believes that Xenia can give her help because she suffered herself and, as a result of this personal experience, she can understand and support another woman, a believer.

In the song, as well as in their letters to Xenia, people call her *matushka*, which is a typical address to a church-going female believer from other members of the believing group. This word is one of the linguistic markers of belonging to a particular social group—in this case to the community of believers. In other words, the saint is a member of this community. She is not the sort of saint who supervises and punishes (like Paraskeva Piatnitsa); she is the sort of saint who feels compassion and helps.

In their letters to St. Xenia, believers constantly represent themselves as poor people who experience the deprivation of something indispensable for normal human existence, such as family relationships, money to survive, or health. They deserve the attention of Xenia not because of their extraordinary piety, but just because of their desperate need for her assistance. In a letter to St. Xenia one can find such words: "As far as I have nothing to give you in return [for your help], help me just because [*prosto tak*]. ... There are zealous slaves of God who apply to you. But there are also the ordinary and weak [like us]" (Iakovleva 2006: 26). The humility of a person is a special quality that increases her chances to be heard by the saint who, according to popular conception, reached sanctity through suffering.

Who are the women who come to the church and why? There are at least three social features typical of the women who participate in religious activities. The first one is their professional position. Many of these women do not have a prestigious profession or have not achieved success in their job (examples include a woman from an account office in the ship factory, a physician working in an outpatients' clinic, a school teacher, a cleaner). Sometimes they have lost their jobs and failed to find a good new job, or have accepted early retirement. In the Church, these women have a chance to start a new life. Some of them find a new job there, working as cleaners or vendors in church shops, or singing in the choir, or as sextons. These positions give them some money, but what is even more important, these new jobs place them in the center of church life. These church workers often pretend to have expert knowledge on different religious questions. Alongside this, many female religious activists use their church activities to interpret dreams and to give necessary information to people looking for some special icon or prayer, or to lead pilgrimages as a kind of social service that is highly respected in their society.

Age, with its challenges, is another rather evident feature of this group. While in the secular world the personal social capital of a woman is often her fertility and sexual attractiveness, which decrease as she becomes older, her status in the religious community depends on her religious knowledge and experience and increases with her age. In the religious context, old age has very positive connotations; only elders can become living saints, or *startsy.*

The third social characteristic shared by many of these women is their loneliness, caused by changes in their family status. Now in their fifties, the family project they participated in as wives and mother has often run its course. The structure of their family has changed radically. Children grow up and build their own separate families; their mother's expertise is not needed anymore. The husband (if he was in the family) has sometimes already died, although more often, he has just left. Sometimes when there is an official relationship with a spouse, in reality the couple is separated. Men escape by drinking and watching TV. They join the virtual community of the TV-addicted or a "male club" focusing on a specific male activity, like car repair or playing chess. It is significant that these husbands often do not share their wives' religiousness. At most, the non-religious husband tolerates his wife's religiosity, considering her to be a freak or worse, mocking her religiosity, hurting her feelings and reducing her self-respect; sometimes he even tries to ban her religious activities. Stories of this sort can be found in the books written by Orthodox writers and recounted by women as part of their life stories (see, for example, a story titled "The Victory over Death" by Father Nikolay Agafonov (1997: 6–23)). The best gift that a husband can give to his wife is his consent to a church wedding ceremony. Martha, whom we encountered early on in this article, proudly explained that her husband (baptized in his childhood but not a religious person) agreed to their church wedding as a present to her for their 50th wedding anniversary.

The majority of women who participate more or less actively in church life take their religious involvement as a sort of cultural activity. For them, the church plays the role of a sort of female club where women find a new social context in which to function. This resocialization gives them an opportunity to enjoy a new social status and a role that is respected in contemporary society.

Conclusion

What does the Church need saints for? The theological answer to this question was given by St. Augustine the Blessed. He argued with a Manichean who contended that Christians had "turned the idols into martyrs" and worshiped them instead of idols. St. Augustine responded, "It is true that Christians pay religious honor to the memory of the martyrs, both to excite us to imitate them and to obtain a share in their merits, and the assistance of their prayers."[34] In other words, for a Christian believer saints are role models and helpers. And it is obvious enough that certain saints are perceived more as helpers than as role models, and vice versa.

Why does the Church need new saints? We suppose that in these saints, images and ideas of sanctity are reconstituted, and the continuing gracefulness of the church and actuality of ancient dogmatic and moral truths are proven. To fulfill this function the profile of a new saint should be up-to-date, and it must be possible to understand the main idea of his or her Christian mission and to imitate the saint's religious deeds in the current social circumstances, or there must be maximal recognizability of his or her social position and life experience. The former meaning creates a perfect role model, and the latter one represents the portrait of an ideal helper—a saint patron for every venerator who hopes that the saint will understand the nature of his or her problem. Ideally those two aspects of the saint's role coincide, but this is often impossible. Moreover, the prospects for the imitation of a saint's life are sometimes very problematic. June Macklin, who considered a similar problem in Latin American Catholicism, noted that according to church teachings, saints "were to be perceived both as model of and models for behavior, which introduced yet another tension into the system: these spiritual overachievers were both imitable, and inherently inimitable" (1988: 70). Indeed, almost any endeavor to imitate a saint's behavior appears to be too conceited for a Christian. One can find a clear example of this idea in the story "Father Serafim" by popular contemporary writer Maja Kucherskaya. She tells us about a woman who decided to imitate St. Xenia and intentionally lost her husband and home. Although the protagonist of the story thought that she acted like her favorite saint, in actuality, her behavior was selfish and irresponsible. By imitating St. Xenia, she turned into the antipode of the saint (Kucherskaya 2004: 220–24). This point leads us to reflect upon the reasons for and receptions of the canonization process.

When canonizing Xenia the Blessed, the initiators of the glorification tried to reconcile the functions of role models and protectors by including the moral message on the religious predestination of wives and widows into the veneration of the popular saint. But St. Xenia's life misfortunes turned out to be closer than the greatness of her Christian devotion to the majority of believers.

Does this mean that the Church did not achieve its aim? We think it does not. Xenia became much more popular. It is the early versions of her life that give to believers a wide potential for interpretation. She is a saint for the urban people; for St. Petersburg citizens in particular; for the aged and the poor; for the single and the separated; for people from lower classes; for women. She is the saint of irregular believers, and a dynamic channel for Church newcomers.

Notes

We wish to acknowledge with gratitude that research for this chapter was supported in part by a grant (09-01-0060) from the Scientific Foundation of the State University—Higher School of Economics (Moscow).

1. Technically, 1988 was not yet post-Soviet, as the dissolution of the Soviet Union officially occurred in 1991.
2. The first two saints on the list are the Great Prince of Moscow Dimitry Donskoi, whose name is closely associated with a famous victory over Khan Mamai of the

Tatar Golden Horde at the Kulikovo battlefield (1380) and with the political independence of Rus', and the greatest Old Russian icon painter Andrei Rublev. In
the Soviet era, Rublev was considered a symbol of ancient Russian spirituality. It
should be added that by Church tradition the sequence of the list of new saints
formally depends on dates of their death.

3. Xenia is the first woman "holy fool" (or a fool for Christ) glorified by the Russian
    Orthodox Church. Fools for Christ with their peculiar ways of behavior constitute
    a special type of saints in Orthodoxy. They pretend to be insane to conceal their
    piety and divine abilities. As secret ascetics, holy fools can practice speaking in
    riddles and unconventional behavior to challenge accepted norms. For more about
    this type of saint, see Ivanov (2006). It also should be noted that Xenia was initially
    canonized by the Russian Orthodox Church Abroad (ROCA) in 1978. That canon-
    ically semi-autonomous Church was founded by Russian post-revolution immi-
    grants as an alternative to the Russian Orthodox Church of Moscow Patriarchate
    in Soviet Russia. As an independent institution, ROCA canonized some persons
    and established their veneration. We will discuss St. Xenia's image in ROCA pub-
    lications later in this chapter. In 2007, the Act of Canonical Unity between the
    Moscow Patriarchate and ROCA was signed in Moscow as a symbol of the reunion
    of both branches of the Russian Orthodox Church.

4. In the Soviet period, secular modern people such as students of the Leningrad
    State University located in the same part of St. Petersburg as Xenia's chapel used to
    visit her grave before taking their exams.

5. In Orthodox Christianity a hymn, dedicated to God, the Mother of God, a saint, or
    a holy event.

6. For more details about publishing letters to Xenia in church publications as an
    advertising strategy by the Church, see Kormina and Shtyrkov (2008).

7. On the history and functioning of Orthodox akathists, see Shevzov (2007).

8. For a discussion of the self-identification of Soviet intelligentsia, see, for example,
    White (2000).

9. The woman's name has been changed to protect her anonymity.

10. The functioning of independent pilgrimage "agencies" and "services" are analyzed
    in more detail in Kormina 2010.

11. For some authors, Xenia seems to be too independent. This can be a challenge
    for the regular Orthodox believer, who has said many times that obedience to a
    spiritual father is the main Christian virtue and an indispensable condition for sal-
    vation. From the early "traditional" variants of the account of her life, it could be
    concluded that it was Xenia's own decision to become a "holy fool." But, as Gip-
    pius argues, "No one can become a Holy Fool of one's own free will and wish. It
    is absolutely necessary to get a special blessing" (2008: 32). And Xenia's confessor
    and spiritual tutor, who allegedly gave her the blessing to become a Holy Fool, was
    found in the remote monastery in the Upper-Volga region: "There is an opinion
    that Xenia spent several years at the Alekseevkaya female cloister that had been
    founded by Theodor of Sanaxar" (Svyataya 2003; Kozlovskaya 2002: 31). St. The-
    odor was the spiritual tutor of that cloister and might have been a preceptor for
    Xenia, if one accepts that idea about Xenia's absence from St. Petersburg for several
    years to visit remote monasteries and receive spiritual instructions from monks.

12. It should be said that the secrecy of the "holy fools'" piety is commonly described in
    the relevant hagiography. See Ivanov (2006: 170–71) and Saward (1980: 16–20).

13. See http://www.interfax-religion.ru/?act=interview&div=206 (accessed 2 November 2009).
14. Trofimov says about thirteen women were canonized for All-Church veneration (1993). In some works, the short list has been enlarged to include locally-venerated saints (Slovar 1862).
15. The information reflects the situation before mass canonization of "new martyrs" in the 2000s when the Church glorified more than 1,500 new saints.
16. Actually it was not a canonization in the proper sense. Yulianiya was a local saint for Murom town. In 1903 her name was included in a Church calendar of Orthodox saints (*Mesyatsslov Vostoka*) (Evgeni 1910).
17. See also Uspenskii (1982: 134–38).
18. On women and icon veneration, see Shevzov (2000: 616, n. 17); on female monastic communities see works by Brenda Meehan-Waters (1986, 1991); see also Belyakova and Belyakova (2001).
19. See Belyakova and Belyakova (2001); Posternak (2004); and Wagner (2007).
20. This motif is borrowed from the official account of the life of Xenia. Although she begged, she accepted only kopeck coins.
21. The response is dated 6 April 2007. See http://www.stihi.ru/comments.html ?2007/05/04-68 (accessed 13 March 2009). The author of the response, Valeria, who is also an amateur poet, changed gender from male to female some fifteen years ago (she is now in her mid 40s). Her narrative about meeting with Xenia looks like a natural expression of her femininity. She has her special reasons to venerate this saint of loneliness and social suffering because she knows very well what it means to be abandoned by society.
22. It should be mentioned here that the followers of the Russian Orthodox Church Abroad who canonized Xenia in 1978 tend to stress her homelessness. The text of the church service which canonized her also reflects this ("Service to St. Xenia" 1978: 155).
23. Accessed 15 December 2008.
24. The attention to what is depicted on holy icons is a rather new phenomenon in Orthodox religious culture. As Sergey Shtyrkov's study about the veneration of icons by modern Russian peasants demonstrates, this type of believer often perceived the holy images as just sacred objects, and simply was not interested in who was painted on the old icons they called *bozhen'ka* ("a little God") and situated in the Red corners of their houses. The name, not the image, of this sacred object revealed its nature and function (e.g., the icon of the Mother of God, "The [Inflammable Bush," helped to extinguish or localize fire (Shtyrkov 2006). It should be said that contemporary urban believers definitely look at the icons they buy in church shops. It seems that the message about speciality of a particular saint now can be read from his or her image rather then from a biography or name.
25. The statement that Xenia's husband was a colonel occurs in every version of her life. We know just one author—Orthodox writer Nikolai Koniaev—who questions this fact. He hypothesizes that the figure of Andrei Petrov unites the traits of several historical personages (Koniaev 2003).
26. See the documentary *In the Name of Love: Xenia the Blessed of St. Petersburg,* made in 2007 (director Elena Plugatyreva) for the Russian TV channel Kultura ("Culture"). The text in the movie is recited by one of the most popular actors of St. Petersburg, Andrey Tolubeev (1945–2008).

27. This motif is repeated in the life story of a non-canonized venerated *staritsa* Matronushka-bosonozhka (barefooted) (1840s–1911), who also lived in St. Petersburg. According to one version of her biography, she became a "holy fool for Christ" after her husband's death in the Russian–Turkish war (1877–78), in which she had served as a nurse. Possibly, this motif was borrowed from the accounts of the life of Xenia.
28. See http://zakonbozhiy.ru/Zakon_Bozhij/Chast_1_O_vere_i_zhizni_hristianskoj/Zhitie_sv._Ksenii_ Peterburgskoi/ (accessed 13 March 2009). The author of the project is Father Serafim Slobodsky.
29. See the documentary *In the Name of Love: Xenia the Blessed of St. Petersburg*.
30. The suicide rate in Russia has almost doubled since 1990 and is now one of the highest in the world; more than 80 percent of those who have committed suicide are men (Gilinsky and Rumiantseva 2004).
31. This is the title of one of the chapters in the book of letters sent by believers to Xenia the Blessed (Iakovleva 2006).
32. In a poem by Natalia Piskunova, Xenia exclaims, "And then I will put on his [Andrei's] shroud and consequently his sins" (see http://www.tropinka.orthodoxy.ru/zal/poezija/piskunov.htm (accessed 20 June 2009)); Dmitri Bobyshev writes that "Blessed Xenia's love ravished him from the somber shadow of Hell" (1981).
33. Translated, this passage reads: *Ksenia Blazhennaya, kak zhe ty terpela! / Ty za vsekh terpela gore i nuzhdu. / Ukrepi v terpenii, Matushka Xenia, / Pomogi mne vynesti tiazhkuyu bedu. Ksenia Blazhennaya, kak zhe ty ustala / Ty za vsekh ustala plakat' i stradat' / Ya v iznemozhenii, Matushka Xenia, / Bez tvoei molitvy mne ne ustojat.*
34 Contra Faustum Manichæum XX, 21

References

Afanas'ev, Alexander N. 1990. *Narodnye Russkie Legendy*. Novosibirsk: Nauka.
Agafonov, Nikolay. 2007. *Doroga Domoi*. Moscow: Sibirskaya blagozvonnitsa.
Basha, Violetta. 2001. "Serdtse Okayannogo Goroda." *Moya Sem'ya* 29.
Belyakova, Elena V., and Nadezhda A. Belyakova. 2001. "Obsuzhdenie Voprosa o Diakonisakh na Pomestnom Sobore 1917-1918 gg." *Tserkovno-istoricheskii Vestnik* 8: 139–61.
Bobyshev, Dmitry. 1981. "Xenia Peterburzhskaya." *Kontinent* 28: 83–86.
Evgeni. 1910. *O Tserkovnom Proslavlenii i Pochitanii Iulianii Lazorevskoy*. Murom: tipolit. M.V. Zvorykina.
Fedotov, George P. 1990. *Sviatye Drevnei Rusi*. Moscow: Moskovskii Rabochii.
Filicheva, Oksana. 2006. "Zapiski dlia Xenii Blazhennoi: Pozitsiia Tserkovnosluzhiteley i Narodny Obychay." In *Sny Bogoroditsy. Issledivanija po Antropologii Religii*, ed. Zhanna V. Kormina, Sergey A. Shtyrkov and Alexander A. Panchenko, 171–83. St. Petersburg: European University at St. Petersburg.
Forest, Jim. 1997. *Praying with Icons*. New York: Orbis Books.
Gilinsky, Iakov, and Galina Rumiantseva. 2004. "Dinamika Samoubiistv v Rossii." *Demoskop Weekly* (June 7–20): 161–62. http://demoscope.ru/weekly/2004/0161/analit01.php (accessed 13 March 2009).

Gippius, Anna. 2008. *Xenia Blazhennaya, Sviatoi Panteleimon*. Moscow: AST.

Iakovleva, Liudmila. 2006. *U Nee Liubvi Khvatit na Vsekh. Divnaya Pomoshch Sviatoy Xenii Prostym Liudiam. Neizvestnye Svidetel'stva Nashikh Dney. Pis'ma Nadezhdy i Utesheniya.* St. Petersburg: Sobesednik Pravoslavnykh Khristian.

Ivanov, Sergey. 2006. *Holy Fools in Byzantium and Beyond.* Oxford: Oxford University Press.

Kanonizatsia. 1988. Kanonizatsiya Sviatykh. Pomestny Sobor Russkoi Pravoslavnoi Tserkvi, Posviashchenny Iubileiu 1000-letiya Kreshcheniya Rusi. Troitse-Sergieva Lavra, June 6–9 1988 g. Moscow.

Kizenko, Nadezhda. 2003. "Protectors of Women and Lower Orders: Constructing Sainthood in Modern Russia." In *Orthodox Russia: Belief and Practice under the Tsars,* ed. Robert H. Green and Valery A. Kivelson, 189 –218. University Park, PA: Penn State University Press.

Koniaev, Nikolay M. 2003. "Russkaya Sviatost' Peterburga (Blazhennaya Xenia)." *Vera-Eskom* 440.

Kormina, Jeanne. 2010. *"Avtobusniki*: The Longing for Authenticity in Among Russian Religious Travellers." In *Anthropology of Eastern Christianities,* ed. Chris Hann and Hermann Goltz, 267–86. Berkeley, CA: University of California Press.

Kormina, Jeanne, and Sergey Shtyrkov. 2008. "Pis'ma Veruyushchikh kak Reklama: 'Vsenarodnaya Priemnaya sv. Xenii Peterburgskoi." *Antropologicheskii Forum* 9: 154–84.

Kozlovskaya, V. 2002. "U Beregov Reki Smolenki." *Pravoslavny Palomik* 4 (6): 30–34.

Kucherskaya, Maya. 2004. *Sovremenny Paterik. Chenie Dlia Vpavshikh v Unynie.* St. Petersburg: Bibliopolis.

Kundysheva, Emilia A. 1995. *"O Chem Ty Plachesh,' Andrey Feodorovich?"* St. Petersburg: Litsey.

Levin, Eve. 2006. "The Christian Sources of the Cult of St. Paraskeva." In *Letters from Heaven: Popular Religion in Russia and Ukraine,* ed. John-Paul Himka and Andriy Zayarnyak, 126–45. Toronto: University of Toronto Press.

Levkievskaya, Elena E. 2001. "Materialy k Slovariu Polesskoi Etnokul'turnoy Leksiki (Opyt Kompiuternoy Obrabotki Vostochnoslavianskoy Dialektnoy Leksiki). Demonologiya." In *Vostochnoslaviansky Etnolingvistichesky Sbornik.Issledovaniya i Materialy,* ed. Olga V. Belova, Elena E. Levkievskaya, Anna A. Plotnikova and Svetlana M. Tolstaya, 379–431. Moscow: Indrik.

Macklin, June. 1988. "Two Faces of Sainthood: The Pious and the Popular." *Journal of Latin American Lore* 14: 67–90.

McLees, Nun Nectaria. 2000. "Life of Saint Xenia of Petersburg." In *A Child's Paradise Of Saints,* 59-61. Indianapolis, IN: Christ the Saviour Brotherhood.

Meehan-Waters, Brenda. 1986. "Popular Piety, Local Initiative and the Founding of Women's Religious Communities in Russia, 1764–1907." *St. Vladimir's Theological Quarterly* 30, no. 2: 117–41.

———. 1991. "Metropolitan Filaret (Drozdov) and the Reform of Russian Women's Monastic Communities." *The Russian Review* 50: 310–23.

Metropolitan Kirill. 2002. "Rossiya—Pravoslavnaya, a ne Mnogokonfessional'naya Strana." *Pravoslavnaya Gazeta (Yeaketerinburg)* 42.

Orsi, Robert. 1996. *Thank You, Saint Jude: Women's Devotion to the Patron Saint of Hopeless Causes.* New Haven, CT: Yale University Press.

Posternak, Andrey. 2004. "Diakonisa: Mezhdu Monastyrem i Mirom." *Neskuchny Sad* 2 (9): http://www.nsad.ru/index.php?issue=10&section=10031&article=252 (accessed 12 May 2011)..

Saward, John. 1980. *Perfect Fools: Folly for Christ's Sake in Catholic and Orthodox Spirituality.* Oxford: Oxford University Press.

"Service to St. Xenia." 1978. *The Orthodox Word* 14, no. 4: 155–89.

Shevzov, Vera. 2000. "Icons, Miracles, and Orthodox Communal Identity in Late Imperial Russia." *Church History* 69 (September): 610–31.

——. 2007 "Between 'Popular' and 'Official': *Akafisty* Hymns and Marian Icons in Late Imperial Russia." In *Orthodox Russia: Belief and Practice Under the Tsars,* ed. Robert H. Green and Valery A. Kivelson, 251–78. University Park, PA: Penn State University Press.

Shtyrkov, Sergey. 2006. "On Perspective of Investigation of Icon Veneration in Russian Popular Culture." Unpublished paper presented at the research seminar of the Collegium for Advanced Studies, Helsinki (November).

Slovar. 1862. *Slovar' Istorichesky o Sviatykh, Proslavlennykh v Rossiiskoi Tserkvi, i o Nekotorykh Podvizhnikakh Blagochestiya, Mestno Chtimykh.* St. Petersburg.

Svidetel'stva. 2006. *Svidetel'stva o Pomoshchi Blazhennoi Xenii v Razlichnykh Nuzhdakh, Bedakh i Skorbiakh.* http://xenia-spb.narod.ru/htmls/help1.htm (accessed 13 March 2009).

Svyataya. 2003. "Sviataya Blazhennaya Xenia Peterburgskaya." *Sankt-Peterburgskie Eparkhial'nye Vedomosti* 30–31.

Toporov, Viktor N. 1995. "Teksty Blazhennoi Xenii Peterburgskoi i ee Kul'ta (po Materialam Smolenskogo Kladbishcha, 70–80 gg. XX v." In *Mif. Ritual. Simvol. Obraz. Issledovaniya v Oblasti Mifopoeticheskogo.* Moscow: Progress.

Trofimov, Alexander. 1993. *Sviatye Zheny Rusi.* Moscow: Entsiklopediya Rossiiskikh dereven'.

Uspenskii, Boris. 1982. *Filologicheskie Razyskaniya v Oblasti Slavianskikh Drevnostei (Relikty yazychestva v vostochnoslavianskom Kul'te Nikolaya Mirlikiiskogo).* Moscow: Izdatel'stvo Moskovskogo universiteta.

Wagner, William G. 2007. "'Orthodox Domesticity': Creating a Social Role for Women." In *Sacred Stories: Religion and Spirituality in Modern Russian Culture,* ed. Mark Steinberg and Heather J. Coleman, 119–45. Bloomington, IN: Indiana University Press.

White, Anne. 2000. "Social Change in Provincial Russia: The Intelligentsia in *Raion* Center." *Europe-Asia Studies* 52, no. 4: 677–94.

Yurchak, Alexei. 2006. *Everything Was Forever Until It Was No More: The Last Soviet Generation.* Princeton, NJ: Princeton University Press.

Zelenin, Dmitry K. 1995. *Ocherki Russkoi Mifologii. Umershie Neestestvennoi Smertiu i Rusalki.* Moscow: Indrik.

Zhizneopisaniya. 1906–1912. *Zhizneopisaniya Otechestvennnykh Podvizhnikov Blagochesiya XVIII i XIX vekov.* 12 vols. Moscow: Izdatel'stvo Afonskogo russkogo Panteleimonovskogo monastyria.

 CHAPTER 10

Built with Gold or Tears?
Moral Discourses on Church Construction and the Role of Entrepreneurial Donations

Tobias Köllner

Introduction

During the socialist period, many of Vladimir's[1] churches were destroyed, fell into decline, or were used for other purposes, such as radio stations or museums. Today, the Russian Orthodox Church (ROC) is the most trusted institution in Russia (Dubin 2006: 84), and there exists a general tendency to restore former church buildings and to erect new ones in places where churches had been before the 1917 Russian Revolution. Although most people favor returning the former church buildings to the ROC, some voice reservations due to the fact that good museums will vanish, and that the newly established churches will be used by only a few parishioners.

The most serious problem the Church faces in the context of its reconstruction is the financing of building activities. According to the Russian Constitution, the state and the ROC are separated and no money can easily be directed to the Church. But since the presidency of Vladimir Putin, the official separation has become blurred, and the ROC is supported by the state in many ways. One way of supporting the ROC is to declare its church buildings as instances of architectural heritage, which enables the ROC to receive state funding for their reconstruction. Nevertheless, the ROC is still highly dependent on donations from private entrepreneurs. In particular, the erection of new church buildings requires substantial donations. In only a few instances have parishioners managed to carry out the restoration of a church building on their own without help from the diocese or from rich businesspeople. In such cases, contributions are made in the form of labor rather than money. The parishioners form a close group of people and many of them spend every free minute on the construction site helping to restore the church.

Charitable giving, labor contributions and donations to the ROC are often morally charged and carry moral meanings. For this reason I connect donations by businesspeople to the sphere of morality. Morality, as Jarrett

Zigon argues in the introduction, can be distinguished into three different but interrelated aspects of morality: 1) the institutional; 2) that of public discourse; and 3) embodied dispositions. In this chapter, I am mainly concerned with the second aspect of morality—public discourses. There are conflicting public discourses pertaining to both types of church-building activities: churches built with gold and churches built with tears. In the first instance, churches built with gold, charitable contributions (*blagotvoritel'nost'*) and donations (*pozhertvovanie, darenie*) are collected from the rich, most of whom are entrepreneurs. But this is not uncontroversial, as some people question the underlying motivations of donors and contrast them with their own penitential[2] labor contributions. By shifting the emphasis away from the beauty or quantity of the erected churches to the arduousness of the labor contributed to build them, those who build churches with their effort and tears are able to claim moral superiority. Consequently, these laborers derogatively depict donations as a way to do penance that is much too easy.

Although both public discourses on church construction are of equal importance in today's Russia, in this chapter I put more emphasis on entrepreneurial donations because entrepreneurs have been the focus of my research. I will show that a combination of religious, moral, and self-interested motivations is characteristic of donations by entrepreneurs. Thus donations can be understood as attempts to compensate for one's sins and as a way to make the possession of wealth more legitimate. Following a more detailed description of churches built with gold I will give a short portrayal of the contrasting discourse, churches built with tears.

The History of Church Donations until the 1917 Revolution

Donations to churches and charity have a long history in Russia. Charitable food donations for people in need were mentioned among the deeds of Prince Vladimir who founded the city of the same name in 995 (Patriarch Aleksii II 2002: 331). In his edict from 996 he ordered the church to do charitable work (in these times called 'societal care' *obshchestvennoe prizrenie,* see also Guliaeva 2003: 126) and in return introduced the church tithe (Patriarch Aleksii II 2002: 331). Charity remained a prerogative of the church until the seventeenth century when the state took over the responsibility from the church (Patriarch Aleksii II 2002: 331). In 1781, a law was enacted which made private donations to various institutions possible (333). As a result of the reforms of 1864 and 1870, the responsibility for charity was handed over to local authorities (city or rural administrations) and charity became dependent on private contributions. At first, donations were given mainly by aristocrats, but the rise of trade and industry in the nineteenth century enabled private merchants and entrepreneurs to participate. By the end of that century, 75 percent of all donations were given by non-aristocrats (ibid.).

In the seventeenth century, older wooden churches in Vladimir were replaced by newer ones built with stone. Even then, some of these churches were financed with donations made by local people. In 1896, 21 charitable societies (*blagotvoritel'nye obshchestva*) and 79 charitable institutions existed in the Vladimir region (Guliaeva 2003: 126–27). These organizations were mainly supported by rich merchants (*kuptsy*) and entrepreneurs (*predprinimatelia*) who owned the newly established industrial factories for glass, steel, and other manufactured goods. Especially famous for their substantial donations were Old-Believer merchants, who formed a substantial part of the merchants' guilds until the revolution. Besides the donations to the ROC and people in need, support for artists was widespread until the revolution. The best-known examples of institutions financed in this way are the Tret'iakov gallery in Moscow and the artists' colony in Abramtsevo.

Local Interpretations of Donations by Clergymen

In contrast to the West, where help for people in need is often linked to religious organizations, the contemporary ROC has tried to avoid taking up a role as a provider of social support. Only in big cities such as Moscow or St. Petersburg is the ROC forced to take a different stance by the threat of competition, mainly from Protestants. In these places, the ROC engages in charitable work by running soup kitchens and providing health care and housing for homeless people (see for example Caldwell (2004) for the description of a soup kitchen).[3] In general, donations are perceived as an opportunity for believers to do good, which secures their own salvation. In order to clarify this point, I would like to cite Father Vladimir[4] who works in an Orthodox school and serves in one of the biggest churches in the city. He is also the person in the diocese who is responsible for donations made to his church. The Orthodox school was situated next to my son's kindergarten, which gave me the opportunity to meet him regularly. After some time, he invited me to the school as well as to the church. His reasons for engaging with me were twofold. On one hand, he was interested in talking about religion in general, and about religion in Germany in particular. On the other hand, he hoped to convert me to Orthodoxy. Here is how Father Vladimir explained the ROC's approach to charity:

> As far as I know, charitable programs [*blagotvoritel'nye programmy*] are very popular in the West. Many publicly known people like art-

ists or politicians perceive it as an honor to take part in such programs. They give considerable amounts to such programs. They fight against AIDS, fight against hunger in Africa and in Asia; in their own countries, they fight against poverty or unemployment.

In Orthodoxy, however, the form for organizing charity is somewhat different. The Orthodox Church considers the first and most important help for people is to put them on the right path. [The Church] says: the most important help for people is to help them to begin to believe in Christ. The most important help for someone is a prayer for him. ...

Because God, He says: "Strive for spiritual gifts" [see 1 Cor. 14:1] first and foremost, because only this will save you. Christ himself is called "true bread" [*istinnyi khleb*]. He [Jesus Christ] says: "Man does not live by bread alone" [*ne khlebom edinym zhiv chelovek*] [see Luke 4:4]. ... We will never overcome misery [*nishcheta*] and poverty [*bednost'*]. This is clear. But I don't know if this is clear in the West. In Russia this has already been clear for a long time. In Russia they tried to build a heavenly Kingdom for a long time, 70 years. They tried to build heaven on earth, to feed all. Communism—this was to give everyone sweets, a piece of bread, and so on. But this is, of course, fraud and deceit [*lozh' i obman*]. And even Christ Himself says: "Poor people will always exist, but the human Son will not be with you forever" [see John 12:8 and Mark 14:7]. He said this before his death, he told his disciples. ...

Our Orthodox Church in contemporary secular society, in Russian society, lately argued very seriously against ... against an understanding of the Church as some sort of a social institution [*nekotoryi sotsial'nyi institut*]. [He describes this view.] Let's say the church—this is a charitable institution, the church is established for people who go to this church and can share their material wealth and they can be sure the wealth is spread correctly. This view on charity is wrong. And our Orthodox Church says: Orthodoxy is not like this. The Church of Christ is first and foremost the mystic body of Christ, first and foremost the illustration [*aktualisatsiia*] of the heavenly kingdom on earth.[5]

Father Vladimir opposes a Western understanding of charity, where donations for different goals are collected in order to overcome misery, poverty, and illnesses. Referring to the Bible, he argues that misery and poverty will always exist and there is no way to prevent them. Rather, donations are perceived as a way of securing one's own salvation, and not as a feasible way to change the world. Consequently, he describes the socialist attempt to care for everyone as "fraud and deceit" because there can be no heavenly kingdom on earth. Therefore, the ROC as an institution does not engage in very much charity work, and it tries to avoid the image of being a social institution which can do something about the rising inequality and poverty in Russian society. Rather, the Church puts emphasis on the next world, for which belief and prayer are most important. Thus Father Vladimir stresses the importance of leading people to the Church and showing them the "right path," which consists of the belief in God. In his view, only the accumulation of spiritual wealth—what he calls "true bread"—is of use for one's salvation.

The interview shows how money is mainly used by the ROC: less for charitable purposes and primarily for the erection of new churches and the adornment (*ukrashenie*) or reconstruction of existing ones. Whereas the churches of Protestant congregations in Russia, as well as elsewhere, are rather plain, Orthodox churches are decorated extensively because they are conceived of as an image of heaven on earth. With this purpose, they herald the good times to come and are thought to attract believers due to their beauty and mystique. In addition to the function of visualizing heaven, Father Vladimir stresses an understanding of the church itself as the mystical body of Christ. This mysticism is not very compatible with a focus on improving the material world through charitable donations.[6]

Another priest also supported the use of donations for the adornment of churches for quite different reasons. According to this priest, it is easy to see the results of money used for the decoration of a church, while no one can control where the money goes if it is used for charitable purposes. Thus he used donations to his parish mainly for the reconstruction or adornment of church buildings in order to avoid accusations of corruption or misuse of the donated money.

In another interview, Father Vladimir is less concerned about donations given as charity than with donations given by rich businesspeople who want to build a church:

> Father Vladimir: Today's businessmen absolutely do not think about it [*votserkovlenie*]. They say: "See, you pray better and so pray." [He continues imitating a businessman:] "See, you need money and I will give it to you so that a bell tower can be bought [*chtoby kolokol kupit'*]. And you will pray for me and everything will be fine with me [*A ty za menia pomolis', pust' u menia budet khorosho*]." This is like a bribe for God [*vziatka Bogu*], yes. But this is stupid, of course, because God does not take bribes. God, He does not need a bell tower. God needs your soul, your heart.
>
> Tobias Köllner: And not the money.

> Father Vladimir: Of course! I will take the money, thank him, and will build the bell tower. And I will pray for this man. But if he himself does not turn to God, hardly anything good will happen. God does not take bribes [*Bog vziatok ne prinimaet*].

In the interview, Father Vladimir describes his perception of the attitude of most entrepreneurs towards the Church. Only a few entrepreneurs really think about religion and the process of inchurchment (*votserkovlenie*), according to his interpretation. *Votserkovlenie* characterizes the process of deeply engaging with the church, and to follow the clergy's prescriptions strictly. Inchurchment addresses the idea that one should work on oneself in order to come closer to the Church and in this way to one's own salvation as the Church perceives itself as the necessary institution for salvation. According to Father Vladimir it means to think about one's soul (*razmyshliat' o svoei dushe*) and to connect one's life to God (*sviazyvat' zhizn' svoiu s Bogom*). He imitates an entrepreneur who orders prayers from him for his soul and in return gives money for the construction or reconstruction of a bell tower. His language is quite explicit when he uses phrases such as "to buy" (*kupit'*) to characterize how entrepreneurs understand their relationship to the Church. In the related context of blessings[7] he coined the term "spiritual service" (*dukhovnaia usluga*) when the person who ordered the blessing did not take part in it himself. Similarly, Father Vladimir depicts donations that are understood as a payment for one's sins as a bribe (*vziatka*) to God if they are not accompanied by a real change in behavior. A real change in behavior, in his eyes, involves the process of inchurchment, and requires that the person starts to think about God and not only about success in business.

Although Father Vladimir does not talk about penance explicitly, his understanding of a change in behavior is based on the concept of penance. Only if the donation is understood as a form of penance and is accompanied by a change in behavior can it bring about salvation. If the person does not turn to God he or she will get no results from the donation because, according to Father Vladimir, God does not accept "bribes." The Church will instead take the money and as a priest he will pray for the donor. The prayer is less for the removal of sins and done more with the intention of turning the entrepreneur to the Church, which, in Father Vladimir's view, is the only way to salvation.

Following Foucault's (1993: 222) distinction between two techniques of self-knowledge in Christianity, auricular confession (*exaugoresis*) and public penance (*exomologesis*), Kharkhordin (1999: 61ff) claims a predominance of the latter in Orthodoxy. This view is supported by Father Vladimir's account of the necessity of a visible change in behavior—a revelation by deeds. In addition, Father Vladimir links penance to the process of inchurchment that always demands new penitential efforts. As I will show in the following sections, the emphasis on public action is inherent in both forms of penance in church construction: churches built with gold and churches built with tears.

Churches Built with Gold (*na zolote*): Motivations for Giving Donations

When I left my field site in August 2007, the first stone was laid for a new church to take the place of one that had been destroyed, during socialism, in 1970. The new church was situated not far from the city center on one of the central squares next to the eternal flame.[8] The church was dedicated to Our Lady of Kazan—one of the most important icons in Russia. The church was "built with gold," as local people told me, because two entrepreneurs, among others, donated money for the construction work. Each of them had donated 10 million rubles (about 300,000 Euros) but this was probably still not sufficient because the expected construction costs were 25 to 28 million rubles (700,000 to 800,000 Euros).

When I attended the official blessing and dedication of the church in November 2008, the construction of the building was completed but inside, the church was still empty—iconostasis, paintings, and icons were still missing. But because the archbishop was pressing and the day of the icon of Our Lady of Kazan was 4 November, the dedication took place on that day, and before the official opening. Many people attended the ceremony and most of them arrived at least one hour before the appointed time. Most of the attendees were elderly women from the surrounding area who, until recently, had to go to the city center in order to attend church. So they were expressing approval for the construction of a new church in their neighborhood.

The archbishop, the mayor, the head of the local faction of "United Russia,"[9] and Gennadii, one of the two donors mentioned above, took part in the official opening ceremony and gave speeches. The archbishop and the mayor thanked Gennadii and all the other donors[10] for their help and praised the new church. When the mayor mentioned Gennadii's name, he asked him to step forward in order to introduce him to the crowd. Gennadii then talked briefly about the work of building the church and the problems they faced, but seemed to be glad when he stepped back again. Afterwards, the archbishop led a prayer and carried out the blessing of the church with holy water, followed by a procession around the church. Towards the end of the official ceremony, the archbishop again expressed his gratitude and gave an icon (Our Lady of Kazan) to Gennadii as a gift. Gennadii thanked him and stressed the importance of the church for the people in this district of the city. Although Gennadii appeared to dislike the publicity, he gave interviews to TV and radio stations as well as to newspaper reporters attending the event.

I would like to distinguish three different aspects of the motivation for businesspeople to give donations: religious, political, and those aspects which Annette Weiner (1992) has termed keeping-while-giving. In contrast to Weiner, many authors (Godelier 1999; Mauss 1925/1990; White 1988) stress the reciprocal aspects of giving. According to Mauss, the notion of reciprocity underlies all gifts and therefore also gifts to gods, "because those gods who give and return gifts are there to give a considerable thing in the place of a small one" (1925/1990: 17). Following this interpretation of the reciprocity of giving, religious motivations for donations are guided by expectations of a return in a next world. Many Russians have a similar understanding and stress the potentially reciprocal nature of donations to the church.

For the second aspect of church donations, political motivation, I underline the increase in influence and power that donations to the Church can bring. Following Bourdieu's ([1983] 2001) argument, donations to the Church can be interpreted as a way to convert economic into social capital that elevates one's social status and prestige in the secular sphere. Increased social status and prestige, then, are transformed into political power by becoming a member of parliament. This perception is shared by many Russians, as I will try to show.

Drawing on Weiner's (1992) account on *kula* exchange I also call the final motivation for donations "keeping-while-giving." Like Parry (1986), she criticizes the assumption of reciprocity in gift-giving because "[d]uring the rise of capitalism, the give and take of reciprocity took on an almost magical, sacred power among Western economists" (Weiner 1992: 2). According to her view, the emphasis on reciprocity in exchanges also gained influence in anthropology and concealed the nature of inalienable possessions. But at issue for her is "not how one gift elicits a return, but rather which possessions the members of a group are able to keep" (26). She even goes a step further and claims that it is "not the hoary idea of a return gift that generates the thrust of exchange, but the radiating power of keeping inalienable possessions out of exchange" (150). Although I would not go so far as to address the motivation to give donations to inalienable possessions alone, at times the idea to give donations to the Church seemed to be a feasible way to prevent pressure from the state's side to take responsibility. Thus it is equally important for me to look at gifts and return gifts as well as at the inalienable possessions that are kept out of exchange. Applied to contemporary Russia, I argue that participation in charitable events and public donations to the church are ways of showing responsibility that allow the donor to keep back other possessions like one's wealth or one's business for him or herself.

Religious Motivation

The first, religious aspect dominates academic and church literature as well as everyday conversations. First and foremost, donations are perceived and described as a form of penance (*pokaianie*) for one's sins. Only through penance does salvation become possible. Historically, the interpretation of donations as a form of penance already dominates. Platonov (1995: 25) argues: "In the consciousness of Russians the idea of penance or atonement (*iskuplenie*) for wealth exists because wealth is always connected to sins." In order to substantiate his claim, Platonov cites Russian proverbs that dominate popular ideas about wealth: "Don't accumulate a belly [wealth], and you won't poison your soul [*Zhivota (bogatstva) ne kopi, a dushu ne mori*]" or "Let your soul go to hell—and you will become rich [*Pusti dushu v ad—budesh' bogat*]" (1995: 25–26). These understandings are, to a certain extent, still valid as the wealth of contemporary businesspeople is often perceived as illegal, and many question their ways of accumulating wealth.

Negative perceptions of wealth are also mentioned in the *Izmaragd*, an anthology from the fourteenth century. It states: "For personal salvation it is better to get rid of wealth, as a wanderer prefers to give robbers his money and save his life; or as sailors, during the storm, throw their freight overboard" (cited in Fedotov 1966: 67). On one hand, wealth is valued in contemporary Russia because many social services, such as health care, education, and housing, are privatized and therefore very expensive. On the other hand, many people still stress the sinfulness of those who became rich. Here, religious and socialist interpretations of wealth and its origins intermingle. Nevertheless, the link between giving charity or donating money to the Church, and penance as the quest for peace for one's own soul or for the souls of one's relatives, is stressed. Prayer, penance, and donations are understood as liberating the soul from sins. There also exists an historic example from the Vladimir region for the link between donations to the Church and salvation. In the seventeenth century a bell was donated to the Assumption cathedral by merchants (Guliaeva 2003: 61); the inscription on the bell reads, "For their souls and for their parents in eternal peace [*Po svoikh dushakh i po svoikh roditeliakh v vechnyi pokoi*]."

Ivan, a former engineer in his mid fifties who now runs a real estate business, also gives a religious interpretation of donations. Here is how he put it:

> And some people really have an interest in religion. They take to books, read; and some go to monasteries; some search for a spiritual teacher (*dukhovnyi nastavnik*) who tells them who Jesus Christ was, why he was crucified, who the Virgin Mary was and ... what is Easter and so on. ...
>
> Then they, so to say, start to study and comprehend, and someone helps them and they understand, understand enough. And these people, who have a lot of success in business, at some time they were criminals (*kogda-to oni zanimalis' kriminalom*). But those who found a spiritual teacher, they really help the church, help to build churches. They help to build, so to say, holy institutions. They occupy themselves with charitable activities. ...
>
> They understood that this is necessary, that the soul can rise (*vrode by i polet dushy byl*), right? They understand: "Apparently I did something wrong in life (*Znachit, chto ia chto-to delal v zhizni ne tak*)."

Ivan describes how some people who have had a lot of success in business, sometimes using criminal methods, came to religion through reading or visits to monasteries. He perceives the role of a spiritual teacher (*dukhovnyi nastavnik*) as crucial, someone who can give them advice and explain Orthodoxy to them. A spiritual teacher can be a priest from one of the local churches or a monk from one of the nearby monasteries. The relationship to spiritual teachers is based on respect, but reflects the personal preferences of the particular entrepreneur. Often these are long-lasting relations that are renewed again and again and require a certain degree of intimacy. In Ivan's view, these spiritual teachers also guide actions by advising charitable work or donations to the church as a form of penance.

In the last paragraph of the quotation above, Ivan explains his view on the underlying reasons for donations and charitable work. Like the *Izmaragd* mentioned above, he has a negative view of wealth, although he himself runs a profitable business. Highly successful businesses are especially suspicious to him and cause him to speculate on connections to criminal methods and sin. He perceives his own sinful behavior as a reason for making donations—"I did something wrong in life"—and accordingly he sees donations to the church as a way of securing his own salvation—so "that the soul can rise."

As a second example I want to come back to Gennadii, whom I already mentioned in the description of the church's opening ceremony. He is in his mid forties and runs one of the biggest construction companies in the region. The church whose blessing I attended was the second church construction to which Gennadii has donated. The first church was built in the cemetery of the city and was complete before my arrival, but rumors about the construction still circulated during my research. The construction work had started in 2004 and the church was finished in 2005. Gennadii himself donated a considerable amount of money to the construction but shared the costs with several other entrepreneurs. I was told that they gave interviews on all local TV channels. Shortly afterwards, elections for the regional (*oblast'*) parliament were held and four of the businessmen who had contributed to the construction of the church were elected to be members of parliament, including Gennadii.

Gennadii himself denies any connection between his contribution to the church and the elections, but mentions a dream that he had:

> I saw myself standing on a hill in white clothes. Other people stood with me in white capes and next to me was a white church. An endless chain of people passed by and bowed to us showing signs of respect. A mysterious apparition.
>
> Later it happened, completely accidentally, that they proposed to me to build [this church]. And why not? There used to be a church there and we decided to rebuild it. Before we got involved they had already tried to build it, about ten years earlier, but they didn't succeed. They collected some money, laid the first stone, but it led nowhere. There was nothing, nothing worked. So, for this reason, there was a ceremony when laying the foundation of the church to insert a box with holy relics [*sviatye moshchi*].
>
> Later there was a meal, such a celebration, and the archbishop, he said: "Gennadii, you can't imagine how those people who are buried here on this cemetery will thank you! They will pray for you [*za tebia molit'sia*]." And I remembered this dream, the endless chain of people. And here in the cemetery, 100,000 people are buried. ...
>
> This is what is important to me. ... I am not interested in public recognition [*priznanie obshchestvennoe*]. I did this for myself [*dlia menia samogo*], and it is possible to share this with other people [*podelit'sia, kak by s liudmi*].

In this part of the interview Gennadii described his dream where an endless chain of people bowed to him. Following the remark from the archbishop he interpreted the people in his dream to be the ones who are buried in the cemetery. When he talked about the 100,000 people buried there he was moved and impressed by the fact that they might pray for him.

Dreams play an important role in Orthodoxy and are thought of as supernatural signs, possibly from God. Many instances can be found where the construction of a church goes back to a dream. Another entrepreneur, a partner of Gennadii who partly financed the first construction, also claimed to have had a dream in which his grandmother appeared and asked him to build a church in the cemetery where she is buried. Both explanations seem to build on traditional interpretations of church-building. An historic example from the Vladimir region of a dream that led to the erection of a church is the famous Virgin Mary Intercession Church (*pokrov na nerli*). In 1155, Prince Andrei Bogoliubskii was on his way from Kiev to Rostov Velikii when his horses stopped suddenly. He had to take a rest, and during the night the Mother of God appeared to him in a dream and advised him to build a church there, which he did soon after.

Furthermore, it is remarkable that Gennadii describes the archbishop addressing him personally and calling him by his first name. Here, the intimate personal relation between them becomes apparent and the archbishop seems to take on the role of spiritual teacher (*dukhovnyi nastavnik*) to Gennadii. According to Ivan's account, the initiative to build the church often comes from the teacher's side and, indeed, it was a suggestion from the archbishop. Both already knew each other and had made business trips to public events together.[11] After the construction was completed, Gennadii received an old icon from the archbishop as a sign of gratitude for his generous donation.

Political Motivation

Besides religious motivations, Ivan the businessperson also mentions political motivations for giving donations. Like others, Ivan sees a connection between entrepreneurial donations and the goal of becoming a member of the regional parliament:

> Tobias Köllner: What connections do you see between religion and business?
>
> Ivan: ... Many of these people who are in business do not understand the core of religion and they felt the need to engage in politics [*u nikh poiavilas' neobkhodimost' delat' politiku*]. They followed the general political trend [*na volne politicheskikh deistvii*]: I will build a church and I will write in the newspaper for everyone: I built a church! ... Yes. And then people will support me in the elections because, you see, I built [a church]. Everyone will [know], especially the pensioners, that is to say the elder voters, and they

are the main part of the electorate. The youth does not come out to vote. ... They [young people] don't go to vote, they just don't. Yes. But those who vote will vote for me. This also is a phenomenon of the relation between business, politics, and religion.

Besides the religious interpretation which Ivan gave earlier, he stresses the political character of donations. He perceives church donations as part of a general rise in the importance of religion in Russia, and he accuses other entrepreneurs of contributing for political reasons. He is especially critical of the practice of making donations public through newspapers or TV. According to Ivan, such public messages are addressed mainly to older generations who are more religious than the average Russian. In contrast to younger people, many of the elder generation vote in elections.

I will use one example to illustrate the importance of being a member of parliament for entrepreneurs. Currently, a regional law exists which prescribes monthly sanitary checkups if one wants to visit a public bath house. As a result, existing public bath houses are in a poor condition because entry fees are low and visitors are rare. One of the entrepreneurs, Gennadii's partner in the second church reconstruction, now wants to open an "aqua park." He dreams of having several different pools and some slides, as he saw in Western Europe. But his plans will only have a chance of being profitable if he is able to change or abolish the law prescribing sanitary checkups. This change is precisely his goal at the moment, and he hopes to be elected in the coming elections. Similar conditions exist in many economic spheres, and building regulations are some of the most complex. Intimate and early knowledge of, or even the ability to influence, regulations therefore can give businesses a competitive edge. Moreover, members of parliaments in Russia enjoy immunity and are therefore not easily charged in the courts. As many legal cases gaining international attention have shown (for example, the forced sale of a gas field by Shell and the case against Microsoft),[12] the outcomes of judicial conflicts are never certain and could always have a political dimension. So entrepreneurs seek immunity in order to be prepared in case of problems arising.

Within the context of political motivations, Yurchak (2002) mentions two other motivational aspects, which are also important. On the one hand, he shows how intimately entrepreneurship can be linked to the concept of governmentality (Foucault 1991). This concept emphasizes "organizing and governing people, institutions, relations, objects, and ideas" (Yurchak 2002: 278). In the Russian context, this applies to people inside as well as outside business. Thus political engagement can be understood as an extension of entrepreneurial governmentality, and therefore an extension of business interests.

On the other hand, Yurchak states that "entrepreneurial agency ... is directed not so much at personal enrichment at any cost as at building a meaningful personal reality" (310–11). Entrepreneurial engagement in politics in this respect can be understood as a way to build something new, to take part in the shaping of a new Russia. Donations to the ROC, which are publicized in this context, serve as a first step meant to guarantee political participation in times of change.

Keeping-While-Giving

In her re-examination of the *kula* trade, Annette Weiner provides yet another reason for gift-giving. She argues, "At issue is not how one gift elicits a return, but rather which possessions the members of a group are able to keep" (1992: 26). Her focus is rather on things one can keep than on gifts that are given away. Following her interpretation, gift-giving is carried out in order to hold back inalienable possessions. Similarly, I perceive donations to the church as a precautionary practice and as a way of protecting one's possessions in a difficult political context. Here, one has to keep in mind difficulties with bureaucracy and the Russian legal system. As long as one's company is small, it is generally ignored, but as a company grows it faces more and more expectations from the state. In June 2007, for example, a conference was held in Vladimir with the topic "social responsibility of business" (*Sotsial'naia otvetstvennost' biznesa*). Many entrepreneurs from well-known and successful local enterprises attended and announced donations to various institutions: to the Russian Orthodox Church, veterans' clubs, sports clubs, schools, and orphanages. It is remarkable that donations were also given to state institutions like schools.

In order to illustrate the connections between the state and businesses, I want to provide an example. One day in August 2007, I was walking along the main street of Vladimir. I stopped in front of one of the big companies from socialist times, which survived the changes but is now privately owned. I took a photo of the building from the street without entering the building. Security men came outside and arrested me. They called the police who took me to the police station. Although I was not accused of espionage, as a foreigner I raised suspicions and was interviewed by the FSB (Russian Federal Security Service) and the OMON (Special Purpose Police Squad). At the beginning, they were quite unfriendly but became more relaxed when they saw the photo I took. It only showed the building with some symbols from socialist times that every passer-by could see from the main road. After two hours of interviews and the writing-up of a report, I was released. So, what was at stake?

When I told the story at work[13] the next day everyone smiled and asked me if I did not know that nearly all the big firms are still producing military goods for the army, or have re-started. The company, which advertises its production of gas and water meters, also produces fuses for bombs and missiles. Another company offers chemicals for civil as well as military use, and yet another firm officially produces oil drilling equipment but is based in a town situated in an area restricted to the military. This overlapping production tells a lot about the relationship between businesses and the state, and it is not strange, then, that all entrepreneurs from bigger companies are members of the same political party—"United Russia," which was formed by former Russian president Vladimir Putin. Accordingly, taking some responsibility for the state's projects (by favoring the ROC, renovating schools, and other activities) is necessary in order to stay in business and to return at least some of the profits made through state orders. Otherwise, sanitary inspections or checks for compliance with fire or tax regulations will be carried out. Thus Caroline Humphrey is right when she points out that "it continues to be impossible to disentangle the 'economic' from the 'political' in postsocialist Russia" (2002: xxii). One example of this entanglement is the case of an entrepreneur who owned an insurance company that underwent a tax inspection during which all his computers were confiscated, and were returned only after several months. During this time, work was almost impossible and he even thought of buying new computers. As this example shows, there are a lot of possibilities for the state administration to interfere in business, if necessary. In order to avoid such actions, entrepreneurs try to show that they care about state priorities by donating to various institutions—among them the ROC.

Churches Built with Tears (*na slezakh*): Notions of Asceticism

After the detailed account I have provided about entrepreneurial church donations, let me now turn to the second, conflicting moral discourse about those donations. Although donations to the ROC by entrepreneurs are widely appreciated by believers as well as by others, they do not go without criticism. As I have tried to show, giving donations is often understood in relation to earlier sinful behavior and is perceived as a cheap attempt to buy off one's sins (*iskuplenie, kompensatsiia*). Thus some believers make a distinction between what they consider to be simply compensation, and what they consider to be real penance. For them, real penance is connected to loss, work, and hardship and reflects ascetic ideals as they are practiced in monastic life, such as fasting, poverty, and manual labor.

Not all parishes receive money from rich businesspeople, and the parishioners sometimes start reconstruction work on their own. In one of the small towns near my main field site a church was restored in this way. Over the course of several years, a group of about 30 parishioners spent very little money but exerted a lot of effort in order to carry out the work. The group, comprised of two-thirds women and one-third men, met on weekends to work and to hold services (sometimes more frequently). Those whom I talked to stressed the close community feeling which arose during those collective activities. This community feeling also provided a reason for people who did not live in the small town to join in with the work. Besides work, services and common meals (*trapeza*) were also held. During my research, the reconstruction work came to an end and after this point only occasional repairs were necessary. These repairs were mainly done by a few men and not by the whole group. As a result the group cohesion changed because people now met mainly during the church services, and the priest sometimes complained when it became too loud: "The church is not for conversations but for prayers!" (*Tserkov' ne dlia razgovorov, a dlia molitv*). But those who took part in the reconstruction still form a cohesive group within the parish, as one could see in their frequent interactions.

Within the group of laborers, I had the closest contact with Igor, who was about 40 years old. I got to know him through Sonia, an acquaintance of mine who worked as a teacher in a religious school of Vladimir and who lived next to Igor in a nearby village. Igor had studied theology for three years at St. Tikhon academy in Moscow, but since he had to provide money for his wife and their four children he could not finish his degree. He currently works as a driver but still wants to finish his studies. Igor underlined the importance that working for the church has for him. He perceives this work as the fulfillment (*ispolnenie*) of the Ten Commandments and stresses the penitential aspect of manual labor for the church. Working for the church, according to Igor, brings special grace (*blagopoluchnyi*) to one's afterlife. For him hard work is part of an ascetic lifestyle, like the fasting he adheres to.

One day Igor was standing with me not far from the church and said: "See, this is our church—not the most beautiful one but built with tears." On one hand, his statement reflects his pride because the group managed to reconstruct the church without any external help. In his view, other churches may be nicer but this is "our church" (*nasha tserkov'*) and it has a special meaning for him—less as a building but more because they put so much effort into it. On the other hand, he points to the penitential aspect of the project when he says the church is built "with tears," reflecting the hardship of their work. Igor is drawing on historic understandings of church construction, wealth, and work, such as the *Nestor Chronicle*,[14] which explains: "Many monasteries were built by the Emperor, by aristocrats, or by wealthy people. But it is different if they are built with tears, fasting, prayers, and vigils. Antonii has no gold, no silver and so he collected tears and fasting. So he said"[15] (Shakhmatov 1916/1969: 202). The *Nestor Chronicle* describes how Antonii,[16] the abbot of the Kievan Cave Monastery, collected "tears" and "fastings" to build churches because he had no gold or silver. Like Igor, the abbot contrasts churches constructed using gold or silver and those built with tears, fasting, prayers, and prayer vigils (*bdenie*).[17] This second option is considered to be the more authentic, so the abbot's statement also implies a critique of the Emperor and the aristocracy. Unfortunately, the circumstances under which the *Nestor Chronicle* was written are not completely clear. Furthermore, the original has disappeared and some parts could have been added or rewritten later. Igor probably became acquainted with the *Nestor Chronicle* and other historic religious writings during his religious studies. In addition, Igor is not only critical about entrepreneurs who donate money without contributing their labor, but also criticizes donations which are made public. If donations are publicized, "one has already received one's grapes," he told me. A similar phrase can be found in the Bible[18] (Matt. 6:16) where Jesus talks about affectation and fast. Igor seems to perceive entrepreneurs who donate money to the church as not particularly religious.

Although many parishioners agreed with Igor's critique of the entrepreneur donors, the portrayal of his own participation in the reconstruction work was contested. One of those who downplayed Igor's contribution to work on the church was Sonia. Although they seemed to be good acquaintances, each of them seemed to claim a leading position within the parish: Igor because he started to study theology in Moscow, and Sonia because she works as a teacher in a religious school and also received religious education. In addition, Sonia led the Sunday religious school for children. Both sustained their claim to a leading role within the parish by sharing their religious knowledge with others. In addition, Igor was accused of having exaggerated his role in the construction work. Due to the fact that the church construction had already come to an end before my fieldwork, I could not evaluate their claims. But it seemed obvious from their behavior that both were competing for a leading role inside the parish and each was trying to outdo the other by showing more knowledge or asserting they had worked more and harder.

The tension between Sonia and Igor elucidates the differences and similarities between the contribution of gold or tears as a form of penance, and allows for an interpretation that bridges the gap between them. One obvious contrast between entrepreneurial donations and labor contributions is the level of sociality involved. Entrepreneurs mainly carry out their projects on an individual level, as the case of Gennadii shows. Although it is the case that about 200 people donated money for the erection of the church, most of the other donors were unknown to him. In contrast to the individual nature of entrepreneurial donations, the construction of a church through labor contributions, such as the project Igor and Sonia participated in, can create a community through the sociality of the building process. This community-building effect of joint labor was appreciated and is certainly one of the reasons why they consider their work to be superior to the donations given individually by entrepreneurs. Nevertheless, the tension between Sonia and Igor threatened the community and meant that it could split up in the future if parishioners join one side or the other. Furthermore, their tension resembles the search for acknowledgement by entrepreneurs, as described in the section on the political motivations for giving donations. Like the entrepreneurs introduced above, Sonia and Igor try to use the community in order to enhance their individual charisma and recognition by publicizing achievements in the spiritual sphere. But in contrast to entrepreneurs both do so through other means like hard work, asceticism, and showing deep knowledge in Orthodoxy. Therefore, I argue that both moral discourses are important as ideals but their actual implementation into practice is far more complex and ambiguous.

Conclusion

In this chapter I have distinguished between two forms of church reconstruction that draw on both local understandings and historic distinctions—one which relies on monetary donations from entrepreneurs, and another which depends on labor contributions by parishioners. Although I am aware of the fact that both traditions are not to be found as monolithic ideal types and in reality there is some overlap, this theoretical distinction is important because it reflects powerful local discourses on morality. Both methods of construction are interpreted as forms of penance, although many believers see a substantial difference between them. The judgment of parishioners mainly rests on respect for ascetic ideals like hard manual labor and an adherence to proper fasting. Monetary donations are perceived by committed believers as a form of penance that is too easy, and are therefore of a different quality than their own penitential efforts through labor, prayers, fasting, and self-restraint. Therefore, donations are often described in slightly disparaging terms, such as compensation (*kompensatsiia*) or atonement (*iskuplenie*). The latter is the Russian translation of the Greek word for ransom (Alfeev 2004: 68–71) and has the word "to buy"

(*kupit'/pokupat'*) at its root, stressing the perception of economic calcula-
tion by those making this type of donation.

Donations are often described as "pure gifts" (Parry 1986; see also Malinowski [1922] 1984: 177–78, on the notion of "pure gift") which are given
without any expectation of profit. Similar to Parry's Indian case, the ideology of non-reciprocity is strong in Russia, and priests in particular try to
avoid any perception of the sale or purchase of spiritual favors and deny
any personal returns for given donations. But in reality, donations do entail
benefits of different kinds for the donors. The most common way to show
gratitude is to hand out certificates to donors. These certificates are often
exhibited in a public part of the office. Sometimes reciprocal gifts, like precious icons, are made, or blessings and prayers take place. Prayers for donors, which are announced publicly during the ceremonies, are ordered in
well-known monasteries for a certain amount of time (forty days, a month,
or a whole year). In addition, donors often get a burial plot at a privileged
place right next to the church. In his description of donations to monasteries in France in the eleventh and twelfth centuries, White (1988) mentions
analogue return gifts. He also points to the aspect of time and stresses the
fact that the church or monastery, as an undying community, could hold
and return gifts forever (26).

Nevertheless, an interpretation of donations and reciprocal gifts from
the church as a commodity exchange is misleading. Drawing on Gregory's
(1982) distinction between gifts and commodities I interpret donations to
the church as part of the former. Gregory states, "[C]ommodity exchange
establishes a relationship between the objects exchanged, whereas gift exchange establishes a relationship between the subjects" (19). Gennadii's relationship to the archbishop clearly indicates the latter. Furthermore, the
value of exchanged gifts and donations cannot be compared. There are no
generally accepted prices assigned to these gifts and the value could only
be described in a rank relation (see also 67–69). It would make no sense
to count the number of prayers exchanged for one donation. Nonetheless,
differences in the status of reciprocal gifts from the church do exist and can
be evaluated in terms of the length of prayers ordered (forty days or a whole
year), or the prestige of the monastery that carries them out. Therefore, I
argue that entrepreneurial donations to the Church include interested exchange of favors as well as disinterested gifts. Both aspects are inseparable
and constitute two sides of one and the same activity.

A recurrent topic for Marcel Mauss was the inalienability of the gift.
Drawing on ethnographic material from New Zealand, Mauss showed how
the life force of a person is embedded in one's personal possessions. Thus
he introduced the notion of the "*hau*," the spirit of a thing, in order to

show the bond of a thing with its original owner, and he applied it to gift exchanges. For Mauss, the *hau* is one explanation that incites the recipient of a gift to offer a counter-gift. Firth made a similar point in noting "that giving is an extension of the self, and hence the obligation is bound up with the notion of the self, its social bonds and social roles" (1975: 10–11). Although I do not follow Mauss' interpretation of the *hau*, his comment that "things exchanged ... are never completely detached from those carrying out the exchange" (33) can be applied to my Russian material. The relation of the donor to the outcome of his donation is often kept alive. Donors do participate in events like anniversaries or in celebrations of the days of saints. During these events, they are located in privileged positions next to representatives of the ROC and from the city or regional administration. The donation establishes a relationship between donor and recipient which is renewed at each meeting. As Mauss noted "the alliance contracted is not temporary, and the contracting parties are bound in perpetual interdependence" (62). Gennadii and the archbishop not only stayed in contact during all these years but restored their relationship with another donation which led to the construction of a second church. Therefore, I understand donations as complex social transactions that are not merely isolated acts, but an ongoing process of social interaction and exchange.

Besides the "unseen fruits" and ecclesiastical favors, a gain in prestige and social status in the secular context can be observed. The post-socialist transition led to changes and inconsistencies in people's status, and the *nouveaux riches* faced a dilemma because there "is a displacement between economic resources and social status" (Sampson 1996: 93). In order to acquire an elite status, entrepreneurs try "to solve the incongruity between newly acquired material resources and lack of cultural hegemony" (94). Donations to the ROC and various other institutions bridge the gap and enable participation in public events that can lead to an increase in prestige. Because the ROC is a trusted institution, donations to the church are preferred and generate moral approval of one's social status. A parallel interpretation has been drawn for France in the middle ages, when "secular princes ... used the foundation of an abbey ... as a means of enhancing their own prestige in the secular world and as a way of establishing, consolidating, and extending their own political power" (White 1988: 30). Therefore, an understanding of donations to the ROC as capital transformation (Bourdieu [1983] 2001) is reasonable. Economic capital is transformed through donations into social capital in the form of higher prestige. And prestige, in turn, is the foundation for political success in elections, which can bring significant benefits.

However, I have also tried to show the limits of these attempts to create a positive image of entrepreneurship and the new elite. Many of the efforts made by businesspeople are not accompanied by an actual increase in prestige, and often entrepreneurs remain morally questionable in the eyes of the public. A discourse that tries to shed positive light on entrepreneurial donations to the ROC is also intersected by conflicting discourses on churches built with tears, socialist notions about trade as speculation, and the immorality of the excessive use of wealth.

Notes

I am grateful to the Max Planck Institute for Social Anthropology which made this research possible by funding it. I would also like to thank Hermann Goltz, Chris Hann, Kirill Istomin, Agata Ładykowska, Anja Sing, Peter Steger, Vladislava Vladimirova, Detelina Tocheva, and Lale Yalçın-Heckmann for their support and helpful comments on earlier versions of this chapter.

1. The research presented in this chapter is based on twelve months of fieldwork in Vladimir, a middle-sized city (350,000 inhabitants) situated 180 kilometers to the east of Moscow.
2. According to Orthodox teachings, the acknowledgement of one's sins in confession (*izpoved'*) calls for compensation through penance (*pokaianie*). Therefore, penitential efforts rather are to be understood as an ongoing process and not as a single event. Often penance is guided by priestly advice.
3. While charitable orthodox organizations like the buses of *Miloserdie* (mercy) and other initiatives are visible in Moscow, at my field site Vladimir, charity-like food collections are seldom organized by the diocese but by the parishioners themselves and distributed among their networks.
4. All names are synonyms but reflect the main features of the real names they replace, for example, as Christian names.
5. All interview translations are my own. I concentrate on the content and do not give word-by-word translation because the quotes are not subject to linguistic analysis.
6. See Weber (1920/1988) for the distinction between religions that are oriented on this world or the next one.
7. In recent years, the blessing (*osviashenie*) of offices became fashionable in Russia among entrepreneurs.
8. The eternal flame, commemorating the victims of World War II, was erected on the former spot of the church. The new church is now situated on the former cemetery grounds.
9. The party United Russia was formed in April 2001 when two parties (Fatherland and Unity Party) were united. Although himself no member of the party, the most famous figure is Vladimir Putin, the party's chairman. Since 2002 the party became more and more important in the city and region of Vladimir, and in 2008 it won about two-thirds of the seats in the regional parliament.
10. Altogether about 200 persons donated money for the erection of the church, but Gennadii and his acquaintance paid by far the biggest share.
11. One of these trips, which went to Italy in order to venerate the relics of St. Nikolai, was organized jointly by the diocese, the city administration, and several entrepreneurs.

212 | *Tobias Köllner*

12. In 2006 Royal Dutch Shell and other partners were forced to sell a majority of the gas field Sakhalin 2 to Gazprom at a price far below the market value. In early 2007 Microsoft lost a copyright infringement case against a teacher who installed illegal downloads on school computers because the case was deemed "too trivial" to be prosecuted.
13. During my fieldwork I worked as a trainee in a local newspaper company whose owner was also the president of a business association. This helped me to get some inside information from a company as well as to come into contact with other businesspeople.
14. Igor never mentioned the *Nestor Chronicle*, and I am very grateful to Hermann Goltz who advised me to check the *Nestor Chronicle* for similar phrases.
15. The *Nestor Chronicle* describes the early years of the Kievan Rus (from about 850 to 1110) and is written in Old Church Slavonic.
16. According to the *Chronicle*, Abbot Antonii moved from a Greek monastic community on Mt. Athos to Kiev in 1051 and settled down in one of the caves. Others monks joined him, and he is considered to be the founder of regular monasticism in the Kievan Rus. He was later canonized (date unknown).
17. *Bdenie* is a religious exercise, mostly practiced in monasteries, where one keeps watch, prays, and concentrates one's thinking and practice on God.
18. Igor never explicitly cited the Bible or the *Nestor Chronicle*. But during his study, he became acquainted with religious literature and obviously makes use of it.

References

Alfeev, Bishop Ilarion. 2004. *Vo chto veriat Pravoslavnye Khristiane? Katekhizicheskie besedy* [In What Do Orthodox Christians Believe? (Catechetical Conversation)]. Klin: Izdatel'stvo Khristianskaia zhizn'.

Bourdieu, Pierre. [1983] 2001. "The Forms of Capital." In *The Sociology of Economic Life*, ed. Mark Granovetter and Richard Swedberg. Boulder, CO: Westview Press.

Caldwell, Melissa L. 2004. *Not by Bread Alone: Social Support in the New Russia.* Berkeley, CA: University of California Press.

Dubin, Boris. 2006. "Legkoe bremia: massovoe pravoslavie v Rossii 1990–2000-kh godov" [Light Burden: Mass Orthodoxy in Russia in the 1990s and 2000s]. In *Religioznoe praktiki v sovremennoi Rossii,* ed. Kati Russele and Aleksandr Agadzhanian. Moscow: Novoe Izdatel'stvo.

Durkheim, Emile. 1915. *The Elementary Forms of the Religious Life.* London: George Allen & Unwin, 1957.

Fedotov, Georgii P. 1966. *The Russian Religious Mind. The Middle Ages: The Thirteenth to the Fifteenth Centuries,* vol. II. Cambridge, MA: Harvard University Press.

Firth, Raymond. 1975. "Themes in Economic Anthropology. A General Comment." In *Themes in Economic Anthropology,* ed. Raymond Firth. London: Tavistock.

Foucault, Michel. 1991. "Governmentality." In *The Foucault Effect: Studies in Governmentality,* ed. Graham Burchell. Chicago: University of Chicago Press.

———. 1993. "About the Beginnings of the Hermeneutics of the Self: Two Lectures in Dartmouth." *Political Theory* 21, no. 2: 198–227.

Godelier, Maurice. 1999. *Das Rätsel der Gabe. Geld, Geschenke, heilige Objekte.* München: C. H. Beck.

Gregory, Christopher A. 1982. *Gifts and Commodities.* London: Academic Press.

Guliaeva, Valentina V., ed. 2003. *Razvitie predprinimatel'stva v Rossii s drevneishikh vremen do 1917 goda* [The Development of Entrepreneurship in Russia from Ancient Times until 1917]. Vladimir: Vladimirskii Gosudarstvennoi Universitet.

Humphrey, Caroline. 2002. *The Unmaking of Soviet Life: Everyday Economies after Socialism.* Ithaca, NY: Cornell University Press.

Kharkhordin, Oleg. 1999. *The Collective and the Individual in Russia: A Study of Practices.* Berkeley, CA: University of California Press.

Malinowski, Bronislaw. [1922] 1984. *Argonauts of the Western Pacific: An Account of Native Enterprise and Adventure in the Archipelagoes of Melanesian New Guinea.* Prospect Heights, IL: Waveland Press.

Mauss, Marcel. 1925. *The Gift: The Form and Reason for Exchange in Archaic Societies.* New York: W. W. Norton, 1990.

Parry, Jonathan. 1986. "The Gift, the Indian Gift and the 'Indian Gift.'" *Man* 21, no. 3: 453–73.

Parry, Jonathan, and Maurice Bloch. 1989. "Money and the Morality of Exchange." Introduction to *Money and the Morality of Exchange,* ed. Jonathan Parry and Maurice Bloch. Cambridge, MA: Cambridge University Press.

Patriarch Aleksii II, ed. 2002. *Pravoslavnaia Entsiklopediia* [Orthodox Encyclopedia], vol 5. Moscow: Tserkovno-nauchnyi tsentr Russkoi Pravoslavnoi Tserkvi.

Platonov, Oleg. 1995. *1000 let Russkogo predprinimatel'stva. Iz istorii kupecheskikh rodov* [1000 Years of Russian Entrepreneurship: From the History of Merchant Families]. Moscow: Sovremennik.

Sampson, Steven. 1996. "Turning Money into Culture: 'Distinction' among Eastern Europe's Nouveaux Riches." In *A la Recherche des Certitudes Perdues… Anthropologie du Travail et des Affaires dans une Europe en Mutation,* ed. Birgit Müller. Berlin: Centre Marc Bloch.

Shakhmatov, A. A. 1916. *Povest' vremennykh let* [A Tale of Bygone Years]. The Hague: Mouton, 1969.

Weber, Max. 1920. *Gesammelte Aufsätze zur Religionssoziologie,* 3 vols. Tübingen: J.C.B. Mohr, 1988.

——. 1990. *Wirtschaft und Gesellschaft. Grundriss der verstehenden Soziologie.* Tübingen: J.C.B. Mohr.

Weiner, Annette B. 1992. *Inalienable Possessions: The Paradox of Keeping-While-Giving.* Berkeley, CA: University of California Press.

White, Stephen D. 1988. *Custom, Kinship, and Gifts to Saints: The Laudatio Parentum in Western France, 1050–1150.* Chapel Hill, NC: University of North Carolina Press.

Yurchak, Alexei. 2002. "Entrepreneurial Governmentality in Postsocialist Russia: A Cultural Investigation of Business Practice." In *The New Entrepreneurs of Europe and Asia: Patterns of Business Development in Russia, Eastern Europe and China,* ed. Victoria E. Bonnell and Thomas B. Gold. Armonk: M. E. Sharpe.

Zigon, Jarrett. 2007. "Moral Breakdown and the Ethical Demand: A Theoretical Framework for an Anthropology of Moralities." *Anthropological Theory* 7, no. 2: 131–50.

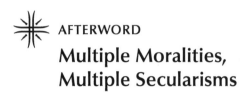

AFTERWORD
Multiple Moralities, Multiple Secularisms

Catherine Wanner

The close analysis of the role of religion in all its guises in fostering certain moral concepts in Russia has much to offer to the study of morality in other societies. Many patterns that are visible in these portraits of constituting communities and recrafting moralities in Russia are widely applicable elsewhere. In nearly all socialist or formerly socialist societies calls for moral renewal can be heard. Such calls are issued as a means to inspire self-transformation as well as social transformation. In the early 1990s, the conventional wisdom of many in the region was that they had fallen into a moral vacuum. Indictments of *bessovestnoe povedenie* (unconscionable behavior) were marshaled to prove that socialism and its atheist policies had disrupted basic understandings of right and wrong and shattered a cultural consensus as to what was proper and appropriate behavior in a variety of situations.

Yet, neither socialism nor its demise destroyed a sense of morality. Rather, socialism itself, compounded by its collapse, simply allowed multiple moralities to flourish. The use of moralities in the plural indicates that there are often several core sets of values and practices to which certain individuals or groups feel an intensely strong commitment. A plethora of new influences, ideas, and possibilities poured into the USSR beginning in the late 1980s, and this enhanced the already fractured sense of morality that socialism had created.

As the Soviet Union collapsed, a variety of religious groups were among the first to offer alternative moral discourses and practices. Many individuals believed that religious traditions and religious practitioners held privileged claims to moral authority. This perception helped religious organizations carve out a place for themselves in society and enhanced their ability to attract adherents to their belief systems. Yet, religion emerged as only one source, albeit an important one, among many sources of morality. Thanks to a vastly expanded and accelerated circulation of ideas, objects, and peoples, diverse and often conflicting understandings of morality at times strained the articulation of consensus, which intensified the struggle and conflicts driven by different understandings of righteousness, justice, and the obligations that individuals have to one another, and that govern the relationship between a state and its citizenry.

Some of the latest ethnographic studies of formerly socialist societies address this phenomenon and analyze the influence of moralities on policy and governance by examining the moral arguments surrounding issues such as women's social activism to assist the poor in Ukraine (Phillips 2008), labor practices in Romania (Kiedeckel 2008), and balancing the competing demands of environmentalism and capitalism in Slovakia (Snadjr 2008). Other recent ethnographies look directly at the sweeping changes emerging in the religious landscape as new communities asserting "non-traditional" belief systems and moralities form (Lindquist 2006; Wanner 2007) and historic denominations reemerge (Naumescu 2006; Rogers 2009). All of these studies attest to the vibrancy of moral questioning that is driven by the multiplicity of moralities currently in play in formerly socialist societies.

Individuals generally have a moral compass that gives clear indicators as to what is "right" for them to do in a particular situation. Those same individuals, however, might disagree with the moral choices others make. Each considers their own actions to be moral but indicts the behavior of others as immoral, when in reality each person is simply following different moral mandates that shape different understandings of virtue and propriety. By identifying those beliefs to which commitments are most fervently held and a set of practices to realize them, the study of moralities offers an opening into how a sense of conscience is formed on an individual level, as well as insight into the making of emotions and the bases for group solidarity on a collective level.

The study of moralities as illustrated in these chapters is also particularly revealing of change in the making. Moral reasoning inevitably takes place in reaction to political and social changes and this is the moment when a reevaluation and shift in moral standards, and sometimes even a breakdown in consensus, can occur. Morality can enter into processes of differentiation, creating visible and palpable cultural and social differences among groups. These differences can be far more profound than other domains that generally have received much more scholarly attention, such as religious affiliation, choice of language, and historical understanding. After the collapse of the USSR, competing and often contradictory understandings of morality were frequently at the root of misunderstandings and cultural conflicts throughout the region.

Some anthropologists, myself included, have used morality in the Tylorian sense of a shared understanding of commitment to certain core values or practices, many of which are prescribed or stem from prescriptions that are attributed to religious traditions (Wanner 2007: 10; Mandel and Humphrey 2002). Morality therefore also implies a commitment in the form of an allegiance to a group that subscribes to the same traditions, canons, and histories and embraces those same values and practices with a similar depth of emotion. Commitment to certain moral understandings and the communities that embrace them is what delivers the self-motivation, even the self-policing, to willingly perform the practices that allow an individual or a community to perceive themselves as moral.

Zygmunt Bauman, drawing on Heidegger, has argued that the essence of morality is *fürsein,* or being for Others, as opposed to ethics, which he characterizes as *mitsein,* or being with Others (Bauman 1993: 13). To act in a moral fashion means to assume responsibility for Others and to do so repeatedly over the course of successive encounters. This commitment carries a significant emotional component. To become moral means to cultivate a certain emotional disposition that prompts a person to react in a predictable and consistent way to injustice. As a Holocaust survivor, Bauman has tried to understand how the twentieth century can be filled with so many examples of uncruel people doing cruel things to Others. This finds an echo here in the atrocities and humiliations that Ieva Raubisko documents in Chechnya or the popular response among women to inexplicable suffering that Jeanne Kormina and Sergey Shtyrkov analyze.

Bauman argues that the ability of bureaucracies to operate independently of an individual's emotional response to others makes cruelty and other forms of immorality possible. Stated differently, collectivities prize rule-following over following one's conscience and as such are a threat to an individual's moral integrity. The mandates for belonging that a collective imposes sometimes hinder an individual from honoring the dictates of his or her conscience.

Moral convictions in the form of a conscience express themselves in terms of bodily reactions. Bodily impulses, Bauman argues (and I agree with him), have the greatest influence in shaping moral reactions. This perspective means that emotion signals a moralized commitment, and the body is a key site where moral beliefs are expressed and even strengthened through disciplining practices that are also aimed at the body. Jarrett Zigon refers to this as "embodied dispositions" in his introduction. The essential point is that morality inscribes itself on the body in the form of emotion. This is illustrated clearly in Alexander Panchenko's essay, in which he shows that group membership has the potential to reinforce a commitment to certain beliefs and practices on the individual level by integrating certain values into the character and disposition so thoroughly that when faced with a quandary, the cognitive process of reasoning can be overshadowed by an instinctive, visceral reaction that is understood to indicate what is undeniably true and moral.

A perspective that privileges the body and emotionalized moral impulses diverges from those asserted by other scholars, such as Joel Robbins, who sees the capacity to engage in moral reasoning as located in reflexivity and rational thought (2004: 315–16). This means that there are no moral impulses and no universal moral truths, only secular claims to moral authority, which always reserve the right to change. For Robbins, bodily sensory responses to situations only have significant meaning *after* there has been a breakdown in the cognitive ability to understand and to make conscious decisions. For Bauman, it is the other way around: Cognition comes into play when emotional and bodily moral dictates are unclear or absent.[1]

Although I too privilege bodily responses as being primary, the point I would like to stress is that when considering morality in conjunction with religion, *both* bodily sensory experiences and cognitive rational thought as forms of moral reasoning are shaped by collective experiences. The collective framing of experience, which includes embodied disciplining practices and patterns of reasoning, leads some emotions to evolve into moral beliefs. Religious traditions, with their canons, laws, practices, and texts, have historically served as one of the primary sources for moral codes that regulate behavior. Religious communities are often the sites where such codes are authoritatively transmitted and used to sanction or restrict certain habits and practices.

In her study of converts to Reverend Moon's Unification Church in the United States, Eileen Barker argues that many converts are idealists who joined the church to express their idealism through action, especially when they perceived idealism and altruism as discounted by society at large in favor of materialism, consumption, and self-advancement (Barker 1984: 242–45). She writes, "The Unification Church offers the potential recruit the chance to be part of a family of like-minded people who care about the state of the world, who accept and live by high moral standards, who are dedicated to restoring God's Kingdom of Heaven on earth. It offers him the opportunity to *belong;* it offers him the opportunity to *do* something that is of value and thus the opportunity *to be* of value" (244). She goes on to characterize converts to the Unification Church as individuals who have a strong sense of service, duty, and responsibility and who are achievers grappling with an unfulfilled yearning to contribute to the greater good of humanity. These converts, she argues, find a means to satisfy yearnings for selfless giving, desires for belonging, and possibilities to consciously do good as members of the Unification Church. In other words, membership in a religious community is perceived among converts as a means to become and sustain oneself as a moral person.

I have written that a similar dynamic exists among converts to evangelicalism (Wanner 2003). In Ukraine, as in Russia today, one hears numerous laments about the need to cheat, lie, or steal just to earn a living, about rampant corruption among government officials driven by self-enrichment over any commitment to pursuing the collective good, and about the ruth-lessness and omnipresence of organized crime. Many who turn to religion do so because they seek to exhibit higher moral standards than those they see in the surrounding society. Sometimes this desire prompts a religious community to advocate a form of total exclusion "from the world." For oth-ers, the desire to live by alternative moralities can become a commitment to exhibit model behavior that offers direction to others, with all of the paradoxes and contradictions that this implies.

The essential point is that communal membership in both of these in-stances and in others helps reaffirm the commitment to and perpetuation of certain moral values and religiously-infused moral practices in the face of hardship, ostracism, and isolation by holding out the reward of self and social transformation and eventual salvation. Community membership can be a means to satisfy emotional cravings for belonging and selflessness as well as the result of a conscious decision to pursue social justice. Com-munal religious life can become a vehicle to encourage commitments to certain values, discourses, and practices and to reaffirm the righteousness of those commitments with such frequency and conviction that the rules to uphold them ultimately become internalized and part of a person's disposi-tion that shapes his or her conscience and acts on his or her body to control behavior. This is why, at this critical juncture of transformation in post-Soviet society, religion has taken on heightened importance for charting the future directions of social and political change. Its pronounced influ-ence over moralities and moral domains means that it plays a key role in shaping the cultural values and practices that reflect these new moralities.

Socialism and Secularism

One of the key ramifications of the emergence of multiple moralities is the simultaneous emergence of multiple understandings of the secular. Moral-ity and secularism cannot be understood independently of one another. The multiplicity of moralities is predicated on a splintering of understand-ings of the secular. The diverse understandings of the role of the secular in Russia and elsewhere in the former Soviet Union have arisen as a result of a softening, a recasting, of Soviet secularization.[2] Religiously infused morali-ties should be considered in conjunction with the official and ideologically infused Soviet moral code as well as with its counterpart, a secular-humanist morality that emerged among members of the intelligentsia in reaction to Soviet state power and perceived injustices. Broadly speaking, Soviet state ideology, secular dissidents, and now religious communities, are three sources, among many possibilities, that provide the foundation for moral codes and understandings as to what constitutes authoritative knowledge and truth, be they ideologically-driven, informed by Enlightenment-era secular-humanistic thinking, or inspired by religious texts.

For decades most scholars assumed that secularization, understood as the decline of religious institutions, was an epiphenomenon of modernization, an inevitable by-product of increased urbanization, education, and bureaucratization. The well-known, three-pronged view of the secularization thesis held currency for quite some time: it claimed that secularization proceeds when, there is first, a reduction in the presence and influence of religious institutions in all spheres of society, such as government and education; second, a corresponding sharp rise in rates of literacy and education, introducing a scientific, rational way of understanding natural phenomena; and thirdly a "privatization" of religious belief.[3] It has, however, since been heartily disavowed, even by those who initially propagated it (Berger 1999; Berger, Davie, and Fokas 2008).

David Martin (1978) has long argued that secularization was not a disinterested concept. It took as a forgone conclusion that the days for religious institutions were numbered. As a theory, then, it suffered from a foundational assumption of unidirectional change leading to a foregone conclusion. This is reflected in Rodney Stark's (1999) infamous assertion that secularization theory was like a hotel elevator that only went down. Yet, it was precisely this understanding of secularization as an inevitable by-product of modernization that was embedded in Soviet ideology and policies.

Each of the dynamics thought to yield secularization was operative in the former Soviet Union: modernization in the form of growing rational and rationalizing bureaucracies, increasing urbanization and education, and an ever-wider embrace of science-based authority, especially in fields such as medicine. Yet, belief in the supernatural and allegiance to religious rituals that appeal to the divine did not vanish during 74 years of socialist rule. The collapse of socialism and the flourishing of religion in the former Soviet Union, among a variety of other events, have made undeniable the claim that secularization does not lead to the eradication of religion. Rather, secularizing processes that draw on particular views of how religion should relate to politics, governance, and public affairs lead to religious change. The forms religious change takes depend on the contours of secularism that have currency in a particular locale at a particular historical moment.

Even when the influence and authority of religious institutions is sharply curtailed, as it was in the USSR, it does not follow that individuals relinquish an interest in religion and become "secularized." Indeed, Soviet history shows us that individuals may still subscribe to religious beliefs and respond to religious sensibilities in the absence of formal religious practices and formal structures of religious authority. This phenomenon is even inherent in Orthodoxy, as evidenced by the concept of *tserkovnost*, or sacred experiences, including forms of belonging, that do not necessarily include collectively practicing religion in a prescribed way in order to consider oneself part of the Church and a believer, as Alexander Agadjanian notes in his chapter included here. In other words, the secularization of a social system or society does not necessarily induce a decline in religious behaviors and beliefs. It simply alters them. To understand the relationship of secularism to morality, I propose that we explore the basis upon which knowledge acquires power. In many respects this is the crux of religion and a key to secularizing tendencies.

Just as there are a variety of sources of morality on offer at any given time yielding multiple moralities, there are many sources of knowledge and means to judge them as authoritative. Secularism implies a particular assessment of authority. If we understand secularization as a process that moves towards a means of knowing, and specifically one that relies on scientific, rational, and verifiable terms to offer explanations and justifications, the supernatural, sensory, and bodily means of knowing, upon which religion and morality rely so heavily, are cast aside as unreliable. Understood this way, secularization is perhaps most of all a process of achieving a certain way of knowing, valorizing a commitment to that means of knowing, and using this as a basis of authority to govern. This parallel harnessing of concepts helps to explain why it makes sense to consider secularization in tandem with morality, and particularly the religious roots of morality.

If the secular essentially elevates and privileges a way of knowing, this can also be inverted and used to show that introducing new forms and ways of knowing can often involve the unknowing of others. As early as the 1920s, the Soviet Union had two great successes: literacy and religious illiteracy. Remarkably, Soviet leaders successfully and rapidly instilled knowledge and ignorance simultaneously. They worked to privilege "scientific knowledge" and to radically disrupt the transmission of supernatural and religious doctrinal knowledge.

There is an ironic twist here because the Bolsheviks considered religion to be the product of ignorance. Religion was seen as an exploitative force by virtue of its ability to trade on ignorance of scientific bases of knowledge. Yet when instilling a secular ethos in public life, early Soviet leaders erased from view, and eventually from memory and conscience, knowledge of religious symbolism and practices. This produced a certain form of ignorance of formalized, doctrinal religiosity, which inversely privileged other bases for authoritative knowledge. This policy had a clear instrumental value politically in that it dislodged the historic role of religious institutions in the region as arbiters of morality. Above all, I think of Soviet secularism as a project of agnotology, or the production of ignorance. Soviet secularism yielded the unknowing of religious traditions, practices and dogma, which, for some, led to an erosion of belief. But belief was not the main target of Soviet state-led secularizing projects. Religious knowledge was.

This is somewhat different that the secularism that one encounters in parts of Europe. Studying France, Danièle Hervieu-Léger (2000) has characterized European processes of secularism as related to memory. She argues that one of the defining characteristics of modernization has been change, which has been highly corrosive of tradition and memory. This process of eroding memory, and not modernization in the sense of urbanization, bureaucratization, and the like, has had enormous ramifications for religion and religious practice in that the "chain of memory" of religious traditions and practices has been broken. This, she argues, is what has diminished the social connectedness and meaningfulness of religion in Europe which has become manifest in a decline in overt religious practice and formal religious affiliation. Thus, the motor of European secularism is the "transmutation of memories" and forgetting and this, she argues, is what has propelled secularism in Europe.

In the USSR, amnesia, or forgetting of formalized religious knowledge, also set in. Yet, the Soviet state played a critical role in accelerating this process, and this remains a critical difference. Institutional mechanisms to offer religious and moral instruction where highly circumscribed, and religious practice, such as it was, was largely sequestered in the home thanks to state sanctions. Yet, this did not necessarily yield an erasure of religious sensibilities or of emotional dispositions, which continued to respond to the transcendent. These sensibilities remained because they were fostered elsewhere in the Soviet Union in political ritual and iconography.[4] The utility of religious moods and motivations in facilitating governance was readily recognized and used to create allegiance and compliance. In this way, the political order undermined religion at the same time that it harnessed religious sensibilities to create new forms of belief that would facilitate governance by yielding ideological conformity.

So, although the three dynamics of modernization that many scholars and Soviet leaders expected would eviscerate religion were indeed operative in the USSR, Europe, and the United States, to name the most obvious examples, the ultimate legacy of Soviet secularism, unlike in Europe or the United States, was the state-led unlearning of religion, its practices, symbols, doctrines, and moral codes, which changed religious practice in particular ways. This process did not necessarily induce a rejection of religion or a rejection of supernatural explanations for various occurrences as an authoritative source of knowing, as these essays depicting a religious renaissance after the fall of socialism demonstrate. Soviet political culture, like elsewhere, used religious moods to more effectively govern, and that kept these sensibilities alive and available.

Rather, Soviet secularization focused on shifting the foundations of knowing away from mysticism and the supernatural and toward the scientific and rational. Indeed, one of the hallmarks of Soviet secularism was that science and humanism could replace the role of religion in forging moral understandings and emotional dispositions for reckoning with the difficult ethical issues that modernization presented. Yet, when the powers of science and technology failed to offer meaningful explanations and insights, their authority as a means of knowing came into question, as did the entire project of state-led secularization. This has led to the emergence, and in some instances reemergence, of new ways of knowing and, by extension, new moralities as well as new understandings as to what constitutes authoritative knowledge. This in turn has affected secularizing tendencies, and in this way, the multiplicity of moralities in Russia has found a counterpart in the secular realm as well.

The chapters in this collection focus largely on the role of religious institutions in articulating moralities and in cultivating embodied practices that integrate these concepts into a person's disposition, and religion is but one source among others. Moral discourses and their related practices have many potential sources. I have noted the interrelated nature of morality to secularism and have suggested that the study of moralities leads to a further area of inquiry, which has only been touched upon here and still awaits closer examination, namely the multiplicity of secularisms. The dynamics and ideologies driving the Soviet experience of secularism are distinct from that of Europe and other regions of the world and merit our attention.

Multiple Moralities, Multiple Secularisms, and the Practice of Anthropology

In closing, I would like to suggest some questions and issues that are relevant to secularisms and moralities, and ones that anthropologists of religion are obliged to contend with when conducting research. Bruce Kapferer (2001: 342) has asserted that anthropology is bound to a secular rationalism whether its practitioners like it or not. I think he is right. But does this commitment to secular rationalism produce shortcomings, especially when the topic is religion? According to Kapferer, "Anthropology is a practice of secularism that must often be anti-secular in an effort to break through what is often a blinding prejudice that can be the self-same limitation of secularism, a secularism that defeats itself and a passion for understanding, in its very secularist zeal" (344). If, as a discipline, we are committed to rational, science-like explanations of social and cultural phenomena that are part and parcel of the secular, how does this affect the way we conduct research on beliefs in the supernatural? Are there not unique challenges to studying religion precisely because one must take seriously supernatural explanations for various events and occurrences and yet describe them in diametrically opposed "rational" terms? The very visceral reactions to moral quandaries and the bodily sensations that declare spiritual experiences as "true" and "real" knowledge must be translated by the anthropologist into a rationalized discourse and analyzed. Yet, certain meanings are often lost in translation and it is imperative for us to consider which ones get lost when the topic is morality and religion.

Is the meeting of multiple moralities in fieldwork, which begins with the moral understandings of informants and those of the anthropologist, and their subsequent translation into another idiom, just another version of translating difference comparable to political or economic differences? Or are there unique challenges to the process of conceptual translation, not least of which are the multiple secular filters that anthropologists and readers use, when analyzing the emotions behind moral and spiritual issues? I believe all anthropologists confront the necessity to engage in empathetic listening, open-minded consideration and careful translation and analysis. Yet, fulfilling these mandates can be particularly challenging for anthropologists of religion. The differences in professed levels of piety, or at least different forms of piety, between anthropologists and the people they study create opportunities for enhanced knowledge as much as they create fortress-like barriers to it. This brings me to the last, and one of the most fraught questions, namely: Is it incumbent on anthropologists, as they analyze in a secular vein the perceptions of supernatural phenomena that inform the multiple moralities and multiple secularisms that exist elsewhere, to reflexively divulge their own moral and secular conceptions in an effort to be upfront about the multiple moralities and secularisms that might exist among the anthropologist and his or her readers? There are, of course, many possible responses to these questions, all of which have their own moral implications for anthropologists.

These questions extend consideration of morality and secularism out of the realm of religion in Russia and bring it into our own practice of anthropology. These issues are worth considering because I suspect that there will be a good bit more moral introspection in the years to come as we continue to rethink the Soviet period and the legacy of socialism. Such inquiries will have distinct implications for the ways we come to know and understand the Soviet past with its particular secularizing practices and attitudes toward knowledge, religion, and morality. Verdicts as to how these questions are handled are likely to have distinct moral overtones. It is these moralized understandings, in all their multiplicity, that will influence the way the religious and political landscape is studied in Russia and beyond.

Notes

1. Importantly, a breakdown in moral consensus does not always lead to inertia and inaction. Rather, without an articulated sense of consensus, however broad, individuals often end up working at cross-purposes, each following their own understandings of righteous behavior. See Wanner (2005) for illustrations of how multiple moralities confront one another in a capitalist arena that is often devoid of legal and other sanctions, save moral ones.

2. For an illustration of the spectrum of secularizations in another context, see Heffner (1998). He argues that the resurgence of Islam in Indonesia has come at the expense of spirit cults and ancestor worship. A more formalized and more abstract Islam-based religious view is supplanting the less doctrinaire and more magical forms of belief and practice. This leads him to conclude that Islam, in some contexts, can be considered an agent of "soft" secularization (1998: 164).

3. See especially Luckmann (1967) for an interesting discussion of the "privatization" of religion, a dynamic also in evidence in the former Soviet Union. Elsewhere Luckmann (1996) attributes the rise of New Age religions, which offer spiritual development without canonized dogmas, a formal organizational structure, and disciplinary systems, among other contradistinctions to more traditional and long-standing religious organizations, to the trend toward individualizing and privatizing religious practice. Notably, New Age religions, which have enjoyed such a resurgence in Russia and elsewhere, offer little in the way of reaching moral judgments and forming identities, preferring instead to rely on individual experiences as sources for authority in these domains. Luckmann concludes that New Age, then, is a consequence of and motor for moral individualism.

4. Alternatively, Michael Bourdeaux (1995) attributes the vast appreciation for the arts in the USSR as a direct result of the closing off of religion as an avenue of aesthetic expression and experience.

References

Barker, Eileen. 1984. *The Making of a Moonie: Choice or Brainwashing?* London: Basil Blackwell.

Bauman, Zygmunt. 1993. *Postmodern Ethics.* Oxford: Blackwell.

Berger, Peter L., ed. 1999. *The Desecularization of the World: Resurgent Religion and World Politics.* Grand Rapids, MI: Eerdmans Publishing Co.

Berger, Peter, Grace Davie, and Effie Fokas. 2008. *Religious America, Secular Europe?: Variations on a Theme.* Burlington, VT: Ashgate.

Bourdeaux, Michael. 1995. "Glasnost and the Gospel: The Emergence of Religious Pluralism." In *The Politics of Religion in Russia and the New States of Eurasia*, ed. Michael Bourdeaux. Armonk, NY: M. E. Sharpe.

Heffner, Robert. 1998. "Secularization and Citizenship in Muslim Indonesia." In *Religion Modernity and Postmodernity*, ed. Paul Heelas. Oxford: Blackwell.

Hervieu-Léger, Danièle. 2000. *Religion as a Chain of Memory*, trans. Simon Lee. Cambridge: Polity Press.

Kapferer, Bruce. 2001. "Anthropology: The Paradox of the Secular." *Social Anthropology* 9, no. 3: 323–44.

Kiedeckel, David. 2008. *Getting By in Post-Socialist Romania: Labor, the Body and Working Class Culture.* Bloomington, IN: Indiana University Press.

Lindquist, Galina. 2006. *Conjuring Hope: Healing and Magic in Contemporary Russia.* New York: Berghahn.

Luckmann, Thomas. 1967. *The Invisible Religion.* London: MacMillian.

———. 1996. "The Privatization of Religion and Morality." In *De-traditionalization: Critical Reflections on Authority and Identity at a Time of Uncertainty*, ed. P. Heelas, S. Lash, and P. Morris. Oxford: Blackwell.

Mandel, Ruth, and Caroline Humphrey, eds. 2002. *Markets and Moralities: Ethnographies of Postsocialism.* Oxford: Berg.

Martin, David. 1978. *A General Theory of Secularization.* New York: Harper & Row.

Naumescu, Vlad. 2006. *Modes of Religiosity in Eastern Christianity: Religious Processes and Social Change in Ukraine.* Berlin: LIT Verlag.

Phillips, Sarah D. 2008. *Women's Activism in the New Ukraine: Development and the Politics of Differentiation.* Bloomington, IN: Indiana University Press.

Robbins, Joel. 2004. *Becoming Sinners: Christianity and Moral Torment in a Papua New Guinea Society.* Berkeley, CA: University of California Press.

Rogers, Douglas. 2009. *The Old Faith and the Russian Land: A Historical Ethnography of Ethics in the Urals.* Ithaca, NY: Cornell University Press.

Snadjr, Edward. 2008. *Nature Protests: The End of Ecology in Slovakia.* Seattle: University of Washington Press.

Stark, Rodney. 1999. "Secularization R.I.P." *Sociology of Religion* 60, no. 3: 249–73.

Wanner, Catherine. 2003. "Advocating New Moralities: Conversion to Evangelicalism in Ukraine." *Religion, State and Society* 31, no. 3: 273–87.

———. 2005. "Money, Morality and New Forms of Exchange in Postsocialist Ukraine." *Ethnos* 70, no. 4: 515–37.

———. 2007. *Communities of the Converted: Ukrainians and Global Evangelism.* Ithaca, NY: Cornell University Press.

Notes on Contributors

Alexander Agadjanian is a Professor at the Center for the Study of Religion at the Russian State University for the Humanities in Moscow. He has recently edited the following volumes: *Laicite/Secularism: International Experience and its Application in Russia and Eurasia* (co-edited); *Religious Practices in Today's Russia*; and *Eastern Orthodoxy in a Global Age.*

Melissa L. Caldwell is Professor of Anthropology at the University of California, Santa Cruz. Her current research and teaching focus on ethics of compassion and charity in Russia, with particular attention to the role of interfaith religious communities in Russia's social welfare sphere. She is the author of *Not by Bread Alone: Social Support in the New Russia* (University of California Press, 2004) and *Dacha Idylls: Living Organically in Russia's Countryside* (University of California Press, 2010), and is the editor of *Food and Everyday Life in the Postsocialist World* (Indiana University Press, 2009). She is currently writing a book on Russian religious charities.

Tobias Köllner holds an MA in Political Science, Sociology, and Social Anthropology. His doctoral dissertation, titled "Orthodox Entrepreneurs. Entrepreneurship, Morality and Religion in Contemporary Russia," was completed in 2010 at the University of Leipzig. Since October 2009 he has worked as a Research Associate at the isw Institute in Halle. He is co-author of the 2010 article "Spreading Grace in Post-Soviet Russia."

Jeanne Kormina is Professor of Anthropology and Religious studies at the Department of Sociology, Higher School of Economics (St. Petersburg, Russia). Her books in Russian include *Rituals of Departure to the Military Service in Late Imperial Russia* (2005); and *Dreams of the Mother of God*, co-edited with Sergey Shtyrkov and Alexander Panchenko (2006). She has also published some chapters in English about Orthodox pilgrimage in Russia.

Agata Ładykowska is a PhD student at the Max Planck Institute for Social Anthropology in Halle. Her research focuses on the intersection of the secular and the religious in education in Russia, with particular attention to the concepts of continuity and change as imagined and used by post-Soviet and post-atheist Russians. She is currently completing her doctoral dissertation and is co-author of the 2010 article "Spreading Grace in Post-Soviet Russia."

Alexander A. Panchenko is a leading research fellow at the Institute of Russian Literature (*Pushkinskij Dom*), Russian Academy of Sciences (St. Petersburg, Russia) and director of the Center for Anthropology of Religion, European University at St. Petersburg. His publications include *Issledovanija v oblasti narodnogo pravoslavija: Derevenskie sviatyni Severo-Zapada Rossii* (Studies in Popular Orthodoxy: Local Sacred Places in North-Western Russia); *Khristovschina i scopchestvo: Folklor i traditsionnaja kul'tura russkikh misticheskikh sect* (Christs and Castrates: Folklore and Traditional Culture of Russian Mystical Sects); "Ivan et Iakov—Deux Saints Etranges de la Région des Marais," and "The Cult of Lenin and 'Soviet Folklore.'"

Ieva Raubisko is a PhD candidate at the Institute of Social and Cultural Anthropology, University of Oxford. Her recent publications include "Proper 'Traditional' versus Dangerous 'New': Religious Ideology and Idiosyncratic Islamic Practices in Post-Soviet Chechnya," in the *Journal of the Anthropological Society of Oxford* (2009).

Kathy Rousselet is Senior Researcher at Sciences Po, Centre d'Etudes et de Recherches Internationales, CNRS, Paris. Her work focuses primarily on social and religious transformations in post-Soviet Russia. She has just co-authored with Alexander Agadjanian "Individual and Collective Identities in Russian Orthodoxy" which appears in *Eastern Christians in Anthropological Perspective* (California University Press); and "Les figures de la Laïcité Post-Soviétique en Russie" in *Critique Internationale* (2009). She co-edited with Alexander Agadjanian *Religioznye praktiki v sovremennoi Rossii* (Novoe Izdatel'stvo, 2006); and, with Gilles Favarel-Garrigues, *La Russie Contemporaine* (Fayard, 2010).

Sergey Shtyrkov is Professor of Anthropology of Religion in the Department of Anthropology, European University at St. Petersburg. He is also a senior researcher at the Department of Caucuses in the Institute of Ethnography and Anthropology of the Russian Academy of Sciences. His publications in Russian include the edited volume Northern Caucasia: *Traditional Rural Community: Social Roles, Public Opinion, Power Relations* (2007); and the co-edited (with Jeanne Kormina and Alexander Panchenko) *Dreams of the Mother of God* (2006). His ongoing research projects concern problems of religious nationalism, particularly in Northern Ossetia.

Detelina Tocheva received a PhD in Social Anthropology at Ecole des Hautes Etudes en Sciences Sociales, Paris, France, in 2005. Since 2006 she has been a research fellow at the Max Planck Institute for Social Anthropology, Halle, Germany. She conducted research on economy and community in Russian Orthodox parish life based on fieldwork in northwestern Russia. She is currently working on the relations between economy and ritual in southern Bulgaria. Her publications include "Spreading Grace in Post-Soviet Russia" (co-authored); and "Frontière Politique, Ethnicité et Clivages Sociaux: Un Exemple Estonien" in *Europa Mon Amour: 1989–2009, Un RêveBlessé.*

Catherine Wanner is an Associate Professor of History and Cultural Anthropology at Pennsylvania State University. She received her doctorate in Cultural Anthropology from Columbia University. She is the author of *Burden of Dreams: History and Identity in Post-Soviet Ukraine* (1998); and *Communities of the Converted: Ukrainians and Global Evangelism* (2007), which won four prizes; and is co-editor of *Religion, Morality and Community in Post-Soviet Societies* (2008). She is currently completing a book on religion and secularization in the Soviet Union. Her research has been supported by awards from the National Endowment for the Humanities, the National Science Foundation, Social Science Research Council, and other foundations.

Jarrett Zigon is an Assistant Professor in the Department of Anthropology at the University of Amsterdam. He is the author of *Morality: An Anthropological Perspective* (2008); *Making the New Post-Soviet Person: Moral Experience in Contemporary Moscow* (2010); and *HIV is God's Blessing: Rehabilitating Morality in Neoliberal Russia* (2011). His articles can be found in *Anthropological Theory, Ethnos,* and *Ethos,* among other journals.

Index

A

Abbot Antonii, 212n16
adat, 108, 114n26
Agadjanian, Alexander, 16, 220
agapè, 159, 163
Aksiuchits, Viktor, 148, 164n6
alcohol rehabilitation, 55
Alexei II (patriarch), 48, 149–151, 192
alms-giving, 53, 86
Anglican Church, 50, 51, 52, 55
anthropology of morality, 6–8, 119–120,
   222–224
   anthropological gaze, 6
   anthropology of virtue, 96
   distinctions between ethics and
      morality, 8–12
   Durkheimian perspective, 6
   epistemology, 97
   ethnographic studies, 215
   fieldwork, 28, 32–42, 67, 77, 81,
      89n8, 147, 212n13
   hagiology and, 168–188
   moral reasoning (choice) approach,
      6–7
   Neo-Aristotelian approach, 6–8
   other-world *versus* this-world, 53
   post-structuralism, 6
   self *versus* deity *versus* society, 53
   structural, 6
   in violence, 95–100
Aristotle, 96
   phronesis, 96
   virtue ethics, 97
artistic support, 193, 224n4
Asad, Talal, 10, 99, 107
asceticism, 180, 186n3, 205–208
"aspects," 8, 12n1

asylum seekers, 55
atheism, 87, 120–121, 171, 214
   orthodox atheist, 28–31
atonement, 208–209
Augustine the Blessed (saint), 184
authority
   loosening, 23
   moral authority, 51–52, 61–62
   priestly *versus* charismatic, 20–24
   science as authority, 219, 222
Avdonin, A. N., 148

B

Baptist Church, 50, 52, 55, 58
Barker, Eileen, 217
Bauman, Zygmunt, 216, 217
bdenie, 212n17
belkhi, 93
belonging, church, 21–22
   flexibility of, 23
Berdaev, Nikolai, 45n6
bespredel society, 4
beznravstvennost', 39–40, 47n13
Bible, 16
   parable of sower, 36, 47n12
Big Return, 18–19
bioethics, 3
blagochinie, 73
blagoslovenie (blessing), 21, 156
blood feud, 103–105, 108–109, 110
Bloody Sunday, 153
bodily impulses, 216
Bolsheviks, 41
borders, church, 23. *See also* belonging,
   church
born-again churches, 44
Born from Revolution (film), 147–148

breakdown, 3, 7, 11, 27, 35, 96, 217,
224n1
range of possibility, 42–44
Brodsky, Joseph, 131
brotherhood, 16
Budanov, Yuri, 114–115n29
Buddhism, 18
bureaucracy, 216, 219

C
Caldwell, Melissa, 3, 8, 10, 48
Cannell, Fenella, 53, 63–64
canonical space, 22
canonization, 146
gender and, 168, 175–178
tsarist family, 149–151, 153
Canonization Commission, 153
capitalism, morality of, 4
Center of the Mother of God, 20
charismatic movements, 20
charity, 53, 192. *See also* social justice
anonymous gifts, 67, 72
grassroots charity, 67–89 (*see also*
grassroots charity)
history of church donations,
192–193
"pure gifts," 209
social status and, 210
terminology of, 69, 71–72
Chechnya, 10, 92–115, 216
achieving justice, 105–109
blood revenge, 103–105, 108–109
civilian casualties, 114n29
rite of remembrance, 100
tradition, 99–105
virtue system, 99
vote 2003, 113–114n23
Chevalkov, Sergei, 128
children, 55
moral growth, 36. *See also* teachers
choice, 6–7, 165n24
Christian Church of Moscow, 54, 56, 57,
58, 59
Christian Democrat Party, 148
Christianity
collaborative relationships, 49–64

consonance with communism,
16–17
doctrinal differences, 58
orthodoxy *versus* orthopraxy, 50–54
social justice, 48–64
"church," 123
church construction, 191–212
architectural heritage, 191
church as mystical body of Christ,
195
"pure gifts," 209
separation of church and state, 191
tears *versus* gold metaphor, 192,
205–208
church economy, 22
Church of Saint Peter, 69–70, 74
foreign aid to, 73
Church of Smolensk Icon of the Mother
of God, 177
Church of the Last Testament. *See* Last
Testament Church
Church of the Mother of God, 70–71,
89n6
Finnish foreign aid to, 76–77, 89n7
German foreign aid to, 76–77
lavka, 76–88
Church of the New Testament, 20
Church on Blood in Honor of All Saints
Resplendent in the Russian Land, 146,
150
church workers, women, 183–184
cleaners, 74–76
cleanliness, 81–82
clothing, 74–76. *See also lavka*
collectivism, 16, 17, 130, 134, 216, 217
in Chechnya, 93
commodities, 209
common ground, 57, 62
communard movement, 132, 137,
143n17
communism
consonance with Christianity,
16–17
Soviet ethos, 130–140
Communist Party, 5, 16
compensation. *See* moral compensation

conformity, 61–62, 63
conscience, 215, 216
continuity, 16–17, 27–46, 163
    break *versus* continuity, 18–24
    versus change, 119–120
    versus discontinuity, 172
    pilgrims and, 168
conversion, religious, 45n1, 157
Cossacks, 162
crime, 164n5. *See also* Russia, post-
    Soviet, moral disorder in
CYF (Commune of Young Frunzentsy),
    133–138

D
Davis, John, 85
deception, 42. *See also* moral camouflage
dhikrs, 101
disabled people, 55, 56
discourse of morality. *See* public
    discourse of morality
dispositional-virtue perspective, 7–8
donations. *See also* charity; church
    construction; clothing; feeding
    programs
history of church donations, 192–193
Douglas, Mary, 81–82
doxa, 49, 52, 60, 63
dreams, 201–202
drug rehabilitation, 3, 55
drunkenness, 180
Dubin, Boris, 154
dukhovnichestvo (spiritual guidance), 21
dukhovnik (spiritual father), 21, 156, 159
dukhovno-nravstvennaia kul'tura,
    113n19
dukhovno-nravstvennyi, 113n19
dukhovnye chada (spiritual children), 21
Durkheim, E., 6, 96

E
ecumenicalism, 49–64
    doctrinal differences, 58
education, 27–46, 219
    textbooks, 40–42
elderly, 56, 57

elders, 19–24, 101–105, 113n22, 155, 183
    powerlessness, 103–105
Elizaveta Fedorovna, 157, 161
embodied dispositions, 7, 10–11, 10–12,
    42–43, 97, 216
entrepreneurial donations, 191–212
    as bribes, 196
    church's attitude, 195–196
    motivations, 192, 197–205
    political ambition, 202–204
epistemology, 97
    epistemological questioning, 3
ethics, 216
    definition, 11–12, 97
    dispositional ethics, 7
    ethical moment, 12, 35, 96
    ethical techniques, 124–130
    ethical transformation, 4
    versus morality, 11–12, 31–32,
        52–53, 97
    virtue ethics, 7, 97
eudaimonia, 98
European Court of Human Rights,
    115n29
evangelicalism, 217

F
family, 3, 10, 157, 162
family values, 5, 16
Fassin, Didier, 97
Fatherland, 70, 157, 162, 163
Faubion, James, 3, 43
Fedotov, George, 175
feeding programs, 54, 57, 59, 62
    soup kitchens, 193
Foucault, Michel, 3, 6–8, 12n2, 43, 98,
    196
freedom, 96, 107, 165n24
fürsein, 216

G
Ganina Yama, 146, 150
gender, 10
    language, 58
German Diakonie services, 73, 89n6
German Evangelical Church, 73, 89n4

Gershon, Ilana, 43–44
gifts
    inalienability of gifts, 209–210
    "pure gifts," 209
    relatedness and, 67
globalization, 3, 150
goodness, 112n12
grassroots charity, 67–89
    anonymous gifts, 67, 72
    clothing, 73
    discrimination, 82–85
    donors, 85
    empathy, 84–85
    foreign aid, 73–74
    housing, 74
    imagined community, 68
    local patterns of support, 73–77
    motivation, 79
    procedure of appropriation, 81–82
    recipients, 79–81
    spiritual services, 72
Great Terror, 146, 163n4
    indifference toward, 148
guilt, 159
gypsies, 82–85, 89n10

H
Habermas, Jürgen, 62
habitus, 99, 107, 111n11
hagiography
    Saint Xenia, 168–188
    tsarist family, 146–147, 153
Heidegger, Martin, 3, 216
Hervieu-Léger, Danièle, 221
historical causation, 19, 21
holy fool, 174, 177, 178–182, 180, 186–
    187n12, 186n3
holy icons. *See* icons
homelessness, 54, 55, 56, 64n3, 187n22,
    193
homes of industry, 86
human dignity, 105–109
human rights, 3

I
icons, 21, 146, 155, 157, 187n24, 198
    Saint Xenia, 169, 177–178, 179, *179*

    of tsarist family, 146, 155
Identification Commission, 148
*In the Name of Love: Xenia the Blessed of
    Saint Petersburg,* 187n26, 188n29
inchurchment, 196
Ingermanlandian Finns, 89n7
institutions, 8–9, 42, 172–173, 174, 192,
    216
interfaith programs, 49–64
Internet, 170
intolerance, 16
Ioann of Kronshtadt, 153
Ipatiev House, 148
irregular believers, 172–175
Islam, 4, 18, 112n16, 224n2
    split religious authority, 20
Ivanov, Igor', 132, 136, 143n19–20

J
Judaism, 4
justice, achieving, 105–109, 114–
    115n29, 216
justice work, 50–64. *See also* social justice

K
Kadyrov, Akhmat-Khadzhi, 105
Kadyrov, Ramzan, 94, 105
Kaluga region of Russia, 146, 147, 157
Kant, E., 96, 98
"keeping-while-giving," 198, 204–205
Kharkhordin, Oleg, 41
Khrushchev, Nikita, 131
Kirill (metropolitan), 48, 173
Kirill (patriarch), 22, 151, 162, 174
Köllner, Tobias, 9–10, 191
Komsomol, 45n3
Korean Methodist Church, 55, 56
Kormina, Jeanne, 10, 216
Kucherskaya, Maja, 185
Kuni, Lula, 106
Kvedaravicius, Mantas, 113n20

L
Ladykowska, Agata, 10, 18, 27, 113n19
Lambek, Michael, 6, 96, 97
Last Testament Church, 8, 18, 120–143
    cosmology, 123

discussion clubs, 128
eschatology, 124
ethical narratives, 129
ethical techniques, 124–130
geographical location, 121–122
members, 121
moral discourse, 124–130. *See also*
    public discourse, moral
New Age beliefs, 120, 121, 123
power relations, 125
sacred algorithm, 128
Soviet influence, 121, 130–140
spiritual circle, 138–139, *139–140*
theology, 123, 142n6
urban culture, 121
lavka, 76–88, 89n8
discrimination, 82–85
donors, 85
motivation, 79
perceptions of, 78
procedure of appropriation, 81–82
recipients, 79–81
resellers, 83–85
lay women, 169
Lemon, Alaina, 82–85
Leningrad State University, 186n4
Levanov, Vadim, 170, 173–174, 180
Levin, Eve, 176
lezginka, 112n14
liberalism, 132, 148, 152, 154
longue-duree, 19
Lutheran Church, 50, 52, 55, 56, 57, 58, 59
lzhestartsys (false elders), 20

M
MacIntyre, Alasdair, 98–99, 104, 111n9,
    111n10
Macklin, June, 185
Mahmood, Saba, 111n11
Maksimovich, Ioann (archbishop), 150
Maloe Zamostie, Russia, 182
market relations. *See* capitalism
marriage, 183–184
martyrs, 146, 187n15. *See also* saints
    patriotism and, 152
materialism *(veshchizm),* 5, 160, 217. *See
    also* capitalism

materialism, Marxist, 37
Mauss, Marcel, 10, 81, 209–210
meaning, 44
Medvedev, Dmitri, 147–149
Melchisedech (bishop), 155
memory, 157, 164n6, 220–221
    secularism and, 221
    transmutation of, 221
Menzel, Brigit, 121
merchants, 193
Methodist Church, 52, 56
Microsoft, 212n12
miracles, 130, 153, 175, 177, 178
mitsein, 216
mladostartsys (young elders), 20–24
modernization, 219
Moldova, 89n10
monarchy, 162
money, 102. *See also* donations
moral, 29, 32–42, 45–46n7, 45n4
    rules and, 39
    in textbooks, 40–42
moral agency, 96
moral authority, 51–52, 61–62
moral breakdown. *See* breakdown
moral camouflage, 41–42
"Moral Code of the Builder of
    Communism, The," 5, 29–30, 42, 130,
    132
    biblical allusions, 16
    brotherhood, 16
    collectivisim, 16
moral codes, 151, 217
    switching, 119
moral compensation, 108, 208–209
moral domain, 7
moral exceptionalism, 62–64
moral indifference, 17
moral perestroika, 147–149, 162
moral pluralism, 17
moral quest, 99–105
moral reasoning, 6–7, 96, 215, 216–217
moral relativism, 17
morality. *See also* embodied dispositions;
    public discourse of morality
    alternative, 218
    aspects of, 8–12, 119

body and, 216
competing moralities, 4
continuity thinking, 27–46, 119, 214
definitions, 96–97, 215–216
double, 17, 40
versus ethics, 11–12, 52–53, 97, 119
institutional, 8–9 (*see also* institutions)
internal motivations, 39, 44, 96, 192, 197–205
moral consciousness, 6, 7
moral debts, 148
moral unreflectiveness, 7, 97, 119 (*see also* embodied dispositions)
morality of society, 6, 40, 44, 96
multiple moralities, 4–12, 214–224
non-Orthodox traditions, 4
perspective of teachers, 34–42
phenomenological approach, 7–8
religious, 17, 119 (*see also* religion)
reproduction *versus* choice, 96
sacred *versus* secular, 4
as sociality, 96
unconscious (*see* embodied dispositions)
war and, 92–115
Morozov, Pavlik, 39–40
Moscow Patriarchate, 149, 168, 186, 186n3
motivations, 39, 44, 79, 96, 192, 197–205
mutual aid, 67. *See also* grassroots charity

N
nationalists, 155
Nemtsov, Boris, 148, 163n4
Neo-Aristotelian perspective, 6–8
Nestor Chronicle, 207, 212n14–16
networking, 55, 56
New Age beliefs, 120, 121, 224n3. *See also* Last Testament Church
New Religious Movement, 18, 20, 119–143
Soviet influence, 120
New Russians, 61
New Soviet Man, 5, 28

Nicholas II, 146. *See also* tsarist family
bloody Nicholas, 147
passion-bearer, 147, 153
versus new martyr, 155
suffering and, 154
normality, 148
novomuchennik, 152
nravopisatel'nyi, 47n8
nravstvennost', 29–30, 32–42, 43, 45n4, 45n5, 47n9
dictionary meanings, 31–32
individual *versus* social, 31–32
secular *versus* religious, 30
in textbooks, 40–42

O
Oedipus, 10
ogoniok, 134
Okudzhava, Bulat, 132
Old Believer Orthodoxy, 4
"On the Rehabilitation of the Victims of Political Repression," 149
Orlovsky, Damaskin, 152–153
orphans, 55
orthodoxy, 50–54
"Orthodox," 21–22
orthodox continuity, 19–24, 27–46, 214
orthopraxy, 50–54, 60
Our Lady of Kazan, 197

P
Pamiat, 155
Panchenko, Alexander, 8, 10–11, 18, 119
Pandian, Anand, 99
paranomic actions, 43
Paraskeva (saint), 175–176
Parish, Steven, 6
passion-bearer, 147, 153
pedagogy, 28
of collaboration, 37
Soviet, 37
of support, 37
penance. *See* repentance
Pentecostal Charismatics, 20
personal interiority, 53
Pesmen, Dale, 5

Petr (father), 155–156, 165n24
phenomenology, 7–8
pilgrimages, 146, 150, 163n3, 168–170,
   169
Piskunova, Natalia, 188n32
pokaianie (penitence), 21. *See also*
   repentance
political repression, 105–109
politics of rightness, 10, 52–53
Politkovskaya, Anna, 111n5
poslushanie (obedience), 21, 156
praxis, 49, 52, 60, 63
prayer, 58, 112n16, 155, 182
   collective prayer, 161
   Saint Xenia and, 170
Presbyterian Church, 55
prisoners, 55
problematization, 3, 43
Progressive Pentecostalism, 54
Protestantism, 4, 51
   collaborative relationships, 49–64
public discourse of morality, 7, 9–10, 42,
   119–120, 214
   chair of wisdom, 126–127, 142n10
   church construction, 191–212. *See
      also* church construction
   egoism, 124
   ethical narratives, 129
   gordynya, 124
   gorenie, 125
   Last Testament Church, 124–130
   moral meetings, 127–128
   mudrost, 125
   podskazka, 125–126
   polianka smireniia, 125
   range *vs.* stability, 119
   revivalist discourse, 86
   sacred *versus* secular, 4
   Soviet, 4–5, 16–17
Putin, Vladmir, 191. *See also* church
   construction

R
rape, 101–105
Rasputin, Grigori, 155
Raubisko, Ieva, 3, 10, 11, 92, 216
reburial of corpses, 147–149, 163n4

reciprocity. *See* relatedness, ethos of
reconciliation, 42
   tsarist family and, 148, 150
Red'kin, Vadim, 123
reflexivity, 44
   reflexive freedom, 96
refugees, 55, 57
regicide, 149, 151, 155
relatedness, ethos of, 67–89, 159
   anonymous gifts, 67
   community of equals, 88
   imagined community, 68
   secular, 67, 69
   secular ethos, 88
   unreciprocated acts, 67
religion, 17
   baptism, 171
   break *versus* continuity, 18–24, 214
   communal membership, 218
   entrepreneurial donations, 191–212
   ethnic associations, 51
   history of church donations,
      192–193
   non-Orthodox traditions, 4
   other-world *versus* this-world, 53
   popular, 170
   privatization of, 224n3
   public discourse and, 3, 7. *See also*
      public discourse of morality
   religious illiteracy, 220–221
   religious return, 18–19
   transmission of, 171–172
religiosity, Russian, 16–24
religious affiliation. *See* belonging,
   church
religious commitment, 27, 155–157, 216
religious conversion. *See* conversion,
   religious
religious culture, 119–120
religious discourse, 119–120. *See also*
   public discourse of morality
religious education. *See* education
religious media, 52
religious pluralism, 49–50
religious publishing, 52
religious revival, 27
repentance, 158–162, 162–163, 164n13

auricular confession, 196
change in behavior, 196–197
"collective person," 151
confession, 211n2
real penance, 205, 207
sin *versus* crime, 164n5
tsarist family and, 149–151
reproductive rights, 3, 5
Riabov, G. T., 147
Ries, Nancy, 87
ritual, 53
Rivkin-Fish, Michele, 5
Robbins, Joel, 6, 7, 217
Rogers, Douglas, 4
Roman Catholic Church, 23, 55, 56, 57, 59
collaborative relationships, 49–64
Romanovs. *See* tsarist family
Rostovon-Don, Russia, 28
Rousselet, Kathy, 10, 18, 146
Royal Dutch Shell, 212n12
Russia, post-Soviet
epistemological questioning in, 3
history of church donations,
192–193
moral disorder in, 147, 158–162.
See also morality
multiple moralities in, 3–12, 17
redemption of Russian Orthodox
Church in, 146. *See also* Russian
Orthodox Church
yearning for tradition in, 147, 154–
158. *See also* tradition
Russia, pre-revolution, 5
morality of period, 71, 86
Russia, Soviet. *See* Soviet Union
Russian Orthodox Church, 17, 62
church building as mystical body of
Christ, 195
church construction, 191–212. *See
also* church construction
collaborative relationships, 49–64,
55
continuity thinking, 19–24, 27–46,
214
criticisms of, 62, 146
decorations on church buildings,
195

ethnic identity and, 51, 68
flexibility of, 23
fundamentalists in, 150
grassroots charity, 68–89
irregular believers, 172–175
moral authority, 51–52, 61–62
new morality and, 151–154
obnovlenchestvo, 88n2
as official religion, 51
orthodoxy *versus* orthopraxy, 50–54
patriarch, 48–49
in post-Soviet Russia, 3
pre-revolution, 5
reconstruction of, 10
revivalist discourse, 86, 88n2
Russian identity and, 18
social work, 55, 59, 68–89, 193–197
spiritual work, 193–197
statistics of membership, 68
theology linked to morality, 8
tsarist family and, 149–154
Russian Orthodox Church Abroad, 147,
150, 155, 186n3

S
sacred algorithm, 128
sacrifice, 112n16, 152, 176
Said-Magomed-Khadzhi Isakov,
104–105
Saint Petersburg, Russia, 147
Church of Saint Peter, 69–70
Church of the Mother of God,
70–71
Saint Tsar, 18. *See also* tsarist family
saints, 18, 21, 153, 185–186n2. *See also
specific saints*
collective values of, 152
female, 175–178
personal relationships, 151
purpose of, 184–185
as role models, 146, 151, 184
Saints of Old Russia (Fedotov), 175
Samoan immigrants (New Zealand),
43–44
Sant'Egidio street ministry, 59
schools
religious subjects in, 28–31

science as authority, 219, 222
Scott, David, 99
sects, 76, 151
secularism, 214, 218–224
self-analysis, 5
self-making, 44, 53. *See also*
  self-transformation
self-transformation, 5, 12n2, 44, 214. *See*
  also self-making
    embodied morality and, 10–11
"Sentimental March," 132
Seraphim of Sarov, 153
sexuality, 5
Shtyrkov, Sergey, 10, 216
Sisters of Mercy, 59
Smolensk Cemetery, 168, 169, 177
sobornost', 15
social justice, 48–64
    history of church donations,
      192–193
    language of, 59–60
    virtual encounters, 55
social relatedness. *See* relatedness, ethos
  of
social status, 210
social transformation, 214
social welfare. *See* charity; grassroots
  charity; social justice
socialism, 214. *See also* Soviet ethos
    secularism and, 218–222
Soviet ethos, 120, 130–140
    atheistic propaganda, 171
    camps, 137
    consonance with Christianity,
      16–17
    hero-identification, 151
    influence of Western Europe, 152
    "last Soviet generation," 172–173
    political ritual, 221
    religious sensibilities, 221
Soviet Union
    collectivism, 17. *See also*
      collectivism
    moral discourse, 4–5, 16–17
    Perestroika, 41. *See also* moral
      perestroika
    Soviet ethos, 120, 130–140

spiritual services, 72, 193–197
St. Xenia of St. Petersburg in her Life
  (Levanov), 170, 173–174
startsy. See elders
suffering, 5, 158, 159, 180
    female, 182–184
Sufism, 101, 112n16
    murid, 109
suicide, 180, 188n30
Sverdlovsk, Russia, 147

T
teachers, 27–46
    as moral authorities, 30
    religious *versus* secular, 28–29
    as sowers, 36–37
telos, 98
textbooks, 40–42
theological diversity, 50
Tishkov, Valery, 95
tithing, 53, 54
Tocheva, Detelina, 11, 67, 182
Torop, Sergey, 120. *See also* Vissarion
tradition, 99, 105, 110, 111n10, 115n29,
  147, 217
    disintegration of, 99–105
    history linked to worship, 158
    transmission of, 171–172
    yearning for, 147, 154–158
"Tsarist Days," 147, 158
tsarist family, 146–165
    canonization of, 149–151, 153–154
    death of, 146, 148
    icons of, 146, 155
    passion-bearers, 153
    procession for, 146, 150, 163n3
    rehabilitation of, 147–149
    residences, 157–158
    significance of worship of, 158–162
    yearning for tradition and, 154–158
tserkovnost' (churchliness), 22, 23, 220

U
UFOlogy, 121, 123
Ukraine, 218
Unification Church, 217
Union of enthusiasts, 132–133

United Russia party, 211n9
urbanization, 177, 219

V
Vedernikov, Vladimir, 128
veruiushchii (believer), 22
"vicarious," 24n1
virtue, 7–8, 96–98, 105
Vissarion, 120, 128. *See also* Last
    Testament Church
Vladimir, (father), 193–197
Vladimir, Prince, 192
Vladimir, Russia, 211n1
Volkov, Solomon, 131
vospitanie, 28, 35, 37
votserkovlenie, 196

W
Wahhabism, 112n16
Wanner, Catherine, 10, 214
war, 92–115
    blood revenge and, 103–105, 108–
        109, 110
    justice and, 105–109
Watson, James L., 53, 60
Weber, Max, 6, 20
Weiner, Annette, 198
welfare programs. *See* social justice
Widlok, Thomas, 96
"work of *dusha,*" 5
work on self. *See* self-transformation

X
Xenia (saint), 168–188, 186n11
    city dwellers and, 177

elderly images of, 178
gender changes of, 179, 187n21
holy fool, 174, 177, 178–182, 180,
    186–187n12
icons of, 169, 177–178, 179, *179*
irregular believers and, 172–175
letters to, 182–183
marriage of, 177, 179, 180–181,
    187n25
matushka, 182
meetings with, 177–178
night religiosity, 174
pilgrims and, 168–170, *169*
popular religion and, 170
song about, 182
stories about, 178–182
suffering, 182–184
target audience of, 171–173
Xenia: The Love Story (Levanov), 170

Y
Yekaterinburg region of Russia, 146, 150,
    162
Yeltsin, Boris, 147–149
Yuliania Lasarevskaya of Murom, 175,
    176, 187n16
Yurchak, Alexey, 172
Yuriev, Zinovii, 128

Z
zapiski, 72
Zemsky Sobor, 150
Zigon, Jarrett, 3, 27, 42, 52, 99, 106,
    191–192, 216